Afghanistan:
to 2015 and beyond

Edited by Toby Dodge and Nicholas Redman

Afghanistan:
to 2015 and beyond

Edited by Toby Dodge and Nicholas Redman

IISS The International Institute for Strategic Studies

The International Institute for Strategic Studies

Arundel House | 13–15 Arundel Street | Temple Place | London | WC2R 3DX | UK

First published December 2011 by **Routledge**
4 Park Square, Milton Park, Abingdon, Oxon, OX14 4RN

for **The International Institute for Strategic Studies**
Arundel House, 13–15 Arundel Street, Temple Place, London, WC2R 3DX, UK
www.iiss.org

Simultaneously published in the USA and Canada by **Routledge**
270 Madison Ave., New York, NY 10016

Routledge is an imprint of Taylor & Francis, an Informa Business

DIRECTOR-GENERAL AND CHIEF EXECUTIVE Dr John Chipman
EDITOR Dr Nicholas Redman
ASSISTANT EDITOR Janis Lee
EDITORIAL Carolyn West, Jens Wardenaer, Dr Ayse Abdullah
COVER/PRODUCTION John Buck
CARTOGRAPHY Steven Bernard
MAP RESEARCH Sarah Johnstone, Jens Wardenaer, Oliver Elliott
COVER PHOTO Jacques Descloitres, MODIS Land Rapid Response Team

The International Institute for Strategic Studies is an independent centre for research, information and debate on the problems of conflict, however caused, that have, or potentially have, an important military content. The Council and Staff of the Institute are international and its membership is drawn from almost 100 countries. The Institute is independent and it alone decides what activities to conduct. It owes no allegiance to any government, any group of governments or any political or other organisation. The IISS stresses rigorous research with a forward-looking policy orientation and places particular emphasis on bringing new perspectives to the strategic debate.

The Institute's publications are designed to meet the needs of a wider audience than its own membership and are available on subscription, by mail order and in good bookshops. Further details at www.iiss.org.

Printed and bound in Great Britain by Bell & Bain Ltd, Thornliebank, Glasgow

British Library Cataloguing in Publication Data
A catalogue record for this book is available from the British Library

Library of Congress Cataloging in Publication Data

ADELPHI series
ISSN 1944-5571

ADELPHI 425–26
ISBN 978-0-415-69642-5

Contents

GLOSSARY

ADB	Asian Development Bank
ANA	Afghan National Army
ANP	Afghan National Police
ANSF	Afghan National Security Forces
CIA	Central Intelligence Agency
COIN	Counter-insurgency
FATA	Federally Administered Tribal Areas
HUJI	Harkat-ul-Jihad-Islami
HiG	Hizb-e-Islami Gulbuddin
IMF	International Monetary Fund
ISAF	International Security Assistance Force
ISI	Inter-Services Intelligence Agency, Pakistan
JeM	Jaish-e-Mohammed
LeJ	Lashkar-e-Jhangvi
LeT	Lashkar-e-Tayiba
LIFG	Libyan Islamic Fighting Group
NATO	North Atlantic Treaty Organisation
NDN	Northern Distribution Network
NWFP	Northwest Frontier Province
OECD	Organisation for Economic Cooperation and Development
SCO	Shanghai Cooperation Organisation
SSP	Sipah-e-Sahaba Pakistan
TAPI	Turkmenistan–Afghanistan–Pakistan–India gas pipeline
TIP	Turkistan Islamic Party

TNSM	Tehrik-e-Nafaz-e-Shariat Mohamedi
TTP	Tehrik-e-Taliban Pakistan
UNAMA	United Nations Assistance Mission in Afghanistan
UNDP	United Nations Development Programme
UNODC	United Nations Office on Drugs and Crime
USAID	United States Agency for International Development

INTRODUCTION

Toby Dodge and Nicholas Redman

In 2010 the International Institute for Strategic Studies (IISS) launched a major research project focused on the future of Afghanistan and its relations with the wider region. This book is a result of that programme. The project began after US President Barack Obama's crucial West Point speech in December 2009 that announced a change to America's policy. By then it was clear that NATO's Afghanistan strategy was not sustainable in its current form. Obama, after a lengthy and fractious Afghan policy review, agreed to send 30,000 extra American troops to the country, but for a strictly delineated period of 18 months. The ramifications of this difficult decision highlighted two competing dynamics at work within US strategy, wider NATO policy and Afghanistan itself. This book examines those dynamics.

On the ground in Afghanistan, violent instability had steadily increased since the invasion and the removal of the Taliban in 2001. Insurgent forces had slowly regrouped and were now striking against both NATO troops and the Afghan security forces with rising cost to human life. In addition, it was clear that the Afghan government was losing legitimacy. The presidential elections in August 2009 had been undermined by widespread fraud and a decline in popular participation. Corruption had escalated significantly and degraded the already weak capacity of the Afghan state. In late 2009, Obama sought to meet these security and political challenges by launching the Afghan 'surge', a counter-insurgency campaign overseen by General David Petraeus, fresh from his success in Iraq, and implemented by General Stanley McChrystal. This counter-insurgency operation was designed to reverse the drift in NATO policy, delivering noticeable success in the fight against the Taliban and boost the rate at which a competent Afghan security force could be built. In conjunction with the military campaign, a civilian surge was to be launched that focused on achieving a steep improvement in government capacity, a reduction in corruption and an improvement in the popular perception of the country's governing elite.

However, Obama's December 2009 speech highlighted a second major dynamic shaping US and NATO policy towards Afghanistan: its increasing unpopularity among the electorates of those countries contributing troops. This led Obama to place a limit on the time that extra American troops could stay on the ground in Afghanistan. In June 2010, British Prime Minister David Cameron also recognised the growing constraints that public opinion placed on Afghan policy when he announced his ambition that UK troops would be home within five years. This move to place a time limit on NATO troop deployments was formalised first at the Kabul Summit in July 2010 and then at NATO's Lisbon Summit in November. The Kabul International Conference endorsed the Afghan government and NATO's Intequal plan for a transition process that would allow Afghans to take full responsibility for security, governance and development. The Lisbon Summit affirmed that 'the irreversible transition to full Afghan security responsibility and leadership' would begin in early 2011. It went on to support 'President [Hamid] Karzai's objective for the Afghan National Security Forces to lead and conduct security operations in all provinces by the end of 2014'.

It was against this background that the IISS launched its Afghan research programme. A series of meetings were held between institute staff, regional experts and government officials from all the countries concerned. It was these in-depth discussions which shaped the research programme's contents and the structure of this book. It was decided that the project would focus on 13 distinct areas, grouped together in three themes. The institute's experts were asked to consider how the reduction in troop numbers after 2014 would impact on their area of research. The first theme would cover the historical background of Afghanistan itself and international involvement in the country. It would also assess the continuation of the United States' post-9/11 policy towards Afghanistan in the light of American history, budget constraints and internal politics. The second research group would focus on Afghanistan itself. It would examine how post-intervention state-building from 2001 had unfolded, how it was likely to be transformed in the aftermath of the new US–NATO policy and, most importantly, what would happen after 2014. Afghanistan's history, especially since the Soviet invasion of December 1979, but in all probability since the second Anglo-Afghan War of 1880, indicates that the country cannot be studied in isolation from its wider region. So the third research group set about analysing the relationship Afghanistan will have with a set of key regional players, certainly its neighbours but also a wider set of states who will have direct influence on the country after 2014.

As research progressed, institute fellows presented and refined their preliminary findings in a number of meetings at IISS offices in Asia, the Middle East and London. This process reached its conclusion in September 2011 when the book's central themes and conclusions were presented at the institute's annual conference, the Global Strategic Review, in Geneva. The cumulative results of this research programme are presented in 13 substantive chapters. Overall, the book argues for a cautious but highly constrained optimism. After assessing the domestic, regional and international dynamics shaping Afghanistan's future after 2014, the book concludes that, on the balance of probability, the country will not rapidly return to civil war. It will not in the main revert to an arena for the proxy conflicts of the regional states. This does not mean Afghanistan is on an uncomplicated trajectory to anything like stability and economic growth: far from it. The country will remain poor, weak and unstable. Its politics will continue to be shaped by civil and military conflict. However, the book argues that this conflict will not result in a speedy state collapse, because the centre of government in Kabul has been reconstituted to the extent that it will manage to hold together, place limits on the ability of the insurgents to operate within the country and on exterior actors who seek to exacerbate internal instability.

The first section of the book places the current and future trajectory of Afghanistan in historical and political perspective. Alexander Nicoll details the history that led up to 2010 Lisbon Summit that set 2014 as the exit date. Centrally, he examines the extent to which future developments after NATO troop withdrawal will represent a reversion to the historical state–society patterns that have governed Afghan politics over the last hundred years. The chapter goes on to detail how the post-invasion Bonn conference chose Hamid Karzai as an interim president and how the legacies of that decision continue to haunt both the man and the office he occupies. Nicoll traces the reconstitution of the Taliban after their initial defeat in 2001, describing how they successfully regrouped, embarked upon an increasingly successful guerrilla campaign and by 2006 represented a complex alliance of ideologically driven madrassa students and jihadist, xenophobic recruits provided by village mullahs allied to sections of the local Afghan community.

Dana Allin, in the second chapter, argues that the Bush administration's campaign in Afghanistan was both under-resourced and far too ambitious. This conscious attempt at re-engineering a nation of almost 30 million people caused strategic over-stretch on a catastrophic scale. By fighting on Osama bin Laden's chosen terrain, the US administration ran the distinct danger of falling into the enemy's trap. Allin argues that the Obama administration, in shaping its own Afghan policy, was very aware of these problems and placed Afghanistan at the centre of a new Obama doctrine, 'a more narrowly focused pursuit of American interests'. This approach is designed to bolster a new public and elite consensus, which will continue to support America's relationship with Afghanistan after 2015, as long as it is not based on large-scale troop deployments but on 'aid, military training and one or two bases from which American soldiers can support the Afghan government and American special forces can continue to target and kill al-Qaeda-linked terrorists'.

Political, economic and coercive dynamics shaping Afghanistan today are then examined, along with their potential to dramatically change in the run-up to and after 2014. Toby Dodge examines the likelihood that the counter-insurgency campaign placed at the centre of Obama's new policy will work. He argues that its success is dependent on solving a number of distinctly political problems. The first is the need to improve the institutional capacity of the Afghan state, its ability to deliver services to the country's population. Given the history and geography of Afghanistan, Dodge thinks this is unlikely. Additional problems concern the declining legitimacy of the Afghan government; revelations of widespread fraud surrounding the presidential and parliamentary elections of 2009 and 2010; and the weakness of Afghanistan's parliament, the Wolesi Jirga. Finally, Dodge looks at the political corruption that continues to undermine state-building.

In chapter four, Nicholas Redman examines the Afghan economy and its prospects for development after 2014. He makes the central point that 'a weak economy, in which poverty is widespread, is inimical to the stabilisation of the state'. However, the Afghan economy has precious few areas for sustainable growth. This is especially the case after 2014, when foreign aid is certain to decline both in absolute and proportionate terms. Against this background, the exploitation of the country's mineral wealth represents one of the few areas of potential growth in the foreseeable future. For most of the population, however, economic activity will continue to be focused on subsistence agriculture, with several hundred thousand Afghans involved in the cultivation of the opium poppy. (Afghanistan is the source of almost 80% of global opium supply.) Narcotics production certainly boosts the country's rural economy, lifts some households out of poverty and stimulates the labour market. However, it also supports a powerful shadow state and will become an even more important source of revenue for warlords after 2014.

Ben Barry, in chapter five, investigates the Afghan security forces and the insurgency, and considers the ability of the Afghan army to hold the territory currently controlled by NATO and the Kabul government after foreign troops leave the country. Barry argues that it was only after 2010 that the International Security Assistance Force (ISAF) received the resources it needed to launch a full counter-insurgency strategy of 'clear, hold and build'. That said, ISAF remains robustly confident about the ability of Afghanistan's security forces to meet this challenge. However, their overall performance remains variable and there are indications of weakness throughout the force, with issues surrounding logistics, planning and management capabilities, the quality of personnel, high levels of illiteracy and inter-ethnic tensions. Barry concludes by suggesting that Afghanistan's eastern region may never be brought under full government control, although it is likely the state will maintain control over the territory already cleared. The Afghan National Security Forces will perhaps lose some ground to the insurgency, but should not collapse.

The sixth chapter is by Nigel Inkster. It examines the various groups involved in terrorism in Afghanistan and Pakistan, and assesses whether the Afghan Taliban would welcome or even tolerate the establishment of al-Qaeda bases in the territory they may control after 2014. Central to this analysis is the interaction between insurgent and terrorist groups operating in Afghanistan and the Pakistani government. In the aftermath of the Taliban's defeat in 2001, such groups were seen by the Pakistani military and intelligence services as a strategic asset whose return to power represented the best insurance against an Indian-dominated Afghanistan. However, the number of terrorist-related deaths in Pakistan between 2003 and 2011 is estimated to have reached 36,741 and this, along with immense American pressure, has forced the Pakistani military to restrict the geographical areas in which Afghan, Pakistani and al-Qaeda militants can operate within Pakistan. Simultaneously, the 'undoubted tactical success of the NATO/ISAF campaign has had the strategic effect of fragmenting the Taliban leadership beyond the point where there is a coherent movement with which to negotiate'. Inkster argues that al-Qaeda now has funding problems, with fewer than 100 of its operatives active in Afghanistan. Mullah Omar, the head of the Taliban, has also shown signs of distancing himself from al-Qaeda. This leaves the Haqqani network, still in receipt of Pakistani support, as the most potent terrorist force operating in Afghanistan.

The book then turns to Afghanistan's neighbours and influential players within the wider region. Each of the chapters evaluates the political, economic and ideological interests of the countries concerned and how these have historically shaped their relations with Afghanistan. The chapters then examine how these interests and policies may change after the drawdown of US and NATO troops. As Nigel Inkster's chapter on terrorism powerfully demonstrates, Pakistan has the greatest capacity to destabilise Afghanistan after 2014. Rahul Roy-Chaudhury provides an appraisal of the concerns that have historically shaped Islamabad's relations with Kabul. He argues that 'the principal strategic interest for Pakistan's involvement in Afghanistan has been the quest for "strategic depth", in light of the power asymmetry with its arch-rival, India'. Pakistan has seen India's policy in Afghanistan as a deliberate attempt to 'encircle' it. In addition, after 2001 Pakistan also became suspicious of the Indian-educated Karzai because he did not bring Islamabad's allies into his cabinet and did not appoint enough Pashtuns to the Afghan National Army. However, against the background of increased terrorist violence at home, Roy-Chaudhury detects a potential positive change in Pakistani policy towards Afghanistan. This is personified by the army chief, General Ashfaq Pervez Kayani, who stated that Pakistan cannot wish for Afghanistan what it does not wish for itself; hence a 'peaceful, stable and friendly' Afghanistan would provide the strategic depth that Pakistan has long sought.

One of Emile Hokayem's two chapters in this book reviews the policy of Iran towards Afghanistan. Hokayem argues that Iran's policy has been guided by 'a pragmatic, cautious and largely opportunistic assessment of its reach and prospects'. Iran's changing attitude to Afghanistan is shaped by its assessment of how events in that country have the potential to affect its own security and, further, how its rivals and enemies may use Afghan territory to destabilise it. The murder of ten Iranian diplomats and a journalist in 1998, when the Taliban took control of the Afghan city of Mazar-e-Sharif, not only caused Iran to mass troops on the Afghan border but has also shaped its long-term goal of halting the Taliban's return to power. However, this is balanced against Tehran's fear that Saudi Arabia will use its alliance with Pakistan to damage Iran through Afghanistan. With this in mind, Tehran has offered overt financial support to the Karzai presidency and limited covert support to those groups fighting to overthrow the government.

Oksana Antonenko, in her chapter, looks at Afghanistan's northern neighbours, the five post-Soviet Central Asian states and Russia. The three Central Asian states that share a border with Afghanistan – Tajikistan, Uzbekistan and Turkmenistan – are mainly concerned about insurgency and terrorism originating from or sustained through bases and safe havens in Afghanistan. This is especially the case as the governments in all five Central Asian countries are committed to preserving secular states and are anxious about the threat of Islamist movements. In addition, Afghanistan represents a possible transport route for these countries to export their raw materials to new markets, while also bypassing their two larger neighbours, Russia and China.

Nigel Inkster, Christian Le Mière and Gary Li, in their chapter on China, argue that until recently relations with Afghanistan were extremely limited. Strategically, Beijing's dominant aim has been to prevent a militant Islamism incubated in the tribal areas of Pakistan and southeastern Afghanistan being exported to the Uighur population of Xinjiang. However, beyond this direct threat, China also worries about the substantial NATO presence in Afghanistan and the US bases in Kyrgyzstan and Uzbekistan being used to encircle it. It has also used its alliance with Pakistan as a counter-balance to its rival India. Beyond the strategic, China has a rapidly increasing economic interest in Afghanistan focused on securing access to its mineral resources. To help secure this myriad of interests China has given a limited amount of development aid to Kabul.

In his second chapter in the regional section, Rahul Roy-Chaudhury examines India's evolving policy towards Afghanistan. New Delhi was an active participant in the 2001 Bonn conference and used its influence to help Karzai gain the presidency. After regime change, India became increasing worried that Islamabad was seeking to engineer a political settlement that would bring the Taliban back into government and further Pakistan's influence in the country once again. It also worried that Afghanistan's weakness could lead to civil war and fragmentation. India has significant 'soft power' in Afghanistan but its attempts to engage systematically, with a leading emphasis on reconstruction work, have made it a target of increased terrorism. In response, the Indian government has curtailed its economic activity and sought to assure Pakistan that its intentions are benign in nature.

In the final regional chapter, Emile Hokayem argues that Saudi Arabia perceives Afghanistan through 'three interlinked prisms: its religious agenda, its relations with Pakistan and its rivalry with Iran'. Riyadh discreetly aided the Taliban's rise to power and consequently there is some evidence to suggest it could use its influence to facilitate peace talks between the government in Kabul and the exiled Taliban leadership, the Quetta Shura. However, Riyadh's relations with the Taliban while in government soured over the group's continued protection of Osama bin Laden as he used his base in Afghanistan to attack Saudi Arabia. While ambiguity continues to surround the Taliban's relations with al-Qaeda, Riyadh will have difficulty improving its relations with the Quetta Shura to the point where it could became an effective mediator.

The book concludes by laying out the arguments for the cautious optimism that emerges from its 12 substantive chapters. The stability of Afghanistan is far from certain and could easily be undermined by mistaken policies pursued in Kabul, Washington or any of the regional states. The conclusions highlight the policy options available to the US, NATO and the international community for encouraging the political, military and economic stability of the country after 2014.

The project has been undertaken in the midst of a complex transition in Afghanistan that is subject to myriad variables. The book seeks to assess the chief variables and, on the basis of that evidence, to provide an assessment of the country's future trajectory. Considering the complexities, the task is a difficult one, but, for the same reason, is worthwhile too. The goal is to draw dispassionate conclusions. Our principal finding is that Afghanistan faces an arduous transition, but not one that is doomed to failure.

CHAPTER ONE

The road to Lisbon

Alexander Nicoll

Nine years after Western countries launched a military intervention in Afghanistan, the leaders of the NATO Alliance met in Lisbon, Portugal, to discuss the future of what had become a troubled mission. Although foreign troops deployed to improve security in the country had grown to a peak of 138,000, it was hard to believe that Afghans were becoming safer. Conflict-related civilian casualties increased by 15% in 2010, as did the number of bomb explosions and suicide attacks carried out by Taliban insurgents.[1] But the appetite of NATO's political leaders to prolong the conflict was apparently on the wane. At their November 2010 meeting in Lisbon, they decided that responsibility for security would be handed to Afghan forces by the end of 2014, with the transition due to begin in 2011.

The summit communiqué said: 'Transition will be conditions-based, not calendar-driven, and will not equate to withdrawal of ISAF troops.'[2] However, David Cameron, prime minister of the United Kingdom, the second-largest contributor of troops to the NATO-led International Security Assistance Force (ISAF), was clear: 'The commitment we have entered into to transfer the lead responsibility for security to the Afghan government by the end of 2014 will pave the way for British combat troops to be out of Afghanistan by 2015. This is a firm deadline which we will meet.'[3] Some other countries had already announced that they would withdraw combat troops. A general move towards the exit could be seen as a logical consequence of the December 2009 announcement by US President Barack Obama that American troops would start to be pulled out in mid-2011.

As 2011 began, the optimistic message from the US military, with 98,000 personnel in Afghanistan, was that increased numbers of troops and aggressive tactics were finally taking a toll on the insurgency. The Pentagon believed that only after the American presence had been sharply increased by the dispatch of more than 60,000 additional troops during 2009 and 2010 did commanders have the resources to execute the counter-insurgency strategy that they believed was the key to success. In a message to his troops in early 2011, US Army General David Petraeus, the ISAF commander and the author of the strategy, said the downward security spiral had been halted during 2010 and that ISAF and Afghan forces had 'inflicted enormous losses' on mid-level insurgent leaders.[4]

Yet the statistics were not promising. A quarterly report on Afghanistan by United Nations Secretary-General Ban Ki-moon, delivered in December 2010, noted that the number of reported 'security incidents' was 66% higher than in the same period a year before. Although the increased 'tempo and scope' of military operations had resulted in the killing and arrest of 'a high number' of mid-level Taliban fighters, the secretary-general wrote that 'anti-government elements were able to sustain high levels of activity in areas into which they had recently expanded, in the north and the northeast'. In other words, the insurgency was spreading. Meanwhile, the use of improvised explosive devices (IEDs) continued to increase, assassinations reached unprecedented levels, and there were an average of three suicide attacks per week. According to the UN's assistance mission in Afghanistan (UNAMA), 2010 saw 2,777 conflict-related civilian deaths and 4,343 injuries, of which more than 75% were caused by insurgents – a 28% increase on the previous year. (For more information on casualties, see Strategic Geography 'Coalition and civilian casualties', p. vi.) There had also been 'widespread fraud and irregularities' in the September parliamentary elections.[5]

The difficulties of 2011 were not at all what had been expected in the months after the fall of the Taliban regime in November 2001. Then, the movement's leaders had seemed to melt away, allowing the forces of the Northern Alliance, a grouping of warlords backed by US bombers and special-operations soldiers, to enter the capital Kabul unopposed. The task of the international community at that point seemed to be to curb the warlords' competing aspirations and nurture the development of a stable government structure, supported by a minimal foreign military presence. However, the Taliban's decision to fall back, regroup and embark on a guerrilla campaign would have been familiar – and ominous – to previous armies who had ventured into Afghanistan over the centuries.

From the start, defence officials in Washington were wary of US military involvement. Paul Wolfowitz, then-deputy secretary of defense, said in November 2001:

> In fact, one of the lessons of Afghanistan's history, which we've tried to apply in this campaign, is 'if you're a foreigner, try not to go in'. If you go in, don't stay too long, because they don't tend to like any foreigners who stay too long.[6]

While it was not true that foreign armies had always failed to subdue the peoples inhabiting what is now Afghanistan, thousands of foreign soldiers – especially British and Russian – have died on Afghan soil. Boston University's Thomas Barfield writes: 'The difficulties that Alexander the Great faced in fighting the mountain tribes in the Kunar Valley in the fourth century BC[E] were not that much different from those faced by the Americans there in the twenty-first century, except that the former dropped boulders and the latter shot rockets from their mountain perches.'[7] And yet, in spite of the lessons of history, modern Western militaries became embroiled in a conflict from which there was no easy exit and in which success was hard to define, let alone to achieve.

The Taliban expelled

Even by the standards of Afghanistan's turbulent and war-torn history, the three decades leading up to the US-led intervention had been tortured and bloody. They had encompassed a republican *coup d'état* against a long-established monarchy in 1973; a communist takeover in 1978; invasion by the Soviet Union in 1979; a ten-year guerrilla war ending with withdrawal of the invader; and years of brutal factional conflict leading to the rise of the Islamist Taliban movement, which took power in 1996. The involvement of Arab jihadists such as Osama bin Laden in the Afghans' struggle against the Soviets in the 1980s had led to the country being used in the late 1990s as a safe haven and training base by bin Laden's al-Qaeda organisation, with the blessing of the Taliban regime. Within a month of al-Qaeda's terrorist attacks on the United States on 11 September 2001, in which 3,000 people were killed, Afghanistan came under attack from bomber aircraft. It was President George W. Bush's first act in his 'Global War on Terror'.

The US quickly decided that it would seek to work with the warlords, though it was handicapped by the fact that al-Qaeda had sought to blunt the likely response to the 9/11 attacks by assassinating Ahmad Shah Massoud, the Northern Alliance's most formidable military commander, on 9 September. The warlords – mostly ethnic Tajiks and Uzbeks – retained their capacity and the militias at their disposal to take revenge on the Pashtun Taliban that had wrested power from them. Central Intelligence Agency (CIA) personnel were inserted to forge alliances with the Northern Alliance leaders, to fund and coordinate the assault on the Taliban, and to build the components of a multi-ethnic government that could replace it in Kabul.[8] A combination of these tactics and air-strikes, many directed by US personnel on the ground, brought about the fall of Mazar-e-Sharif by 9 November, swiftly followed by other northern cities, including Kabul. The Taliban and foreign fighters made a stand at Kunduz until it fell on 22 November. Attention then switched to the Taliban's southern heartland, where the city of Kandahar fell to a combination of US forces and militia groups, one of which was headed by Hamid Karzai, previously an exile in Pakistan. The Taliban's leader, Mullah Omar, fled to Pakistan. In December, according to accounts by people who took part in an attack on a mountain hideout at Tora Bora, close to the border with Pakistan, al-Qaeda leaders, including bin Laden, were cornered, but managed to escape into Pakistan. The Taliban regime was removed within a short space of time and with a relatively small military presence on the ground.

Meanwhile, the Northern Alliance of warlords had taken control in Kabul amid intensive international diplomatic efforts to deal with the aftermath of the conflict. Representatives of all the main groups in Afghanistan, with the exception of the Taliban, assembled in Bonn, Germany, under the auspices of the United Nations. Pashtun tribes were represented by the Rome group, centred around the exiled former king, Mohammed Zahir Shah, then living in the Italian capital. While the warlords had, with the help of the United States, seized power and had tens of thousands of troops, foreign governments saw it as important that the country's new temporary leader be a Pashtun. The conference therefore settled upon Karzai, who belonged to the Rome group, but was seen as weak by the Northern Alliance. Under the Bonn Agreement reached on 5 December, he was to head a 30-member interim administration which would govern while preparations were made for a Loya Jirga, or gathering of elders, who would elect a transitional administration. This in turn would govern while overseeing the writing of a new constitution. Once the constitution was approved by another Loya Jirga, elections would be held by mid-2004.[9] The parties also agreed to invite an international force to bolster security and to help in establishing and training new armed forces. The International Security Assistance Force (carefully named so as to be clear that it was not responsible for keeping the peace) began to be deployed under British command on 20 December, under UN Security Council Resolution 1386. The resolution strictly mandated it 'to assist the Afghan Interim Authority in the maintenance of security in Kabul and its surrounding areas'.[10] The interim administration took power on 22 December.

Thus, just 102 days after the 9/11 attacks, Afghanistan's government had been ousted and replaced, and the country had been wrenched on to a path towards democracy. Billions of dollars of external assistance had been pledged. Al-Qaeda's leaders had been expelled from the country, and the Taliban had disappeared. These were extraordinary achievements. However, the warlords of the Northern Alliance held sway in Kabul, holding top cabinet positions. The defence portfolio, for example, was given to Mohammad Qasim Fahim, who had 30,000 troops in the capital, compared with ISAF's target strength of just 4,800. As so often, the seeds of future problems were contained in the initial arrangements. The conflicting interests and priorities of both domestic and foreign partici-pants eventually set Afghanistan on the road to its present state of disarray.

Most importantly, the primary interest of the United States military in Afghanistan in 2001 and 2002 was to pursue al-Qaeda and the remnants of the Taliban. Under the leadership of Donald Rumsfeld as secretary of defense and with a number of neo-conservative Republican officials in its senior echelons, the Pentagon favoured using American military power for decisive effect, but leaving responsibility for the aftermath to Afghanistan. Past involvements in Vietnam and the Balkans had convinced these officials – and many military officers – that US armed forces should be involved in state reconstruction only to the least possible degree. Other parts of the American govern-ment, and particularly the State Department, favoured devoting greater resources to assist in the rebuilding of Afghanistan. But the difference in this case may have been more of scale than of fundamental approach: according to accounts of the policy debate, the main practical difference on military matters appears to have been whether international troops should be deployed to bolster security in cities other than Kabul. In any case, Afghanistan rapidly became almost incidental to the post-9/11 policy discussions of the Bush administration, in which key figures steered attention towards what they considered to be a much greater priority: removing Iraqi leader Saddam Hussein. Political scientist Seth G. Jones quotes Richard Armitage, deputy secretary of state at the time:

Afghanistan was really an accidental war for much of the Administration. No one wanted to do it. And once it became clear the Taliban was likely to fall, senior Pentagon officials wanted to turn to Iraq as quickly as possible.[11]

The military dispositions as of early 2002 began were therefore as follows: the British-led ISAF, building up to modest strength but with a remit only to help in assuring security in the capital; some 9,000 American troops deployed under *Operation Enduring Freedom*, based at Bagram air base north of Kabul and focused on pursuing al-Qaeda and the Taliban in the eastern and southern mountainous areas along the border with Pakistan; and elsewhere in the country, the still-active forces of rival warlords, each keen to advance their own positions in the new government arrangements. Most importantly, the Northern Alliance leaders lacked sway in Pashtun-dominated areas, and it was not clear that Karzai had the authority to exert the government's writ there. The entire Pashtun area lacked established leaders, having previously been dominated by the Taliban, which had temporarily supervened old tribal hierarchies because it had a strong leadership structure.

Power balances

While the arrangements agreed in Bonn proceeded as planned, the first years after foreign intervention were characterised by jostling between the new leaders, each keen to consolidate his local power base. The planned constitutional changes were unprecedented, but subsequent developments represented a reversion to historical pattern.

From 1747 to 1978, Afghanistan had been ruled by Pashtun leaders from the Durrani tribes. Each dynastic monarch's rule depended on securing supremacy first over his own tribal rivals and then over other tribes, ethnic groups and territories, which in 1747 extended well beyond the country's present borders.

Pashtuns are estimated to make up some 42% of Afghanistan's present population, Tajiks 27%, Hazaras 9% and Uzbeks and Turkmens a total of 13%, with smaller groups making up the remainder (see Strategic Geography, p. x).[12] With this diverse ethnic make-up, and in an overwhelmingly rural country of peasant smallholdings, in which much of the terrain was mountainous and remote, the concept of central government has almost never been as concrete as in other nation-states. Rather, it was a matter of ensuring loyalty. Dominance meant maintaining the fealty of the main cities, where local rulers tended to be similarly embroiled in their own battles for control. There was a degree of federalism involved, since it was not possible to exercise actual control over every part of the country.

Only one ruler, Abdul Rahman Khan, emir from 1880 to 1901, had succeeded in imposing strict control over the whole country, and he did so with utter ruthlessness and with the backing of substantial subsidies and weapons supplies from the British. He established elements of the state that lasted for a century, but Barnett R. Rubin summarises his position as follows: 'A Pashtun ruler using external resources to reign over an ethnically heterogeneous society while manipulating that social segmentation to weaken society's resistance.'[13] Later, as Russian and American aid to Afghan monarchs replaced that of the British, the traditional mode of government persisted. For Durrani rulers, this was never a matter of securing the support of ordinary Afghans and mobilising them into a cohesive state system. According to Rubin:

> The political elite did not rule the people of Afghanistan by representing them and managing conflicts ... Rather than incorporating the various sectors of the population into a common national political system, the political elite acted as an ethnically stratified hier-

archy of intermediaries between the foreign powers providing the resources and the groups receiving the largess of patronage.

For thousands of years, Afghanistan had been a target for foreign invaders because it was located on the route to the famed riches of India. But it came especially into focus in the nineteenth century as it stood between the competing imperial aspirations of Russia and Britain, and thus became the chessboard for their 'Great Game'.[14] It was because of Britain's constant concern that Russia had designs on its Indian empire that a British/Indian army advanced into Afghanistan in 1839 with the intention of creating a buffer. Under brief British occupation, state structures were imposed that had the effect of drastically cutting payments to tribal leaders, and this prompted a revolt, particularly by Ghilzai Pashtun tribes in the southeast and Kohistani Tajiks from north of Kabul. The result of the ensuing rebellion against the 'infidels' was ignominious retreat in 1842 and a massacre from which, as the story goes, only one British officer out of an army of 4,500 British and Indians made it back to India alive (though in fact some others were captured and survived). In spite of this humiliation, however, Afghanistan henceforth came under British influence as successive Durrani rulers – their position undermined by family feuding and by the role that other tribes had played in the rebellion – received British aid to stay in power.

Britain's second military venture into Afghanistan followed a similar course. Provoked again by Russian diplomatic forays, Britain took Kabul in 1879 and imposed direct rule, but again faced a rebellion by the Ghilzai Pashtuns and Kohistani Tajiks. Looking again to withdraw, the British unsuccessfully tried to divide the country into two parts, north and south, and the outcome of ensuing manoeuvres among tribal strongmen was the emergence of Abdul Rahman as ruler. He depended on British support, and thus the indirect (as opposed to the 'forward') approach to controlling Afghanistan won a long-running policy debate in London and Calcutta. Afghanistan could not be coloured on a map as part of the British empire, but was a client state as far as its external dealings were concerned.

Though Abdul Rahman proceeded without scruple to establish firm control over all Afghanistan's tribes and ethnic groups, the two Anglo-Afghan wars had shown the potential of tribal forces to undermine the Durrani Pashtun monarchy. Rubin writes:

> During both British invasions, tribalism re-emerged as a potent force that weakened the state in its battle with the khans for social control. The balance of power between state and tribes – in contemporary terms, the degree of autonomy of the state from social forces – repeatedly shifted, often because of changes in the relations between the state and the international system.[15]

Abdul Rahman – and his son and grandson who followed him – made extensive efforts first to unify and centralise the state and later to modernise it. He increased taxes on the Ghilzai Pashtuns, and inflicted extraordinary losses in defeating their ensuing revolt. He then established control over the Uzbek/ Tajik north by defeating a cousin on the battlefield. His army subdued the Hazaras, who are Shia and occupy mountainous central Afghanistan, and the then-non-Muslim Kafir community in the east. While dependent on British money and arms, he cast himself as an Islamic leader protecting Afghanistan from foreign infidels – although Britain, by imposing in 1893 the Durand Line, which is still the de facto border, deprived him of territories that now form part of Pakistan. Meanwhile, he sought to neutralise future threats to his own dynasty from within his own tribe, and to reinforce the supremacy of the Pashtuns, crushing the power of regional leaders. He thus was the first ruler of the nation-state that exists today. Barfield, however, questions the degree to which the country was fundamentally changed. The economy, he notes, remained subsistence-based, and the social structure of distinct kinship groups at village and provincial level (*qawms*) was unchanged. Barfield writes:

> Afghan rulers were historically forced to work within a political system that was more federal and consultative. Though this older system of politics did appear to have been wiped out during Abdul Rahman's rule, it had not really disappeared but rather reappeared in new guises. For the next century and more, successive regimes that attempted to model their governments and style of rulership on that of Abdul Rahman's inevitably found themselves challenged by this tradition – in some cases, resulting in state collapse.[16]

These themes – the separation of the people from rulers in Kabul, and the tribal structures that gave local power – were to reassert themselves in the twenty-first century. In 2001 Karzai, a Durrani and the leader of the Popalzai tribe, came to office not through bloody feuding with fellow Pashtuns, but as a result of a selection process over which the United States had a very strong influence. His father had been assassinated by the Taliban in 1999 and he had worked in the anti-Taliban resistance from Pakistan. From the start he faced a difficult struggle to win authority over the Northern Alliance leaders who dominated his cabinet, as well as other Pashtuns. As Amin Saikal wrote, 'Karzai himself has no national standing. Before his assumption, as a compromise choice, of the interim leadership, few people inside and outside Afghanistan had ever heard of him ... He cannot claim acceptance either among non-Pashtun Afghanis, or among the tribally heterogeneous Pashtuns.'[17] He was certainly not in a position to impose control as had Abdul Rahman, but he did have the substantial backing of the United States and other countries, as well as military support, and he had considerable scope to exert patronage to build his authority and government. He was duly elected head of the transitional administration in 2002 and then became the first elected president of Afghanistan in 2004.

In the aftermath of regime change, there was a massive return of refugees from Pakistan and Iran and a general outpouring of enthusiasm for the freedom that citizens could now enjoy, at least in Kabul and other relatively well-governed cities.[18] In addition to the steps towards a new democratic constitution and state structures, a new Afghan National Army (ANA) was founded. A programme of disarming and demobilising fighters was launched, a new currency introduced and a development programme begun. But there was dissatisfaction with the speed of disbursement of foreign aid, and with the low proportion of aid money that reached Afghans, as well as with the amount that was given to be distributed by the Afghan government rather than directly by foreign agencies. The first two years were also characterised by frequent armed clashes and factional fighting in the north and west between the forces of rival warlords. The country's opium crop, an important financing source for warlords, began a steady climb. Meanwhile, in the south and east the United States pursued Taliban and al-Qaeda elements, for example in *Operation Anaconda* in March 2002 when US and coalition forces attacked fighters who had regrouped in the mountains at Shah-e-Kot near Gardez, inflicting heavy casualties. In July 2002, a prominent anti-Taliban Pashtun leader from the east, Abdul Qadir, who had been made a vice president in the transitional government, was assassinated by gunmen. By 2003, the number of attacks on foreign troops, aid workers, Afghan officials and teachers was rising. The Taliban had returned.

Taliban reborn

The Taliban (meaning 'seekers' or 'students') had sprung up in Kandahar in 1994, apparently in spontaneous disgust at the brutal civil war and power struggles that followed the withdrawal of Soviet troops in 1989 and the fall in 1992 of the Moscow-backed Najibullah regime. During the Soviet occupation, the United States and other countries had heavily funded seven mujahadeen resistance groups based in Pakistan. These parties were in no sense unified. Each of them was given recognition by Pakistan's Inter-Services Intelligence (ISI) directorate – and thus access to American funding and other support – purely with Pakistan's own regional objectives in mind. Among these goals – apart from stopping the spread of communism – were the prevention of any Indian influence in Afghanistan, support for Muslim fundamentalism, and the heading off of any possibility of the creation of a 'Pashtunistan' nation which would subsume Pakistan's own substantial Pashtun population. For the backers of the mujahadeen groups, building a strong post-war Afghanistan was a second-order priority, and after the fall of Mohammed Najibullah in 1992, the flow of aid from both Russia and the United States to Afghanistan was cut off.

The mujahadeen groups subsequently fell into years of warring among themselves. This left the way open for the Taliban, especially in Kandahar. Peter Marsden writes: 'Kandahar experienced virtual anarchy from 1992 until the Taliban takeover as the various Mujahedin commanders fought for control of the streets and reduced much of the city to rubble.'[19] Mullah Omar, the Taliban leader, who had fought (and lost an eye) with one of the mujahadeen groups, led a movement to bring purity and Islamic justice – a popular message in the Pashtun south-ern provinces that the Taliban quickly came to dominate. The goal was to rid the country of the mujahadeen commanders who, Omar said, were 'corrupt, Western-oriented time-servers' and to establish an Islamic state practising sharia law.[20] Many thousands of Afghan children had been brought up in refugee camps and were educated in traditionalist Pakistani madras-sas where teaching was based on a strict interpretation of the Koran. These proved a plentiful recruiting base for the Taliban. As the Taliban took over government in Kabul in 1996, the preoccupation with purity was manifested in, among other things, strict codes for dress and beards, a ban on music, and restrictions on the education, employment and behaviour of women. Punishments were severe.

Just as the country's recent chaotic history – especially in the Pashtun south – had made it fertile ground for the Taliban in the mid-1990s, so too did weak government and insecurity lay it open to the revival of the Taliban after the installation of Karzai's government. Antonio Giustozzi recounts how, at the national, provincial and local level, many official posts were given by Karzai to militia commanders and strongmen who needed to reward their own followers with allocations of yet more jobs and patronage so as to consolidate their positions. The people promoted by Karzai would jostle with each other – again, Kandahar was an example as three strongmen, includ-ing Karzai's brother Ahmad Wali Karzai, constantly struggled for control over the city. Giustozzi writes:

> Afghanistan's sub-national administration developed after 2001 strong patrimonial traits, looking even

less institutionalised than that of the Taliban, of the leftist governments of the 1980s and of the monarchy and republic in the 1960s and 1970s. The system was geared for accommodating strongmen and warlords endowed with their own power base and resources, not for allowing functionaries loyal to the central government to consolidate the influence of Kabul.[21]

If perennially weak government was one factor, so too was the continuing availability of young Afghan men educated in Pakistani madrassas. Those brought up in refugee camps were much less likely to be respectful to village and tribal elders. The Taliban has steadily grown since 2002 following a recruitment drive instigated by Mullah Omar, the head of the group's leadership in exile, the Quetta Shura, named after its base in the capital of Pakistan's Baluchistan province. According to Giustozzi, by 2006 the Taliban constituted a 'complex opposition alliance' comprising ideologically driven madrassa students; jihadist, xenophobic recruits provided by village mullahs; allies among local communities; and some mercenaries.[22] A series of interviews with Taliban fighters in districts around Kandahar, carried out for the Toronto newspaper *Globe and Mail* in 2007, reveals a variety of motivations, including a desire to drive out the non-Muslim foreigners, inspiration by deaths in families or of other civilians caused by foreign bombing attacks, and the need to protect opium crops, which were their families' sources of income, from official eradication efforts.[23] While generalisations about the rise of the Taliban are dangerous, the areas in which it was able to establish a strong presence most easily appear to have been those where government was ineffective, tribal structures were undermined, infighting among strongmen and tribal groups was persistent, educational standards were lowest, and where there were particular grievances, for example over eradication of poppies. In some areas, all of these conditions could be found. But the Taliban's rate of progress through the country was not uniform (as illustrated by 'The Taliban strikes back', Strategic Geography, p. ii), and varied from district to district.

The way that the Taliban operated was also not uniform, depending on the precise group involved and the circumstances and logistics in each area. David Kilcullen argues that the Taliban are not a unified group, and are also not the only group to contend with. He writes: 'Any attempt to describe a "Taliban operating system" is to some extent a caricature, a distorted snapshot of one stage in the constant and rapid evolutionary process of a highly adaptive social movement.'[24] Nevertheless, it appears that a broad description can be given of the tactics used by the insurgents to increase their influence. Small teams were sent across the border from Pakistan to spread propaganda in villages and threaten those opposed to them, often with the use of 'night letters', threatening messages delivered to a property during the night. A campaign of assassinations of people accused of collaborating with the government or foreign forces began in 2003. Among the targets were officials, clerics, doctors, teachers, judges and NGO workers. The Taliban repeatedly attacked the posts of Afghan police, army and pro-government militias. It employed suicide bomb attacks. Together, these tactics were intended to demoralise the Afghans ranged against them. In addition, the Taliban continually stepped up the level of attacks on foreign troops, with growing use of IEDs. While the insurgents suffered heavy casualties from ISAF and US military action, air-strikes against them also caused civilian casualties, further boosting the insurgents' cause. Core Taliban fighters were trained in Pakistan and sent over the border in units, and returned there at the end of their assignments. As Kilcullen notes, these would be foreign to any area in which they were fighting, unless it happened to be their home valley.[25] They therefore cut across tribal networks, as members of units could come from different tribes, and could even include non-Afghans, such as Chechens or Arabs. Other fighters were recruited locally in villages and assisted the core groups. The next stage, once the Taliban had sufficient presence in an area and was confident of adequate local support, was to set up a 'shadow' administration. The most important element of this was a judicial system, which the government in Kabul had failed to establish. Giustozzi writes that, although Taliban justice was rough, 'the system offered a greater degree of predictability and reliability than the arbitrary behaviour of government security forces'.[26] Meanwhile, the Taliban carried out an extensive propaganda campaign using CDs and DVDs, as well as contacts with the media – a big change from its distaste for Western technology in the 1990s.[27]

The nature of the insurgent groups and their links with Pakistan will be addressed later in this book. As well as the Taliban per se, the insurgency includes two groups which date from the anti-Soviet resistance: the Haqqani network, claimed to be responsible for a number of high-profile attacks; and Hezb-i-Islami Gulbuddin, led by Gulbuddin Hekmatyr, who held the title of prime minister during the post-Soviet civil war period. While the precise associations between these three – and with al-Qaeda, whose leaders are believed to be still in Pakistan – are hard to determine and probably ever-shifting, the nature of the links seems less relevant if an attempt is being made to assess the overall spread of the insurgency. The fact is that the insurgency has spread from small beginnings in 2002 to affect large parts of Afghanistan – initially from border areas close to Pakistan, then through the Pashtun-dominated areas of the south and east, and later more widely to parts of the north and west.

As the insurgency grew, certain positive steps were also taken. The passage to democracy set out in the Bonn Agreement was successfully accomplished. To some extent, the power of the Northern Alliance warlords within the government was blunted, for example as Karzai managed to shift Ismail Khan, for long the dominant figure in Herat, out of the provincial governorship and into a ministerial post in Kabul. The Tajik leader Fahim, appointed defence minister in 2001, was moved out of the vice presidency and the defence ministry in 2004. Efforts were made to improve infrastructure, for example with the paving of the road from Kabul to Kandahar, and there was some progress elsewhere in development, although continuing inadequacies in the aid process were evident. However, the pace of growth of the Afghan National Army was slow and the police, lacking training, were ineffective.

Escalation

While foreign diplomats, military officers and aid workers were aware of the developing insurgency, it was not until 2006 that violence erupted to a sufficient extent to capture the attention in international capitals, where the chief preoccupation was the war in Iraq. By then, there had already been modest increases in the number of foreign troops, and an extension of responsibilities. US forces deployed under *Enduring Freedom* fluctuated around 20,000 from 2004 to 2006, and Washington was planning to reduce the numbers as other countries assumed more responsibilities. In 2003, NATO was given command of ISAF, and the force's mandate was expanded beyond Kabul.[28] In 2004, its operations were extended to northern provinces, in 2005 to the west, in 2006 to the south and the east. This last move gave ISAF responsibility for the whole country and meant the absorption of most of the American troops under NATO command. The number of

ISAF troops rose to 6,250 in 2004, and 8,500 in 2005. Both ISAF and the US established a series of Provincial Reconstruction Teams intended to boost development in particular areas with military support.

From 2006, the campaign entered a new phase as the Taliban's build-up of influence across the south and east enabled it to step up its attacks significantly, while ISAF also increased the scope of its activities. In particular, ISAF marked its assumption of responsibility for the south with the addition of some 10,000 troops and a substantial expansion into areas that had seen few, if any, foreign troops and very little progress in terms of government, police presence and development – and in which the Taliban was already well established. British troops were sent to Helmand province, Canadian forces to Kandahar, and Dutch and Australian troops to Uruzgan. John Reid, the UK defence minister at the time, sought to draw a distinction between the task of the US-led coalition, which had been to 'go and chase and kill the terrorists who did so much to destroy the twin towers in that terrible attack', and the UK mission in Helmand. 'We would be perfectly happy to leave in three years and without firing one shot because our job is to protect the reconstruction,' said Reid – a remark for which he was later ridiculed. However, he also made clear that this was a dangerous mission as 'terrorists will want to destroy the economy and the legitimate trade and the government that we are helping to build up'.[29] The growing presence of the Taliban throughout the south would certainly make ISAF's task a challenging one. For example, the *New York Times* reported in May 2006 that Uruzgan, Helmand and Kandahar provinces 'have been increasingly overrun by militants this year, as large groups of Taliban are reportedly moving through the countryside, intimidating villagers, ambushing vehicles, and spoiling for a fight with coalition or Afghan forces. Insurgents also have the run of parts of Zabul, Ghazni and Paktika provinces to the southeast, and have increased ambushes on the main Kabul–Kandahar highway'.[30]

As the Taliban stepped up attacks with IEDs and suicide bombers, as well as assassinations and kidnappings, some areas saw intense combat in 2006 between Taliban fighters and coalition forces. There were battles in districts near the city of Kandahar, and British forces became embroiled in efforts to hold small garrisons in towns within Helmand province. This escalation was set against a background of continuing political disquiet in many Western countries about the war in Iraq, and this negatively influenced the cohesiveness of foreign forces in Afghanistan. As the demands of combat grew, differences between NATO allies over 'caveats' – restrictions placed by some European governments on the activities in which their troops were authorised to engage – became rancorous. Meanwhile, there were mounting frustrations among Afghans about corruption in government, the slow pace of development, and the presence of foreign troops – for example, riots broke out in Kabul on 29 May 2006 after a traffic accident involving a US military truck.[31]

The heightened combat prompted arguments both within NATO governments and between NATO allies about strategy and tactics. Commanders on the ground were contending with unrealistic demands from their capitals to promote reconstruction and development, which they were unable to execute because of the growing insurgency, and the absence of aid officials, who were deterred by the lack of security.[32] Where they were able to build links with local elders, military officers very often found themselves in the midst of tribal rivalries that could obstruct their efforts. American commanders had access to substantial amounts of money that they could direct towards reconstruction projects, and were able to use these funds to advance tactical goals, but improvements that were made often could not be sustained.[33] NATO leaders, meeting in Riga, Latvia, in November 2006, acknowledged all these problems in agreeing that a 'comprehensive approach' was needed, 'involving a wide spectrum of civil and military instruments, while fully respecting mandates and autonomy of decisions of all actors'.[34] However, the realities of the situation in Afghanistan, with growing violence, absence of effective central and provincial government, a lack of unified military strategy, and the difficulties of channelling aid, meant that such an approach was almost impossible to put into practice.

The years after 2006 saw continuing expansion of the conflict with rising incidence of violence, a spread of violence to areas of Afghanistan further away from Pakistan, and growing casualties among Afghans and foreign troops. There was a series of high-profile Taliban attacks, including a bomb at Bagram air base while US Vice President Dick Cheney was visiting it; the kidnap of 23 South Korean Christian missionaries, two of whom were killed, leading to the withdrawal of all 200 Korean troops from the coalition force; the killing of scores of people by suicide bombers, for example at a dogfight near Kandahar; an attack on the Serena Hotel in Kabul, popular among foreigners, in which six people were killed; and a bomb at the Indian embassy in Kabul, in which more than 50 people were killed. In April 2008, gunmen opened fire on Karzai at a military parade in Kabul, killing three people but failing to hit him.

Foreign military forces did score successes, such as the killing in 2007 of Mullah Dadullah, a senior Taliban military commander. Their numbers increased to a total of about 65,000 by the end of 2008. But as US President Barack Obama entered office in January 2009, there was no sign that the insurgency was being quelled. A new approach was needed.

Strategy change

Obama had campaigned on ending the war in Iraq, which he had opposed. It was very important for him to achieve a measurable result in the war in Afghanistan, which he had supported. He immediately dispatched 17,000 more troops to add to the 36,000 Americans already deployed, and ordered a strategy review.

While the conclusions of the initial review were quickly to be overtaken by events, it did contain several significant elements. The first was to bring the mission back to its original objective. The review stated that 'the core goal of the US must be to disrupt, dismantle and defeat al-Qaeda and its safe havens in Pakistan'. Secondly, the review explicitly linked Afghanistan and Pakistan as key to achieving US policy goals. Thirdly, it did not set defeat of the Taliban as a target. Rather, it said that 'the Taliban's momentum must be reversed' and that the 'priority missions' of US military forces were, firstly, to secure the south and east so that al-Qaeda could not return and the Afghan government could exert control of these areas; and secondly, to mentor Afghan security forces so that they could take the lead and foreign forces could wind down their operations.[35] These proved to be enduring themes as Washington's policy altered again.

The trigger for the next change was the appointment of a new military commander. By now, all foreign troops in Afghanistan fell under an American general as ISAF commander. General David McKiernan was replaced in June by General Stanley McChrystal, a former special-forces officer. He initiated his own review of the campaign, and it quickly became apparent that he would argue that he could only achieve success with the addition of a large number of troops. McChrystal embraced the counter-insurgency doctrine written – in light of experience in Iraq – by General David Petraeus, then head of Central

Command, the regional military command for the Middle East and Central Asia. In a memo leaked to the *Washington Post* in September 2009, McChrystal said the campaign was under-resourced. 'Almost every aspect of our collective effort and associated resourcing has lagged a growing insurgency,' he wrote. ISAF's strategy must be 'credible to, and sustainable by, Afghans'. The key to its approach would be 'protecting the population' – long an important tenet of counter-insurgency thinking. Therefore, ISAF needed to study more closely the peoples of Afghanistan 'whose needs, identities and grievances vary from province to province and from valley to valley'. McChrystal wrote: 'We have operated in a manner that distances us – physically and psychologically – from the people we seek to protect.' The pursuit of 'tactical wins', he said could cause civilian casualties or unnecessary damage, which would be self-defeating.[36]

McChrystal's assessment had several immediate results. The first was to reduce the use of 'kinetic' tactics – including air-strikes – that risked civilian casualties, one of the main factors inciting local hostility. The second was to make ISAF much more unified under a strong central command, replacing a looser structure in which troops of different nations had essentially pursued their own strategies in the provinces for which they were responsible. By far the most important element, however, was McChrystal's request for 40,000 additional American troops. This, according to military officers, would enable ISAF to execute the true counter-insurgency approach of 'clear, hold and build', under which areas would be cleared of insurgents and then held so that confidence could be built among local people in the strength and effectiveness of the Afghan government. Previously, the tendency had been to take areas, but then to cede them to the Taliban for lack of the resources needed to hold them.

The commander's request caused an intense policy debate in Washington, in which requests for a range of options from Obama, and contrary views expressed by senior administration officials, were met with implacable resistance from the Pentagon.[37] On 1 December 2009, after three months of discussion, Obama announced that he would send 30,000 more troops to Afghanistan. With several more thousand pledged by other nations, McChrystal obtained almost all that he had asked for.

There remained, however, a number of questions surrounding his strategy. The first was that the entire approach depended on there being credible and effective government at the national and local levels – something that had not existed in Afghanistan for decades, and had never existed there at all in the sense understood in Washington. The Obama administration made no secret of its frustration at levels of corruption, exemplified even as the US review was under way by Karzai's blatant rigging of the 2009 presidential election, from which he emerged the victor. The strategy also depended on the growing strength of the Afghan army and police forces, whose present and future capabilities remain open to question.

Secondly, McChrystal's strategy in itself set very challenging targets. Bob Woodward quotes a member of McChrystal's review team as saying: 'The kind of COIN (counter-insurgency) doctrine that they're talking about requires a level of knowledge that I don't have about my home-town.'[38] Scepticism on this score was reflected in the views of Vice President Joe Biden, who advocated a switch to a policy dubbed 'counter-terrorism plus', under which the emphasis in Afghanistan would be less on combat and more on training Afghan security forces, and Washington would instead put more focus on Pakistan and al-Qaeda. Doubts such as this, as well as the growing unpopularity of the war in Afghanistan, prompted Obama to add an essential caveat to his announcement of a troop surge. Soon after the number of troops reached a peak, they would start to be reduced. By mid-2011, he said, 'our troops will begin to come home. These are the resources that we need to seize the initiative, while building the Afghan capacity that can allow for a responsible transition of our forces out of Afghanistan.'[39]

Thus was the stage set for NATO's decision in November 2010 to set a target date for the end of combat operations. The clear intention was that Afghanistan should not turn into another Vietnam. Yet the plan to seize the initiative was not easy to execute. Efforts in 2009 and 2010 to 'clear, hold and build' in parts of Helmand and Kandahar provinces took longer than ISAF had hoped. In fact there were signs of a return to a more 'kinetic' approach in the wake of McChrystal's removal in June 2010, after he made injudicious remarks to a reporter for *Rolling Stone* magazine, and his replacement by Petraeus. Night raids conducted by special forces were claimed to have killed hundreds of mid-level Taliban commanders. The Taliban were reported to have a presence in almost all provinces of Afghanistan – and, from this position of strength, seemed in no mind to enter into serious discussion about reconciliation or integration into some future government. The situation was not promising: although ISAF troops could win every military encounter in which they engaged, they seemed no closer to achieving success. While foreign politicians, officials and military officers all agreed that the solution to Afghanistan's problems was not a military one, Western countries had been drawn inexorably into a conflict that used up ever-greater resources and inflicted an increasing number of casualties among their troops.

CHAPTER TWO

US policy and Afghanistan

Dana Allin

On 2 May 2011, American Navy SEALs penetrated the walled compound in Pakistan where Osama bin Laden was hiding, and killed him. President Barack Obama's decision to launch the operation was a risky one: there was only indirect evidence that bin Laden was actually in the Abbottabad compound; if the mission had failed, with American deaths and Pakistani victims, Obama would have been pilloried as relentlessly as Jimmy Carter was after an analogous failure 31 years before. But the mission did not fail.

Seven weeks later, Obama announced that 33,000 American troops would be withdrawn from Afghanistan by September 2012. It meant that his bid for re-election would take place after the reversal of America's escalated deployment, announced in late 2009. In his speech, Obama said that 10,000 troops would be leaving before the end of 2011. This was at the accelerated end of the options with which the president had been presented; both the out-going Defense Secretary Robert Gates and Afghan commander David Petraeus, who took up his post as head of the CIA in September 2011, had argued for a slower drawdown.

The killing of bin Laden did not lead directly to this Afghan withdrawal schedule, but it did make it easier. Both fit well with an emerging Obama doctrine of muscular but more narrowly focused pursuit of American interests. That doctrine, which is more readily justified than implemented, rests on Obama's apparent conviction that the United States has become strategically overextended, and needs a process of managed retrenchment that will help it to achieve an economic restoration at home. In this regard, killing bin Laden was an achievement of huge symbolic importance, because the Saudi terrorist had cost the US dearly. Indeed, in the final decade of his life, bin Laden pursued a strategy against America that he had learned – or at least thought he had learned – during the demise of the Soviet Union. Bin Laden's formative experience was in organising support – and fighting in at least one battle – for the anti-Soviet resistance in Afghanistan. 'We, alongside the mujaheddin, bled Russia for ten years, until it went bankrupt,' bin Laden later asserted. This was a somewhat potted version of history – the USSR's collapse had many internal and external causes unrelated to its war in Afghanistan – but it is worth pointing out that bin Laden's narrative was not very different from the one propounded by leading American triumphalists.[1] In any event, as Daveed Gartenstein-Ross and others have noted, the leader of al-Qaeda on more than one occasion made explicit comparisons between his campaign against the Soviets and his plans to bring down the United States. He boasted he would repeat the anti-Soviet success by 'bleeding America to the point of bankruptcy'.[2]

This strategy was based on a highly exaggerated perception of American weaknesses. One must concede, however, that bin Laden had shown shrewd insight into the national psychology that would compel the United States to respond, even if he potentially misjudged how far Washington would go and how much treasure and blood it was able to expend in reaction to the attacks of 11 September 2001. A rough reckoning of the financial costs of war in Iraq and Afghanistan, together with massive upgrades to general counter-terrorism and homeland security, comes to more than $5 trillion over the past decade. Arguably, there were also huge indirect costs stemming, as Ezra Klein has written, from the Federal Reserve's decision to cut interest rates to counter both a possible 'fear-induced recession' as well as high oil prices after the Iraq invasion. 'That decade of loose monetary policy may well have contributed to the credit bubble that crashed the economy in 2007 and 2008.'[3]

These are economic costs; in human terms, the American reaction to 11 September took a heavy toll. The wars in Iraq and Afghanistan caused many deaths and injuries and degraded America's moral reputation at Abu Ghraib and Guantanamo. In broader strategic terms, the United States was weakened by being drawn into land wars in the Middle East and South-Central Asia. The costly American reaction was not precisely inevitable.[4] Still, as Klein observed in reflecting on bin Laden's death, the Saudi terrorist had made 'a smart play against a superpower':

> We [the US] didn't need to respond to 9/11 by trying to reshape the entire Middle East, but we're a super-power, and we think on that scale. We didn't need to respond to failed attempts to smuggle bombs onto airplanes through shoes and shampoo bottles, but we're a superpower, and our tolerance for risk is extremely low.[5]

All in all, bin Laden laid a trap that he could be reasonably confident America would walk into. Assuming office, Obama appeared to be aware of this trap, and determined to get out of it. His speeches and interviews conveyed the necessity to restore a balance between international commitments on the one hand, and American capabilities and resources on the other, a requirement that he thought his predecessor had virtually ignored. At West Point in December 2009, where he announced an escalation of the war in Afghanistan, the president also insisted that war would be fought with a clear understanding of America's limits:

> As President, I refuse to set goals that go beyond our responsibility, our means, or our interests. And I must weigh all of the challenges that our nation faces. I don't have the luxury of committing to just one. Indeed, I'm mindful of the words of President Eisenhower, who – in discussing our national security – said, 'Each proposal must be weighed in the light of a broader consideration: the need to maintain balance in and among national programs'.[6]

This speech was a classic expression of Obama's 'small-c' conservatism, aimed at restoring balance to American foreign policy. The president and his advisers took pains to emphasise the relationship between current and future resources and various kinds of deficits. They stressed the fiscal deficit and the strategic over-commitment embodied in two ongoing wars. They also highlighted a moral deficit embodied in the Bush administration's official sanction of torture, abuses at Abu Ghraib and Guantanamo and the invasion of Iraq, as well as close ally Israel's occupation of the West Bank. They also identified an attention deficit caused by the over-commitment in the Middle East to the detriment of other interests and concerns, especially the key strategic theatre of Asia-Pacific. On top of these deficits, moreover, the United States still faced a terrorism threat that constituted, potentially, a huge uncovered liability. Al-Qaeda was still a strategic-level threat, not so much because of the physical damage it could inflict, but because of political consequences from any significant terrorist attack: it was not just that Obama could lose the next election, but that the United States could egregiously lose its balance, as was perceived to have happened after 2001.

Against al-Qaeda, the new administration from the outset had moved aggressively to ramp up the intelligence war, of which the most tangible products were drone killings in Pakistan, Afghanistan and Yemen. Though legal under the UN mandate that followed 11 September,[7] these targeted killings inevitably caused collateral civilian deaths and a great deal of anti-American anger. Against this contribution to the moral deficit, the administration could be reasonably satisfied that it was keeping al-Qaeda's leadership on the run, its command-and-control degraded and its capability to attack the United States limited.

The shadow of Vietnam

The killing of Osama bin Laden, while not quite constituting the elusive victory in the war on terrorism, was nonetheless an event of huge importance. It raised the hopeful possibility that Americans could now put a weakened al-Qaeda into some kind of reasonable perspective: still a serious security problem, to be sure, but not an existential challenge. The American approach to jihadist terrorism would become, in other words, something closer to the national approaches of various European states and societies that confronted Red Brigade, Red Army Faction, Irish Republican and other terrorist movements from the 1970s through the 1990s.

This is not to deny the important distinctiveness of Islamist terrorism. There are aspects of al-Qaeda that lend themselves to the Bush administration's more heroic call to arms for a 'long war'. Certainly bin Laden himself saw the conflict in these terms and had war aims that were not amenable to a negotiated settlement. The horrific spectacle of al-Qaeda's attack on lower Manhattan and Washington understandably left Americans with the realisation that in this new kind of terrorism, they faced a truly strategic-level foe that had to be defeated, rather than a criminal or security problem to be 'managed'. And there was something to this intuition, at least insofar as the terrorists who destroyed the Twin Towers were known to have been seeking nuclear and biological weapons – and had demonstrated, through the scale of their 9/11 slaughter, that they would not hesitate to use them if they could.

And yet, by consciously waging 'war', America was fighting on the enemy's chosen terrain. Those who argued for a less dramatic definition of the struggle against al-Qaeda were arguing, in part, that this would be a better way to isolate the movement and deprive it of potential support among wider Islamic communities. Obama certainly saw substantial withdrawal from Iraq as necessary, in part because he wanted to stop feeding the jihadist narrative. But with the Iraq War substantially over, and bin Laden now dead, a nagging question became more urgent: what was America doing in Afghanistan?

In trying to approach this question rationally and dispassionately, the Democratic president was, in certain respects, hoist by his and his party's own political petard. Democrats for generations have struggled against voters' judgements that they are not as tough as Republicans when it comes to confronting America's enemies. In criticising George W. Bush's foreign policy in general and the Iraq War in particular, the Democratic politicians took great and repeated pains to emphasise that they were not pacifists. Obama was an Illinois state senator when he opened his speech to a 2002 anti-Iraq War rally in Chicago with the declaration: 'I don't oppose all wars ... What I am opposed to is a dumb war.'[8] It became a standard Democratic argument that one of the big problems with Bush's rush to war in Iraq was that it caused the administration to neglect the more important, and more justified, war in Afghanistan. It was, after all, from Afghanistan that the 11 September attacks were planned and directed.

In his 2004 campaign to unseat President Bush, Senator John Kerry hit frequently at the frustrating and embarrassing battle of Tora Bora, in which American commanders were convinced that they came close to capturing or killing bin Laden, only to have him slip away through the mountains into Pakistan. Kerry claimed that preoccupation with and preparations for Iraq meant inadequate force levels in Afghanistan, including Tora Bora, where the US relied on anti-Taliban Afghans under the banner of the Northern Alliance.[9] Obama carried the same argument into the 2008 presidential campaign.[10] Such statements expressed a recognisable liberal internationalist perspective that was based as much on moral reasoning as strategic logic. Having helped to arm the mujahadeen fighters, the United States was deemed to have abandoned Afghanistan as the fall of the Soviet-backed regime gave way to a devastating, decade-long civil war. Upon their return to Afghanistan after 9/11, it seemed incumbent upon the United States and its allies to do the right thing this time. Above all, it could not let the country again fall victim to the mediaeval cruelties of Taliban rule.

Such liberal interventionism had been tested in the Balkan interventions of the Clinton administration, and was a topic of debate in the 2000 presidential campaign. Republican candidate George W. Bush and his advisers argued that the United States should not squander finite strategic resources on quixotic projects of nation-building. 'We don't need to have the 82nd Airborne escorting kids to kindergarten,' was Bush adviser Condoleezza Rice's memorable way of arguing that US troops should not be tied down in lengthy Balkans missions.[11] Vice President Al Gore, the Democratic candidate, responded with a full-throated defence of what the United States and its European allies had accomplished with military interventions and extended peace-keeping missions in Bosnia and Kosovo.[12] Bush may have won the election, but the Democrats seemed to win that particular argument insofar as the new administration decided against a precipitous withdrawal of American troops from the Balkans, on the grounds that such a move would be too unsettling to alliance relationships.

In their military responses to 11 September, however, the Bush administration continued to exhibit an allergic attitude towards heavy commitments of infantry forces to what it deemed to be unnecessary projects of social engineering. The initial war in Afghanistan was not so much a US invasion as the application of air power and special forces to tip the balance in favour of the Northern Alliance, in Afghanistan's ongoing civil war. (Even many years later, Bush's second defense secretary, Robert Gates, expressed misgivings that a larger military footprint might repeat the Soviet Union's failed campaign to pacify the country.) For the invasion of Iraq, civilians and officers in Donald Rumsfeld's Pentagon were beguiled by a misleading view of what 'transformational' technologies could accomplish with a relatively small number of troops.[13]

In both cases, arguably, but certainly in Iraq, the United States suffered real debacles born in part out of an egregious mismatch between war aims and invested resources. The Democratic critique of this mismatch was largely correct, and it was elaborated in detailed work by a RAND Corporation team under veteran diplomat James Dobbins, an accomplished

Balkans and Afghanistan hand who observed that, when it comes to nation-building, there is a direct relationship between input (in terms of troop numbers and other resources) and output (in successful peace, stability and development).[14] These RAND studies helped establish a rule of thumb that successful nation-building projects required one soldier or police officer for every 40 to 50 of population being protected.

By the middle of Bush's second term, however, the partisan line-up on the question of a large-versus-small military footprint for nation-building had been jumbled. To some extent this was because the main justification for invading Iraq – Saddam Hussein's nuclear-, biological- and chemical-weapons programmes – turned out to be groundless. By default, the president turned to his other, grander rationale – using American military power to spread democracy in the Middle East. This had always been part of the package, but it seemed increasingly ridiculous as Iraq descended into a savage sectarian war. What saved it, especially in Republican eyes, was the success of the 'surge' of American forces in Iraq that, after 2006, seemed to turn around a losing war.

The calming of Iraq's civil war happened thanks to other positive factors, including the revulsion of Sunni tribal leaders in Anbar province at the savage behaviour of their al-Qaeda allies, and their recruitment by US military commanders, through cash payments and other blandishments. But the new strategy implemented by Gen. Petraeus, focused on protecting civilians as much or more than killing insurgents, was also important. President Bush and his dwindling supporters felt vindicated, and Senator John McCain, the 2008 Republican candidate for president, used the surge's apparent success to argue that Obama, who had opposed the escalation in Iraq, lacked the judgement to command America's military establishment.

Besides partisan politics, there were military politics. Petraeus was the most visible of a group of dissident officers who challenged what they regarded as the Pentagon's faddish fixation on an information-technology driven 'revolution in military affairs'. In the view of the dissidents, this fixation had left America unprepared for real wars in urban settings such as Iraq, where no amount of computer-networked information dominance could compensate for the US army's essential cluelessness about the language, culture, motivations and politics of the insurgencies it was trying to suppress and the nation it was trying to build and sustain. As then-Colonel H.R. McMaster, a dissident defence intellectual allied with Petraeus, argued in *Survival*:

> thinking about defence was driven by a fantastical theory about the character of future war rather than by clear visions of emerging threats to national security in the context of history and contemporary conflict. Proponents of what became known as military transformation argued for a 'capabilities based' method of thinking about future war. In practice, however, capabilities-based analysis focused narrowly on how the United States would like to fight and then assumed that the preference was relevant.[15]

According to McMaster, 'self-delusion about the character of future conflict [had] weakened US efforts in Afghanistan and Iraq as war plans and decisions based on flawed visions of war confronted reality'. This included the reality that Iraq and Afghanistan were wars of counter-insurgency that required winning the support of the local peoples who constituted the greatest stake in the struggle. This meant living among them, rather than barrelling past or over them in intimidating armoured vehicles, and convincing them that the Americans were not occupiers but rather protectors. This, in turn, required large numbers of well-trained troops.

Without quite saying he had been wrong about the Iraq surge, the new President Obama made clear that he wanted to learn from its successes and apply them to Afghanistan. Yet, in the series of Afghan strategy reviews that he commissioned for the first year of his administration, a rather awkward question emerged. Though no one would have put it quite this way, the question was essentially this: what if the Bush administration had it right the first time?

The point of the question was not to challenge the now-conventional wisdom that the Bush administration neglected Afghanistan and woefully mishandled Iraq. Yet it is arguable that the Bush administration's initial instinct of avoiding an ambitiously defined Afghanistan mission was the right one. The case would go something like this: the United States had suffered a devastating attack for which the Taliban regime, as al-Qaeda's host, was partly responsible. But Mullah Omar, the Taliban leader, probably did not know about the 11 September attacks before they happened, and Washington's initial response came in the form of an ultimatum to hand over bin Laden and other key al-Qaeda leaders, or wait for the destruction of the regime. Implicit in this ultimatum was the possibility that Omar and the Taliban would comply, and that the United States and its allies would then have left the Taliban and Afghan people to their own devices. Admittedly, the scenario was never very probable. But, had it transpired, would it have been reasonable to argue that the United States had failed to respond adequately to the 11 September attacks?

The argument, in other words, is that strategic-level acts of terrorism may indeed require a strategic-level response: in effect, regime change.[16] But to go even further, by attempting to re-engineer a society and a nation of almost 30 million people, is to risk strategic over-stretch on a catastrophic scale, thereby falling into the classical terrorist's trap. Arguably, the US should have helped destroy the Taliban, and then left.

This is not to suggest that the Bush administration pursued anything resembling such a narrowly defined strategy. On the contrary, under Bush an incoherent and under-resourced war in Afghanistan drifted for seven years. The US was joined in this drift by NATO allies, and for much of that time Afghanistan was argued about as a test of Alliance solidarity without any clear or common understanding of what the Alliance was trying to achieve there, or whether it was achievable. Likewise, Obama came into office promising to do a better job, though without having undertaken a forensically rigorous examination of what that job actually was or should be. To his credit, having responded in his first months in office to what his military officers said was a general deterioration on the ground with an order to reinforce troop levels with another 17,000 soldiers, he insisted that before the next escalation there would be such a forensic examination.

That policy review took place during autumn 2009, and created inside the administration the most intense argument of Obama's first term, an argument that the *Washington Post*'s Bob Woodward narrated meticulously in his book *Obama's Wars*.[17] One faction included Petraeus, who was now US Central Command (CENTCOM) commander, the Chairman of the Joint Chiefs Admiral Mike Mullen, and the newly appointed commander in Afghanistan, General Stanley McChrystal. These officers used the Iraq experience to push for a fully manned counter-insurgency campaign aimed at winning over the Afghan population and reversing the Taliban's momentum. McChrystal wasted no time in touring Afghanistan immediately upon his appointment, and drafted a lengthy and dire assessment of a war that was on the verge of being lost. The classified assessment was leaked to Woodward, who published it in the *Washington Post*, to the great consternation of the White House. Without another 40,000 troops, McChrystal concluded, the US and its allies faced 'mission failure'.[18]

The contending faction, led by Vice President Joe Biden, and including many of Obama's top political advisers, considered any Afghan escalation to be unavoidably under the shadow of Vietnam, strategically incoherent and not discernibly connected to any overriding American interest or purpose. The United States had been drawn into Afghanistan by al-Qaeda's attack on the United States, but al-Qaeda in the meantime had been driven out of Afghanistan and into Pakistan, where its leadership enjoyed de facto sanctuary. Nothing that the US could do in Afghanistan would change the reality that the military and especially intelligence leadership of a precarious Pakistan was playing a double game: fighting with considerable heroism and sacrifice against Islamist militants in tribal areas, yet at the same time hedging with continued support for the very Taliban that it had helped create in the first place. How to change Pakistan's behaviour was an excruciating problem, but banging America's head against the door in Afghanistan had little to do with solving that problem. The nightmare scenarios for American interests included a takeover of the state and its nuclear weapons by the Islamist militants that Pakistan had nurtured as weapons against India, or an Indo-Pakistani nuclear war. Indeed, the former was potentially one catastrophic avenue to the latter. Pakistan's behaviour was said to stem from its fear of being left alone with a huge and conventionally superior India. But Obama himself, according to Woodward's account, noted the contradiction in arguing that America had to stay in Afghanistan to reassure Pakistan against another strategic abandonment, since the ostensible

American *purpose* in Afghanistan was to strengthen a Karzai government that Pakistan considered an Indian puppet, and was determined to undermine. Strengthening the Karzai government was a losing proposition in any event, according to the Biden faction. Kabul's intractable corruption and misgovernance was a primary and renewable source of Taliban strength.

Against the generals, Biden and his allies argued strenuously for a more limited strategy that they dubbed 'counter-terrorism plus'. In essence, it was a strategy for maintaining major American military bases and supporting the Kabul government in those places where its writ plausibly ran, but not attempting to pacify all of Afghanistan or train a massive 400,000-strong army. Instead, the Americans would train a more realistically sized force and otherwise focus on destroying terrorists, both those few remaining in Afghanistan and the more numerous groups in Pakistan. Negotiations and some sort of power sharing with the more reconcilable elements of the Taliban would be encouraged. Among other virtues, this was seen to be a strategy that could be replicated in other places where al-Qaeda established itself, including Somalia and Yemen (whereas the idea that the US would repeat its Afghan counter-insurgency and nation-building efforts in Somalia, Yemen and any place else that the terrorist group popped up was simply preposterous).

The Vietnam comparison can be a careless cliché. But the problem of civil–military tensions that constrained Obama's decision-making did have an instructive precedent in the early 1960s. Recent scholarship supports the contention that President John F. Kennedy was determined to avoid an all-out war in Vietnam, and in fact rejected at least five separate appeals from his military and strategic advisers for a major deployment of American troops there. Kennedy had been a junior naval officer and war hero in the Second World War, and he had an arguably healthy contempt for the senior generals who were calling on him to escalate.[19] Obama, by contrast, lacked the prestige-enhancing background of military service, but did try to avoid being boxed in by the military. It was not easy. The president and his political advisers became intensely frustrated by the Pentagon's refusal to present him with realistic options other than the generals' preferred package of 40,000 more troops. They also were concerned that military commanders were using their connections in the press and the Republican Party to pre-empt the conclusions of the policy review. This concern came to a head in October 2009, when the then-Afghan commander General McChrystal delivered a speech at the London headquarters of the IISS. Asked in general terms about Biden's preferred counter-terrorism strategy, McChrystal called it 'short-sighted' and said it would lead to 'Chaos-istan'.[20] According to Woodward's account, McChrystal's comments marked a seminal moment for the White House staff. What better proof that the military was on a 'search-and-destroy mission aimed at the president?'[21]

For policy reasons Obama did, of course, need to take military advice seriously, and for political reasons he could not afford an open break with his commanders. The die was probably cast when both Defense Secretary Gates and Secretary of State Hillary Clinton came down in support of the more ambitious strategy. More generally, the decision was constrained by a form of status-quo bias: however fallacious it might be to argue on the basis of already sunk costs, it was difficult to abandon an eight-year military effort without investing in one more try.

In the end, the president approved another 30,000 troops, most of what the military had asked for. But he also tried to establish his own authority and a more narrowly defined mission through a six-page, single-spaced 'terms sheet' that he dictated himself. The intent would be to 'degrade', rather than defeat or destroy, the Taliban. There would be no country-wide counter-insurgency effort, Obama insisted, and there would be no unrealistic commitment to train a massive army of 400,000 Afghan troops. The mission was to be limited in geography and time. By July 2011, the terms sheet stated, 'we will expect to begin transferring lead security responsibility from these [US] forces to the ANSF [Afghan National Security Force] and begin reducing U.S. forces to the levels below the extended surge'.[22]

It was a nuanced outcome, starting with ambiguity about what the July 2011 date actually meant, and it opened the president to criticism from all sides. Hardline backers of the war complained that any deadline, however soft, would embolden the enemy to simply wait for America and its allies to leave.[23] War sceptics feared the date was too elastic to set any serious limit on the American commitment; moreover, since they suspected the president of sharing their scepticism, they accused him of squandering more money and more lives on a hopeless cause.[24] The president's terms sheet stated that the 'total cost for this option in Afghanistan is about $113 billion per year for those years in which we sustain nearly 100,000 troops in Afghanistan'.[25] For how many more years, the sceptics asked, could Washington justify spending more than $100bn on this war?

What Afghanistan costs

This kind of accounting is not generally applied to America's military activities. The US defence budget, almost as large as all other countries' combined spending, has long existed in a kind of magical kingdom where the normal rules of political bargaining over finite resources do not apply. Could this be changing? There is certainly a recent precedent for squeezing US defence spending in real terms to the point of significant impact on the federal fiscal balance. The post-Cold War peace dividend reduced the military share of American GDP from 5.62% in fiscal year 1989 to 2.98% in FY1999. Over the same period the national (federal) budget deficit fell from 2.8% of GDP to zero and then a 1.4% surplus.[26] Modest tax increases and strong economic growth played the largest role in this fiscal improvement, but the impact of restrained defence outlays was far from negligible. It would be difficult to argue, moreover, that these Clinton-era budgets weakened the United States militarily, for they funded the armed forces that helped topple the Taliban and then invaded Iraq.

In contrast to the Clinton prosperity, of course, the United States is now making spending decisions in a climate of auster-ity, created in 2008 by the worst financial crash since the 1930s. This age of austerity has had and will continue to have profound consequences for the United States, its alliances and international politics. It will have an effect on the allies' rela-tions with each other – throwing the future of the euro and the EU integration project into some doubt, for example – and on the transatlantic place in the wider world. It has thrown the question of respective geopolitical weights of transatlantic versus Asia-Pacific into sharper focus.

To be clear: this is not because the United States is insolvent in any common-sense meaning of the term. Its medium-term budget deficit would be mostly erased if Washington returned to Clinton-era tax rates.[27] Thus, the fundamental problem is political and ideological: one of the two major political parties in the United States has adopted the position that in an already historically low-taxed country, it is nonetheless a matter of unyielding dogma that taxes must always go down and never up. Of course, operating according to such dogma can bankrupt a country. And beyond politics, the United States does indeed face a significant long-term budget and debt problem beyond

2020. If one could erase the effects of the tax cuts, and discount the costs of two wars, there would remain the genuinely difficult problem of health-care costs for the elderly, which drives most of the long-term deficit.

So the austerity is a real and limiting condition of international politics for the foreseeable future. And while entitlements such as health care and social-security pensions for the aged are the most significant drivers of long-term indebtedness, they are also the most difficult to address. Political gravity therefore draws attention to the remaining, so-called 'discretionary' spending. And while the military budget constitutes 20% of the federal budget, it is more than half (57%) of discretionary spending.[28] Under these circumstances, Afghanistan by summer 2011 became an ineluctable subject of budget scrutiny. In FY2011 budgeted outlay for Afghanistan was $106bn, and this certainly understated the true cost that includes such expensive commitments as long-term care for the severely wounded. Such annual expenditures are an order of magnitude greater than Afghanistan's GDP – roughly $14bn – an anomaly that raises the further problem of America training and equipping an Afghan National Army that Afghanistan will never be able to support from its own resources.[29] 'Money is the new 800-lb gorilla,' a senior Obama administration official told the *Washington Post*'s Rajiv Chandrasekaran. 'It shifts the debate from "is the strategy working?" to "can we afford this?" And when you view it that way, the scope of the mission that we have now is far, far less defensible.'[30]

There are other categories of costs. One is opportunity cost. As Chandrasekaran noted, the 'nearly $1.3bn on military and civilian reconstruction operations in one district of Helmand province — home to 80,000 people who live mostly in mud-brick compounds — [was] about as much as it provided to Egypt in military assistance'.[31] And while one might quibble about how much of America's aid to Egypt should take the form of military assistance, it is hard to ignore the question of whether $100bn directed towards Egypt's faltering economy would secure a better return for America's strategic interests, by fostering the democratic aspects of the Arab Awakening, than spending the same amount in Afghanistan. Of course, it is inconceivable that the United States would extend that sum as aid to Egypt – for FY2012 the entire US foreign aid budget is $47.1bn – and it is unlikely, in any event, that the Egyptian economy could properly absorb such funds.[32] The comparison does say something, however, about how easy it is for the US to get sucked into indefinite war without performing a rigorous analysis of cost-versus-benefit, and opportunity cost.

Another cost is political. By summer 2011, opinion polling showed sagging public support for the war. Congressional Democrats were becoming restless; in June 2011 the House of Representatives came close to passing a resolution calling for a fixed timetable for withdrawal. The vote was 204 to 215, compared to 162–260 on a similar resolution the year before. Even some Republicans have started to express doubt, including presidential candidate Mitt Romney, who argued in a New Hampshire debate that 'it's time for us to bring our troops home as soon as we possibly can, consistent with the word that comes to our generals that we can hand the country over to the [Afghan] military in a way that they're able to defend themselves.' Romney added: 'we've learned that our troops shouldn't go off and try and fight a war of independence for another nation. Only the Afghanis can win Afghanistan's independence from the Taliban.'[33] To the extent that Obama's thinking about Afghanistan includes political calculations, those calculations are inevitably complicated. Compared to the dismal economy, Afghanistan's impact on the president's re-election chances is likely to be marginal. It would be an excellent thing for him, no doubt, to be able to show voters that troop levels were going steadily down. Yet a resurgent Taliban, and the suggestion of an American defeat, would be irresistible and potentially effective banners for his Republican opponent to wave against him. In the final analysis, the American domestic politics of the Afghan war are hard to measure, but nor should they be considered a mere nuisance or distraction from America's real strategic and moral interests in the war. Politics is, ultimately, the only mechanism through which a democracy can establish a viable long-term strategy, and decide whether a war is worth fighting.

Finally, there are human costs to the protracted presence in Afghanistan. Obama's 'surge' pushed troop levels over the same symbolic threshold of 100,000 that President Lyndon B. Johnson crossed in Vietnam the year after his November 1964 election victory. American combat fatalities in Afghanistan rose from 155 in 2008 to 317 in 2009, topping out at 499 in 2010, the year of the surge. By way of comparison, during 1965, the year that US troop numbers in Vietnam were escalated, 1,863 Americans lost their lives. That figure exceeds all of the American deaths in Afghanistan since 2001. (It should be remembered, however, that the ratio of severely wounded to combat deaths is much higher in Afghanistan than it was in Vietnam, because of advances in battlefield medicine.) Just as the drawdown will ensure the number of troops in Afghanistan never matches the 500,000 deployed at the height of the Vietnam War, it is equally implausible that American casualties will near the 58,000 Americans who died in Vietnam between 1959 and 1973.[34]

Yet there is a moral trap in such comparisons, a temptation to assume that the human sacrifice in Afghanistan is acceptable compared to the extreme losses inflicted in Vietnam. The intensity of combat in Afghanistan is much lower than Vietnam, but it is a real war with real costs, and the United States cannot escape the question of whether it is justified in strategic and moral terms. Morally, the question is complicated by the difficulty of balancing real Afghan casualties, including civilians killed in errant NATO air-strikes, with hypothetical deaths in the civil war that could continue and even intensify upon an American and NATO withdrawal.

Whatever the moral judgement, however, it is hard to conceive that America will continue to fight a war in Afghanistan with 100,000 troops for another five years without a broad consensus that it is essential to US strategic interests. And notwithstanding his 2009 decision to escalate, Obama at the same time made his view clear that those US interests, though significant, were limited. This view, together with his June 2011 drawdown announcement, seemed consonant with a rough public and elite consensus. It also seemed likely that the drawdown would continue, slowly but steadily through 2014, when there will be well less than half as many American and allied troops in the country. A complete withdrawal is not in the cards for the foreseeable future, but whatever happens on the battlefield and regardless of whether Taliban fighters can be induced to trade weapons for power sharing, America's relationship with Afghanistan after 2014 is likely to consist of aid, military training and one or two bases from which American soldiers can support the Afghan government and American special forces can continue to target and kill al-Qaeda-linked terrorists. Resetting Washington's strategic balance will mean a scaling back of ambitions, which is likely to frustrate advocates of state-building and 'counter-insurgency plus' alike. Obama reportedly summarised the revised engagement thus: 'This is neither counter-insurgency nor nation-building. The costs [of doing either] are prohibitive.'[35] It is hard to imagine the circumstances under which he would change that position.

Republican critics will accuse him of telegraphing a lack of will to the Taliban, inviting the insurgents to wait America out. The accusation is fair, but the alternative is not so clear. And it cannot be assumed that a Republican president inaugurated in 2013 or 2017 would set a fundamentally different course. It is, in any event, almost impossible for a large, transparent democracy such as the United States to effectively bluff about commitments and goals that go – as Obama put it at West Point – 'beyond our responsibility, our means, or our interests'.

CHAPTER THREE

Domestic politics and state-building[1]

Toby Dodge

US President Barack Obama announced the end of the tempo-rary surge in operations in Afghanistan on 23 June 2011, vowing to withdraw by December 2012 all the 33,000 extra troops sent to the country as part of his review of Afghanistan policy.[2] However, those involved in conducting the US government's review of Afghan policy were divided into two camps. On one side was the Pentagon, supported by Secretary of State Hillary Clinton, which advocated the ambitious counter-insurgency (COIN) solution. They were opposed by Vice President Joseph Biden and the then-US Ambassador to Kabul Karl Eikenberry, who argued that counter-insurgency could not deliver success and hence called for a much more modest approach.[3] The terms in which Obama announced the end of the surge indicated that, after 18 months of the COIN campaign, those advocating a more modest counter-terrorism approach had regained control of America's Afghanistan policy. However, they are confronted by the same challenges identified by Eikenberry in his critique of the COIN campaign in 2009. Then, Eikenberry focused on the political and governance problems involved in attempting to rebuild the Afghan state. Firstly, he argued 'there is no political ruling class that provides an overarching national identity that transcends local affiliations and provides reliable partnership' for the American effort in Afghanistan. Of possibly greater importance, he stated that those advocating COIN

> underestimate how long it will take to restore or establish civilian government ... it is likely to be slow and uneven, no matter how many US and other foreign civilian experts are involved. Many areas need not just security but health care, education, justice, infrastructure, and almost every other basic government function. Many have never had these services at all.[4]

Clearly, Obama has now reduced the danger to the US of Afghanistan becoming a political and military quagmire, both undermining and negatively defining his presidency in a comparable way to the role that the Iraq War played during the administration of George W. Bush. However, Afghan state capacity and the legitimacy of its post-invasion ruling elite are yet to be addressed by those now steering the ISAF operation towards the exit. In his June 2011 speech, Obama studiously avoided mentioning the issues surrounding the civilian 'surge' and the need to reconstruct the Afghan state. Instead, he focused purely on the military counter-terrorism successes that had been delivered. He also gave clear backing to the NATO deadline for the handover of control of security and governance to the Afghan government in 2014. Further troop reductions, he said, would follow the removal of the initial 33,000, driven by the 2014 deadline.

If Afghanistan is to be sustainably stabilised before and after 2014, then the US government, its NATO allies and the new Afghan ruling elite it empowered will need to find answers to five major political difficulties that have bedevilled the country since the collapse of the Taliban regime in 2001. The first concerns state-building; the second, the government's electoral legitimacy; the third is the constitutional power of Afghan President Hamid Karzai; the fourth pervasive political corruption; and the fifth the barriers that may well stop substantive peace talks from succeeding.

Militarily, with its technical superiority, massive resources and post-2007 track record in Iraq, the US has both the capacity and the strategic blueprint to significantly degrade the Taliban's ability to destabilise the country. However, the generals in charge of implementing the campaign plan linked to Obama's Afghan policy – initially Stanley McChrystal, then David Petraeus and from July 2011 John Allen – have always stressed the dominant role that politics will have to play if their strategy is to succeed. McChrystal and Petraeus assign such a central role to the reconstitution of state capacity and government legitimacy because of their adherence to what they have labelled 'classic' counter-insurgency theory.[5] So Afghanistan's future stability after 2014 will depend on the possibility of finding solutions for five essentially political problems.

COIN doctrine and the possibility of success in Afghanistan

In spite of the US military's rediscovery of counter-insurgency in 2006–07, 'classic' approaches have remained fairly constant since the end of the Second World War. Like McChrystal and Petraeus's approach to Afghanistan, they stress the primacy of the political over the military, the need for close coordination between the civil and military wings of the campaign, the centrality of intelligence-led operations and the need to separate the insurgent from the wider population.[6] McChrystal and Petraeus's main point of departure from classic approaches is not doctrinal; it is instead the shoring up of an imposed government in post-invasion Iraq and Afghanistan, rather than the defence of an existing indigenous government.[7] This quasi-imperial form of expeditionary warfare raises profound issues about whether an exogenous force can be seen as legitimate by the population it has committed itself to 'protecting'. As Eikenberry highlighted in his cables from Kabul, it is thus essential that the Afghan government allied to NATO be perceived as autonomous of American control, legitimate in the eyes of its own population and effective in delivering government services to those it is fighting to control. As Stanley McChrystal argued in May 2011, 'The key is the Afghan government. It needs to be viewed as a legitimate representative of the Afghan people, otherwise we will be seen as occupiers.'[8]

McChrystal and Petraeus have placed David Galula's influential approach to counter-insurgency at the centre of their thinking.[9] Galula emphasised that rebuilding state capacity, the 'machine for the control of the population', was the key to success.[10] This approach identifies weak or illegitimate government as the root cause of rebellion. It creates space for violent opposition to organise and mobilise an alienated population in support of their attack upon state power. Under this rubric, counter-insurgency begins to look a lot like 'competitive state-building'. Both sides of the conflict are engaged in a struggle to increase the power and reach of their coercive and civil institutions as they fight to gain control of the largest section of society.[11] The problem for the Afghan state after 2001 was that, having been built under occupation, it can be damned by its opponents as being exogenous. For the US military, the answer to this critique is that sustainable legitimacy can be delivered through the 'provision of basic economic needs', 'essential services' and the 'sustainment of key social and cultural institutions'.[12]

This stress on the legitimacy and the capacity of the Afghan state means NATO's approach to Afghanistan from 2011 to

2014 and beyond is hugely dependent upon President Karzai and his cabinet. However, since his appointment in December 2001, the Afghan leader's increasingly mercurial approach to rule has had a detrimental effect on both the legitimacy and capacity of the Afghan state. This reached its peak when Karzai's domestic political credibility was severely damaged after the widespread fraud that surrounded his re-election in August 2009. Repeated allegations of financial fraud directed at those in the president's inner circle and family have also taken their toll.[13]

Beyond electoral politics, the increase in US troops stationed in Afghanistan was supposed to be accompanied by a 'civilian surge', a redoubled attempt to dramatically increase the non-military capacity of the Afghan state. In 2011, this triggered a shift in policy to focus on building stronger, more viable local-government structures, as well as reforming the central institutions of the state in Kabul. However, pervasive political corruption across Afghanistan's ruling class has done a great deal to hinder, if not reverse, attempts at reconstructing the state since the overthrow of the Taliban in 2001. For NATO's policy to deliver results that remain sustainable after 2014, for the 'civilian surge' to stand any chance of success, anti-corruption measures in Kabul would have to show demonstrable progress. Finally, during 2010 and into 2011 there was a growing consensus both in Afghanistan and internationally that sustainable stability could not be achieved without successful negotiations with a resurgent Taliban. This aimed to reintegrate at least some of their senior commanders into the political process in return for a disavowal of violence. Key Taliban leaders, meanwhile, have shown little taste for engaging in substantive negotiations to end the violence; nor indeed has the ruling elite in Kabul expressed a readiness to share power with them.

The Afghan state before 2001

Following the 'classic' approach to counter-insurgency, NATO's policy for delivering sustainable stability in Afghanistan foregrounds the political. This focus on politics has two major interlinked aims: improving the capacity of the Afghan state to deliver governance and services to its population; and demonstrating the legitimacy of Afghanistan's ruling elite.[14] The first problem this policy has to overcome is geography. Three quarters of Afghanistan's population live in rural areas. In addition, the population is 'scattered across geographically peripheral areas of mountains, steppes and deserts'.[15] For state institutions to occupy a meaningful and positive position in the majority of the population's lives, robust and coherent institutions need to be built that can deliver services and resources to populations that have historically been inaccessible to the state. This is a key prerequisite for a successful COIN campaign.

Beyond geography, the history of the state in Afghanistan and attempts to increase its capacity pose, if anything, an even greater challenge for NATO's counter-insurgency campaign. In April 1978, a successful communist *coup d'état*, the 'Sawr revolution', was launched in Kabul. This brought to an end the rule of the Musahiban dynasty, but more importantly marked a watershed in state–society relations with the new Marxist government unsuccessfully attempting to use state institutions to transform Afghanistan's rural society. The resulting revolt led to the Soviet invasion of 1979.

A wider historical examination of state–society relations in Afghanistan reveals a more nuanced and balanced relationship between the state based in Kabul and its rural hinterland. Historically, Afghans sum up the state's relations with its own population by referring to the 'six-mile rule', the distance from major urban centres that government development funding was thought to reach.[16] Beyond limited state capacity, governments in Kabul before 1978 survived by mediating between competing groups within Afghan society. Rulers would accept the limits of their power to transform rural Afghanistan and, in return, those areas would offer their loyalty to a state in Kabul with limited powers. Periodic attempts to expand the capacity of the state into rural areas of the country would thus trigger violent revolts.[17] This mediatory role of the Afghan state was based on the de facto delegation of informal authority to Afghan society and recognition of the distinct limits of governmental power.[18] These limits were indicated by the sources of government funding. In the early 1970s, out of 50 developing countries surveyed, Afghanistan had the second-lowest capacity to raise taxes domestically. It meant the Afghan government has always relied on external aid to fund its limited activities. From the late 1950s until the coup of 1978, 40% of government spending was financed from overseas.[19]

Problems with state-building after 2001

Some of the institutions of the state, with their base in Kabul and offices in Afghanistan's major cities, managed to survive the bloody Afghan civil war that began four years after the Soviet withdrawal. When they finally seized control of Kabul in 1996, the Taliban ruled the capital through a six-man Shura, but continued to run the country from Kandahar. They occupied the old ministerial offices in Kabul but attempted to purge non-Pashtuns from the senior ranks of the civil service.[20] Their approach to governance was straightforward, if minimalist:

> Religious law and madrassa-trained religious judges provided a judiciary; state administration was cut to a minimum both in Kabul and in the provinces; no state budget existed; the educational system was cut down

to religious madrassas and a limited number of state schools, very few of which admitted girls.[21]

When US and Afghan forces took Kabul in November 2001, the state institutions they inherited were shaped by two contradictory dynamics. Firstly, they had been deeply scarred by the legacy of 23 years of misrule and revolt. The Communists had overestimated the power of the institutions they had taken over in the coup, and attempted to instigate an ambitious land-reform programme. This brought state institutions into a fatal collision with a largely autonomous rural society.[22] The civil war that raged from 1992 until the Taliban secured dominance across the majority of the country likewise did great damage to the state, its institutions and personnel. Finally, the Taliban, through purges and neglect, added to the decomposition of an already weak nationwide system of governance. However, the state itself did not disintegrate completely. In 2001 there remained 240,000 civil servants on the government payroll[23] who were judged to have a

> reasonable commitment and discipline to deliver services ... a corporate memory (although fast disappearing) that knows how a functioning system can work, and ... processes in place (albeit cumbersome) that when operational do function.[24]

However, the civil service and the remnants of the state institutions it ran were organised in a highly centralised fashion that recognised neither the historical realities of state–society relations in Afghanistan nor the massive degradation these institutions had undergone since 1978. The question for the US, the UN and the Afghan elite concerned which was the most effective and realistic way to rebuild state capacity?

In December 2001, Hamid Karzai was flown back to Kabul and sworn in as the president of the Afghan Interim Authority. Afghanistan's first post-Taliban cabinet drafted an ambitious 'National Development Framework' and placed the National Solidarity Program at its heart. This sought to delegate developmental decision-making to the village level, with small grants given to communities to spend in the ways they thought best. The cabinet also drafted the government's first budget and set about rebuilding its ministries.[25]

However, the approach to rebuilding the Afghan state developed in a somewhat schizophrenic fashion. On one hand, Lakhdar Brahimi, as Special Representative of the Secretary-General for Afghanistan and then head of the United Nations Assistance Mission in Afghanistan (from 3 October 2001 to 31 December 2004), pioneered what he termed a 'light footprint' for the international community in Afghanistan. Brahimi argued that a greater international presence in the country was 'not necessary and not possible'. It was thought that a large foreign military presence would trigger a popular revolt.[26] This assumption coincided with the Bush administration's deep suspicion of 'nation-building' and an extended US commitment to Afghanistan.[27]

However, in spite of this 'light footprint', international donor agencies, the returning Afghan exiles and the first government pursued different and contradictory approaches to reconstituting Afghan state capacity.[28] The gargantuan ambitions involved in these various projects flew in the face of previous successful indigenous models of Afghan state practice. They also overestimated the ability of the international community to deliver the funding needed in the short, let alone medium, term. Finally, they did not take into account the incapacity of the myriad non-governmental, governmental and international organisations to coordinate among themselves when attempting to deliver reconstruction and then development aid.[29] This disorganised and contradictory approach led to individual donor agencies funding pet projects, rather than directing their resources to rebuilding the state.

Predictably, the results of this schizophrenic approach to state-building were meagre to say the least. Until late 2009, the dominant focus of capacity-building remained overbearingly centralist, 'all budgetary and most staffing decisions' were made in Kabul as part of a national planning process. This left little or no room for the provincial outposts of ministries or their governors to make autonomous policy decisions specifically tailored to the realities of the regions.[30] Government officials working outside Kabul therefore had little incentive to court local support since their continued employment and promotion remained disconnected from the areas in which they worked. As Thomas Barfield and Neamatollah Nojumi put it:

> Large-scale corruption and bad decision-making are the inevitable by-products of a system in which a governor knows his time of service will be short and that he owes no responsibility to the people he governs.[31]

Even in Kabul, the initial progress in reconstructing government capacity made by the first post-2001 government proved unsustainable. By 2005–06, Afghan ministries could only spend 50% of the money allocated to them in the national budget.[32] In 2006, the Ministry of Finance was described as 'broken at every level'.[33] Illiteracy, lack of advanced education and competition from high-paying NGOs meant the government had only a small pool of potential applicants from which to recruit staff.

Since 2001, the inefficient reconstruction of the Afghan state has directly hindered the ability of the counter-insurgency campaign. For example, throughout 2010, Kandahar Province was the focus of a major ISAF counter-insurgency operation aimed at driving the Taliban from the area. Once the military side of the COIN operation – the shaping of the battlefield, the clearing of insurgents and the holding of territory – was over, the civilian aspect of the campaign, the rebuilding of civilian capacity, was very slow to arrive. By November 2010, only 40 Afghans were working in Kandahar city's government, leaving 80 jobs unfilled,[34] even though ISAF head David Petraeus was actively lobbying the Afghan cabinet to bring council staff up to full strength. This weakness is indicative of the US reconstruction effort only starting to focus on provincial government in late 2009. In addition, as more effort was put into building provincial government, the Taliban stepped up their campaign of assassinating and intimidating local government employees.

The weakness of non-military Afghan government capacity was meant to have been addressed by a 'civilian surge' placed at the centre of President Obama's new policy in 2009. However, as this book goes to press, it has delivered neither the resources nor successes required. The deployment of US development aid is hugely skewed to the south of the country, with roughly 77% of the USAID budget for 2009–10 being spent in the south and east of the country.[35] Secondly, in spite of a new focus on local government capacity-building, some estimates indicate that by March 2011, two-thirds of the 1,110 American civilians working for the US government in Afghanistan were still based in Kabul.[36] By June 2011, of the 1,300 civilians working for the US government in Afghanistan, only 380 were stationed outside Kabul.[37] The time taken to hire, train and deploy personnel has certainly hindered civilian reconstruction. Security concerns have also obviously restricted the US embassy's ability to post its employees outside the capital. It places narrow limits on the role that foreign personnel can play once they have been deployed. Provincial Reconstruction Teams are heavily restricted, for example, not just in how they can travel through the regions for which they are responsible, but also in who they can meet. However, a greater problem is that the US government's ability to deliver military capacity into a COIN campaign far outstrips its ability to build non-coercive infrastructure. This 'government in a box' approach, linked as it is to the application of COIN doctrine, radically underestimates the difficulties of building sustainable civilian governmental capacity, especially at the geographic periphery of the state. The ramifications of this civilian–military mismatch are not hard to predict. As Generals McChrystal and Petraeus have repeatedly stated, COIN campaigns are won and lost politically, not militarily, thus the slow progress made in constituting Afghan government capacity at a regional and local level does not bode well for the stability of the post-2014 government in Kabul.

One possible adjustment to NATO, the UN and the Afghan government's approach to building the Afghan state has emerged during 2010–11. Starting towards the end of 2009, there was a concerted attempt to shift the focus of state-building from ministerial headquarters in Kabul to the provinces. This started with a 'District Delivery Program' which laid the foundations for what became, over time, a more comprehensive sub-national governance programme. In March 2010, Karzai signed the 'Sub-National Governance Policy'.[38] The new policy set out an ambitious 15-year timetable for transforming governing structures to deliver greater administrative autonomy and capacity into the provinces. However, sceptics within the Afghan government pointed out that the first step in this process, which would see the devolution of money for local government hiring, would take at least two years.[39]

The shift to a more local approach to state capacity-building in Afghanistan is a recognition that the ambitions encapsulated in the original plans for reconstructing the state were out of step with the realities of Afghan history and the international community's abilities. However, political power remains highly centralised not only in Kabul, but in the hands of the president. There has been little evidence that Hamid Karzai or the government he runs has any intention of developing real political or economic autonomy down to the provincial, let alone local, level in Afghanistan. In addition, the renewed focus on building sub-national governance began very late in NATO's occupation, meaning that the resources allocated to it will, along with US and international aid more generally, start to tail off within a relatively short period of time after the programme started. That said, the tensions between national and sub-national state-building are becoming an issue of political debate in Afghanistan and may well feature in the 2014 election campaign.

Government legitimacy and the problems with Afghan elections

The counter-insurgency doctrine promoted by Generals McChrystal and Petraeus and placed at the centre of ISAF's campaign plan focuses on government legitimacy as the central pillar of any success. This can be won for the government by building comprehensive state institutions that deliver services to the population in return for their support. The 'competitive state-building' at the heart of counter-insurgency poses historic and geographic problems when applied to Afghanistan, because the state's direct intervention into the lives of rural Afghans has been perceived as unwelcome, illegitimate or, because of the terrain, impossible. A second and possibly more straightforward source of legitimacy is through the ballot box, making the government directly responsible to the population through regular, free and fair elections.

The Afghanistan constitution, drafted in 2003 and approved by a Loya Jirga in 2004, makes it very clear where governing responsibility lies within the Afghan state, by giving the president the lion's share of executive responsibility. Under Article 64 of the constitution, the president appoints all cabinet ministers, the attorney general, the head of the Central Bank, the national security director, judges, military officers, police and national security as well as other high-ranking officials.[40] Concentrating this much power in one pair of hands was justified at the time by the need for the centralisation of executive decision-making. Many of Afghanistan's new political elite believed the state had become so fragmented by civil war that there was no alternative. However, it also personalises the government's performance and links it directly to the character traits, actions and abilities of just one man. This makes the five-yearly presidential elections crucial for the legitimacy of the state.

Hamid Karzai did not face a real electoral test until the first presidential elections in October 2004, having been appointed as interim president by a Loya Jirga. With all the advantages of incumbency, Karzai won an impressive victory, taking 55.4% of the vote, with his nearest rival gaining only 16.3%.[41] However, Karzai's attempt at re-election in August 2009 posed a more difficult challenge. His supporters, worried about the challenge he faced from his most coherent rival, Abdullah Abdullah, engaged in widespread and obvious electoral fraud.[42]

In Ghazni, Paktia, Paktika and Kandahar provinces, there was massive ballot stuffing for Karzai and his allied provincial council candidates in entire districts. The massive scale of fraud surprised even some in Karzai's camp, suggesting that his supporters may have overcompensated after public surveys showed the president's lead shrinking ahead of election day and also as partial results were released.[43]

The irreparable damage this did to the electoral legitimacy of the presidency and the whole Afghan government was compounded by the investigation the Electoral Complaints commission carried out into the elections. After two months, the Commission disqualified nearly 25% of the votes cast, thus triggering a second round run-off between Karzai and Abdullah. The illegitimacy of the electoral process, President Karzai and the government was then underlined when Abdullah refused to take part in the next round, citing fears that it too would be tainted by electoral fraud.[44]

One of the few new Afghan institutions empowered under the constitution to place limits on the office of the president is Afghanistan's lower house or parliament, the Wolesi Jirga. It has the ability to accept or reject Karzai's budget and his choice of cabinet ministers. In January 2010, the Wolesi Jirga rejected 17 of the 24 people proposed for ministerial appointments. Two weeks later, the parliament rejected ten of the new list of 17 proposed. Beyond the parliament's limited powers, the weakness of political parties in the lower house also hinders its ability to organise, act collectively and hold the executive to account. Secondly, there have been persistent rumours that parliamentary votes on key issues are influenced by widespread bribery.[45] Finally, when votes have consistently gone against Karzai, he has resorted to using presidential decrees announced when the parliament is not sitting, votes in the upper appointed house, and judgements from the Supreme

Court to circumvent the Wolesi Jirga. The ten people rejected by parliament for cabinet posts were still able to take up their positions when the president simply labelled their appointments 'temporary'.[46]

In the run-up to the Wolesi Jirga elections on 18 September 2010, there were hopes that a comparatively efficient and transparent campaign could help to re-legitimise the Afghan government and show the country had moved beyond the controversy of the 2009 elections. To begin with, competition for the 249 seats appeared to be fierce, with 2,545 candidates registering.[47] In the capital, because of its comparative security, 662 people competed for 33 seats. However, the campaign was disorganised, partly because political parties were underrepresented. A new law governing political parties, passed in September 2009, required Afghanistan's 110 parties to re-register in order to compete in the elections. Only 25 managed to do so by the deadline and government inefficiency left only five licensed in time for the elections. These five were the only parties permitted to have their candidates' affiliations mentioned on the ballot paper.[48] Secondly, intimidation and insecurity limited the ability of candidates to campaign outside Kabul. When researcher Tina Blohm visited the southwest province of Paktika, which borders Pakistan, she found that only six of the 22 registered candidates were present in the province and only two were actually campaigning.[49]

Two major dynamics, fraud and violence, undermined the election's outcome. Instability led to a government announcement in August 2010 that it would reduce the number of polling centres for the elections from 6,300 to 5,900.[50] This raised fears that the Pashtun areas of the country, where violence was at its worst, could be disenfranchised. On the day of the election a further 461 polling centres were closed because of security fears and 63 were directly attacked. In comparison with the October 2009 presidential elections, violence had increased. ISAF registered 380 attacks (100 more than the previous year), whereas the Afghanistan NGO Safety Office recorded a 56% increase in attacks.[51]

Even greater damage to the electoral process and its legitimacy was caused by widespread and systematic voter fraud. This resulted in Afghanistan's Independent Electoral Commission rejecting 1.3 million of 5.6m ballots cast; it then disqualified 21 of 249 successful candidates.[52] Those who were excluded organised demonstrations across Afghanistan. The exclusion of a number of Pashtun candidates triggered President Karzai's intervention and his attempt to use an investigation by the attorney general to overturn the commission's judgement.[53] However, after muscular diplomatic negotiations, the election result and the exclusions were unchallenged and the parliament opened on 26 January 2011. This could not distract the attention focused on the dramatic reduction of Pashtun parliamentarians in the new Wolesi Jirga.

The electoral turnout itself may indicate that, after numerous cases of electoral fraud, democracy is no longer delivering legitimacy to Afghanistan's ruling elite. With no reliable voter registration tally, the size of the electorate is hard to gauge, with estimates ranging from 10.5m to 12.5m. In the September 2010 parliamentary elections, 3.6m ballots were cast, compared to 6.4m in the previous poll in 2005. This dramatic and disturbing decrease is mirrored in the presidential elections, with 7.4m votes cast in 2004 compared with 4.8m in 2009.[54] The population of Afghanistan is apparently losing its appetite for voting. Given the widespread corruption among the country's political elite and their continuing inability to deliver government services, this is hardly surprising. However, reduction in the legitimacy of the government bodes ill for the success of the ongoing counter-insurgency campaign and its ability to win the hearts and minds of ordinary Afghans.

The problem of the presidency

President Karzai and his cabinet are central to the delivery of progress during the period of transition running up to full Afghan control in 2014, as the current system of government places a great deal of executive authority in the office of the president. Karzai is not only personally responsible for appointing his cabinet, but also the 34 provincial governors, 400 district sub-governors and all government officials down to the level of district administrator.[55] Doubts about his ability to handle this level of authority became widespread after his election in 2004. These were fuelled by leaked diplomatic cables from the US embassy in Kabul and its ambassador Karl Eikenberry. A report from the embassy placed Karzai 'at the centre of the governance challenge'. It stated that he struggled to strike 'the correct balance between institutional and traditional (that is, tribal) governance'. Ambassador Eikenberry was if anything even blunter, doubting whether Karzai would ever lose the habit of blaming the US for everything that went wrong in Afghanistan. Eikenberry went on to say that Karzai was unable 'to grasp the most rudimentary principles of state-building' and had two competing personalities, one 'paranoid and weak', the other 'an ever-shrewd politician'.[56]

Karzai's approach to governance became clearer by August 2010, when it was revealed that the Presidential Palace had amassed a fund estimated at between $10m and $50m, which Karzai used to buy loyalty from Afghanistan's politicians. The money came not only from Afghan businesses eager to curry favour with the president, but also from the country's allies and neighbours. In October 2010, Karzai himself admitted that his Chief of Staff Umar Daudzai received biannual cash payments from Iran of £625,000 for this slush fund.[57] To some degree, Karzai has co-opted a number of potential opponents through the deployment of this largesse and strategic appointments to lucrative government jobs. This has delivered a tenuous balance of power in Kabul. However, he has by no means ensured those opponents' sustained dependence on him, nor achieved a monopoly over the power of patronage.

Karzai's approach to politics has had damaging effects. In June 2010, two of the most highly respected members of his government abruptly left. The departures of the Interior Minister Hanif Atmar and Chief of Intelligence Amrullah Saleh were initially explained as a result of their failure to prevent Taliban attacks during a three day 'Peace Jirga' held in Kabul that month. However, it soon became apparent that the men had been sacked or had resigned because of long-running tensions between themselves and President Karzai. Karzai claimed he had lost trust in both men. The sackings may have been caused by the shifting basis of the President's political coalition. Saleh, who was one of the longest-serving members of the government, came to prominence because of his links to murdered Northern Alliance commander Ahmad Shah Massoud. The Northern Alliance had been a key pillar of Karzai's ruling coalition following their seizure of Kabul in 2001. However, since 2007, Karzai has attempted to reduce their influence within government as he has reached out to the Pashtun population. In 2009 this attempt at reworking his political base triggered the presidential campaign of Abdullah Abdullah. Considered against this background, Saleh's departure may well have been linked to the president's strategy of reducing the influence of the Northern Alliance within his government. In addition, Atmar, a Pashtun, was seen as a future political rival to Karzai. Both he and Saleh were viewed by Karzai as close to the US and were suspected and envied for this reason. As two of the most effective senior members of the government, their removal has clearly had a detrimental effect on the coherence of Afghanistan's security forces as the country moves towards complete Afghan control. It also indicates the depth of the long-held suspicion harboured by Karzai about the country's armed forces, which he perceives as disloyal.[58] For more on the power-brokers and influential figures in Afghan politics, see 'Who wields power?', on p. xi of the Strategic Geography section).

Vesting so much power in the office of the president has also hindered state-building efforts and undermined the political legitimacy of Afghanistan's ruling elite. State–society relations are highly personalised, at a time when the success of NATO's counter-insurgency campaign is heavily dependent upon the creation of independent, legal–rational state institutions and their ability to deliver services to the whole of Afghanistan's population. But the country's constitution enshrines this personalisation of the state and its power. The constitution places almost no constraints or oversights on Karzai's rule. The system used to elect members of the Wolesi Jirga directly hinders the ability of its members to collectively oversee the actions of the president or place meaningful constraints on his power. The appointment of the attorney general, which is in the gift of the president, has been used to stifle legal investigations that threaten to curtail his room for manoeuvre. All in all, the political system set up in the wake of regime change appears almost tailor-made to alienate Afghan society from the state, hinder state-building and thus directly undermine NATO's counter-insurgency campaign.

Political corruption

Endemic, politically motivated corruption has caused considerable damage to the ongoing attempts at rebuilding the Afghan state. The influence of criminal patronage networks within the Afghan government is such that it poses a serious threat to the viability of the state. Corruption affects every aspect of the state's interaction with Afghan society. At the lowest level, policemen on the streets of Kabul demand money from drivers to let their cars through the numerous checkpoints that have been set up across the capital. A police officer who aspires to be appointed a district officer will often have to pay as much as $50,000 to a superior to be assured of promotion.[59] In a survey carried out in 2010, Integrity Watch Afghanistan found everyday bribery of government officials had doubled since 2007, with ordinary Afghans having to pay an average of $156 in bribes each year to access government services.[60] Overall, the US government reported in September 2010 that 80.6% of Afghans polled believed corruption affected their daily life.[61]

Although President Karzai has repeatedly acknowledged that pervasive corruption is a serious and destructive problem, little has been done by his government to limit its corrosive effects. Attorney General Mohammed Ishaq Aloko has been repeatedly accused of stalling, obstructing or halting criminal investigations into senior government officials charged with corruption. Many of Afghanistan's ruling elite acknowledge the scale and damaging effects of corruption in private and are increasingly concerned about the threat of state fragmentation and failure. Nevertheless, those with the power to challenge corruption perceive the short-term risks of taking action against the problem as outweighing the long-term risks of civil war. High-level government hostility to the investigation of corruption was revealed in a raid on the New Ansari Money Exchange (a Hawala, or money exchange, which ensures remittances are paid) in Kabul in January 2010. The police raid found that it was responsible for shipping government officials' private resources to Dubai, as well as handling the wealth of drug smugglers and money for the Taliban. A phone-tap set up by Afghan and US investigators caught Mohammad Zia Salehi, the head of administration of the Afghan National Security Council, offering to stop the investigation if those connected to the New Ansari Hawala would give his son a new Toyota car worth $10,000. Salehi was arrested in July 2010. However, he reportedly rang President Karzai from his prison cell and was driven away from the jail by a car sent from the Presidential Palace. The Anti-Corruption Unit, the Afghan government organisation that led the investigation and arrested Salehi, had its power and autonomy sharply curtailed on the orders of the attorney general. The prosecutor responsible for the case, Fazel Ahmed Faqiryar, was forced into retirement in August 2010 and then charged with libelling members of Karzai's cabinet.[62] From 2007 to 2010, Hawalas were responsible for shipping $3bn of untraceable money from Kabul airport to Dubai.[63]

With such a poor Afghan government record in tackling corruption, it is little surprise that NATO recently set up its own organisation to tackle the problem. Shafafiyat, or 'Transparency', became fully operational in October 2010. It aims to coordinate between the international community and the Afghan government to tackle corruption. This involves ensuring ISAF's own approach to contracting does not exacerbate the situation while deploying enhanced NATO resources and personnel to bolster and support Afghan anti-corruption campaigns. Such is the importance NATO has invested in this initiative that it placed one of its most respected generals, H.R. McMaster, in charge of Shafafiyat.[64]

However, the pervasive nature of political corruption may have at least two drivers in Afghanistan. The first, targeted by Shafafiyat, is the weakness of the judicial system and its lack of autonomy from the ruling elite. This could be termed 'inefficient corruption', that which exists because the chances of getting caught are minimal or worth the risk. The second source of could be termed 'politically efficient corruption'. This is the use of government resources by senior politicians as a tool of rule, tying small sections of the Afghan population personally to them by offering unfair access to state resources. By its very nature, politically efficient corruption, the use of state resources to build a political constituency, means that corruption is sanctioned from the highest levels of the Afghan state. Its existence is central to the ruling strategy of the governing elite in Kabul and its reduction would be seen as a direct threat to them. The governing elite has a complex calculation to make between the undoubted damage that corruption is causing to the coherence of government institutions and their own legitimacy, versus the central place it plays in their strategy to stay in power. It is hard to believe, given the origins of this type of corruption, that the Shafafiyat initiative could make significant headway without a complete transformation in the modus operandi of those in power. This leaves the Shafafiyat vulnerable to mounting resentment from the governing elite and accusations that it is a vehicle for foreign domination of the Afghan state.

The problem with peace talks

Given that increasing the legitimacy of the current Afghan government and the capacity of the state has proved so difficult, it is unsurprising that the possibility of a negotiated settlement with the Taliban was increasingly explored during 2010 and 2011. President Karzai announced his proposed peace plan at a major international conference in London in January 2010. This involved plans for a 'Peace Jirga' in Kabul and additional funding to drive reconciliation forward through demobilisation and reintegration of low-level Taliban fighters. Karzai also backed an amnesty law and encouraged the UN to remove five senior Taliban leaders from a 'watch list' of 137 of the movement's current and former leaders.[65]

In the early stages this initiative was greeted with scepticism by the US, as it was not yet clear what the outcome of the troop 'surge' would be. This was a source of profound tension between the Afghan government and NATO about policy towards the Taliban.[66] Karzai and the United Nations stressed reconciliation: direct peace talks with the Taliban and a peace settlement involving the integration of at least some senior Taliban commanders into the governing elite. The US government initially favoured a similar model to the one used in Iraq, promoting reintegration. This would try to fracture the Taliban from the bottom, offering its foot soldiers promises of amnesty, cash payments and employment. Secretary of Defense Robert Gates argued that the Taliban had to be placed under such intense military pressure that negotiations would be preferable to facing a defeat on the battlefield. In March 2010 he clearly believed that point had not yet been reached.[67]

In June 2010, Karzai attempted to galvanise support for the Afghan government's approach to peace talks with the Taliban by holding a three day 'National Consultative Peace Jirga' in Kabul. 1,600 handpicked delegates were assembled in the capital to give their blessing to the $160m plan to provide employment for those who left the insurgency.[68] After heavy lobbying from the government, the Jirga elected the former president Burhanuddin Rabbani as its chair. However, Afghan opposition to negotiations soon became apparent as key members of the country's governing elite, led by Abdullah Abdullah, and a number of MPs and senators, pulled out of the Jirga.[69]

At the time the Peace Jirga appeared to represent a victory for those advocating reintegration not reconciliation, with the plan's author, Mohammad Masoom Stanekzai, stressing that it was highly unlikely that the Afghan government would open up a dialogue with senior Taliban commanders.[70] This scepticism appeared justified when the Taliban managed to fire several rocket-propelled grenades at the tent in which the Jirga was being held. Although the head of the National Directorate of Security, Amrullah Saleh, was forced to resign because of this security lapse, he subsequently let it be known that the prospect of releasing reconciled Taliban fighters from jail was a 'tipping point' in his relations with the president. 'Negotiating with suicide bombers will disgrace this country,' he argued after losing his job.[71]

By July 2010 it was evident that the United States government had changed its approach to negotiations with the Taliban and was now actively facilitating them. Sustained reports of informal discussions between the Afghan government and senior Taliban commanders were confirmed by Karzai in October. Gates, Clinton and Gen. Petraeus all confirmed that the US now supported negotiations.[72] In September, Karzai attempted to build on the momentum surrounding plans for peace talks by announcing the 'Process of Peace, Reconciliation and Reintegration'. This set up a High Peace Council under Rabbani to lead all of the government's negotiations with the Taliban.[73]

Behind these public initiatives, it was clear that all sides were engaged in confidential, if limited, discussions, to see whether substantive peace talks were possible. In April 2010, reports began to circulate that both Karzai and the then-head of the UN in Kabul, Kai Eide, had opened up negotiations with the senior Taliban commander, Mullah Baradar and representatives of the Taliban's leadership in exile, the Quetta Shura. In September, General Petraeus confirmed that senior members of the Taliban had indeed approached the Afghan government about the possibility of peace talks. Petraeus added in October that NATO had 'facilitated' negotiations between the government and the Taliban. Far less formal but more public talks were held in the Maldives in November.[74] The killing of Osama bin Laden in May 2011 may have added momentum to the process. Bin Laden had developed a close personal relationship with Taliban leader Mullah Omar. This tied the Taliban, which was essentially fighting a geographically confined war, into the global ambitions of bin Laden's own jihadist struggle. With bin Laden's removal, the link between the 'Arab Afghans' and their Taliban allies appeared to have loosened, allowing peace talks with the Quetta Shura to focus on national issues.

Despite the different initiatives, both domestic and international, during 2010–11, there were few signs that these proposals and informal talks would lead to an immediate breakthrough or sustained and structured negotiations. Numerous informal talks about talks were held, but the Taliban insisted that formal talks would depend upon acceptance of their central non-negotiable demands: an unambiguous timetable for the complete withdrawal of all US forces and the release of all Taliban prisoners held by the US and Afghan governments. There also appeared to be little substantive incentive for the militant groups to take part in reconciliation talks, particularly in light of the general lack of confidence in the Afghan government to deliver prosperity and security. Doubts that peace talks could deliver meaningful reconciliation were exacerbated by the killing of Afghan High Peace Council head and former president Rabbani in September 2011.

Afghan politics and state capacity after 2014

Once Barack Obama announced the end of the troop surge in Afghanistan and gave his backing to the 2014 transition plan, responsibility for the future development of the country was placed very firmly in the hands of the Afghan government. It must find solutions to the political and governance problems that continue to undermine the stability of the country. The Afghan state, reconstituted after 2001, is still caught between two antagonistic dynamics, the centralising ambitions of its ruling elite and the constitution they wrote, and the reality of a very weakly institutionalised state struggling to deliver services to the vast majority of its population. Now that both the exogenous military and civilian assistance to Kabul has peaked and will rapidly decline, Afghan politicians may have to temper their centralising state-building ambitions and settle for a more modest presence for the state across rural society. Overall, the experience of state-building in Afghanistan gives the international community cause to be modest about its collective capacity to leave sustainable indigenous institutions in place after violent interventions.

CHAPTER FOUR

The economy, the budget and narcotics

Nicholas Redman

The fortunes of Afghanistan's economy are inextricably bound up with political stability, security and the strengthening of state structures. A weak economy, in which poverty is widespread, is inimical to the stabilisation of the state. Economic growth alone can provide the jobs and food security that will underpin a transition away from a war economy. Development of exports and domestic industry are essential if the current-account deficit is to be reduced to a safe level, removing a major risk to macroeconomic stability. Moreover, only growth in the licit economy can sustainably provide the rising tax revenues on which rest President Hamid Karzai's aspirations to increase the capacity of the state and its authority across the country. Finally, economic development in Afghanistan could increase the incentives for neighbouring states to work constructively with the Afghan government, rather than pursuing divisive or damaging policies.[1]

Foreign aid has been a principal driver of economic growth since 2002. It will inevitably decline in absolute and proportionate terms after 2014, if not earlier, though the most likely trajectory is for a rapid decline rather than a precipitous collapse.

Thus, Afghanistan will face a strong fiscal contraction just as it takes primary responsibility for its own security. The construction sector will suffer as reconstruction projects wind down. Services will also suffer, in particular the transit and security industries that have enjoyed multi-billion-dollar contracts to deliver and protect the 6,000–8,000 convoys per month that have been needed to supply US forces in the country.[2] These contractionary fiscal effects will principally affect the towns and cities, which have been the main Afghan beneficiaries of foreign aid since 2001.

The post-Taliban economy

Analysing the Afghan economy is far from straightforward, because of long-standing concerns over the reliability of data, which were exacerbated by the Soviet withdrawal in 1989. The 1990s was largely a data-free decade. Ten years after the foreign military intervention reopened the country to international organisations, there is still uncertainty over basic questions such as the size of the population: US officials admit a broad range, of between 26 million and 30m.[3] While a census was under way as of September 2011, the Afghan Central Statistics Organization has previously estimated the population at 24.9m (see Strategic Geography, p. x). Furthermore, GDP data do not capture the country's huge illicit economy, which is almost certainly larger than the licit one. Opium poppy cultivation is the leading economic activity, employing an estimated 3.3m people.[4]

Afghanistan was an economy based on subsistence agriculture that underwent a partial industrialisation during the Soviet occupation, the fruits of which were almost entirely destroyed by the conflicts that followed the Soviet withdrawal in 1989. As a result, agricultural output fell by 45% in less than a decade and imports of Soviet grain increased.[5]

Despite the inflow of billions of dollars in development aid since 2001, poverty rates remain high. The Afghan government assessed the poverty rate in 2008 as varying from 34% at harvest time to 42% in leaner times.[6] Moreover, a further 20% of the population were assessed to be only just above the poverty line.[7] The Asian Development Bank concurs with this assessment: it puts the poverty rate at 36%.[8]

The country's physical infrastructure is in scarcely better shape than its human capital. Most of the asphalt and concrete road network, built in the 1960s and 1970s with US and Soviet financial assistance, was largely destroyed by three decades of war, as were the country's electricity lines, gas pipelines, water-distribution and sewerage systems, and bridges. The process of reconstructing this infrastructure has been slow and arduous. A national road network is of particular importance for Afghanistan because it has no rail network, despite being surrounded by countries with railways. The lack of accessible, reliable transit infrastructure is a major impediment for Afghanistan, both in terms of uniting the country politically and for economic growth. Decent transit infrastructure is strongly associated with trade expansion, export diversification, the attraction of foreign direct investment and GDP growth. The World Bank-sponsored 2010 Logistics Performance Index (LPI) ranking, which includes an assessment of the quality and usability of trade and transport-related infrastructure, ranks Afghanistan 143rd out of 155 countries, with a lower score than Pakistan or Tajikistan.[9]

In the years following the ouster of the Taliban, economic growth in the country increased briskly, in line with expectations for a country with such a low starting point. Per capita annual income nearly doubled between 2002 and 2007, from $147 to $289. Aid and reconstruction has played a sizeable role in this, equivalent to 40% of GDP. High inflows and large-scale security spending fuelled demand for goods and services, including construction. In the second half of the decade, economic growth averaged 10.4% annually but demonstrated considerable volatility, lurching from 13.7% in the fiscal year 2007/08 to 3.6% the following year and 20.9% in 2009/10.[10]

The volatile performance in growth, which is further explored on p. xvi of the Strategic Geography section, under-lines the extent of the country's reliance on agriculture, which is highly dependent on rain falling in the right quantities at the right time of the year because of the destruction of irri-gation systems and poor water management. GDP growth is closely correlated with agricultural performance. A good cereal harvest of approximately 6m tonnes in 2007 helped to propel GDP growth that year to 13.7%, whereas a poor harvest of around 4m tonnes in 2008 contributed to GDP growth of just 3.6% in the fiscal year 2008/09. The following year, a record harvest of around 6.8m tonnes helped to push GDP growth to a breakneck 20.9%.[11] Agriculture's importance is not immediately obvious from a glance at national accounts data. According to the Asian Development Bank, agriculture's share of GDP in 2009 was 32.5%, compared with 22.1% for indus-try and 45.4% for services.[12] However, these numbers fail to reflect the dominance of agriculture within the economy, because swathes of industry and services are directly linked to agriculture. Manufacturing is dominated by food, beverages and tobacco. A significant part of economic activity in trans-port, trade and services involves the delivery of agricultural produce for processing or to market. As a consequence, it is probable that at least 50% of the economy is directly tied to agriculture, which is by far the largest sector by employment.

Exports, consisting principally of carpets and fruit, play a very small role. Balance-of-payments data for 2010 show exports of $2.63 billion and imports of $9.15bn, creating a huge current-account deficit that was largely covered by current transfers of \$6.17bn.[13] Without donor inflows, the current-account deficit would have been 54% of GDP in 2009/10, rather than the officially recorded 3.6%.

The role of foreign aid is of considerable concern, in light of the inevitable reduction in aid flows as foreign troops leave the country in preparation for the late-2014 handover of responsibility for security to the Afghan government. Foreign aid's share in the economy has fallen in recent years, from 60% of GDP in 2007/08 to 50% in 2009/10.[14] Non-security grants are expected to drop from 30% of GDP in 2007/08 to just 9% in 2012/13 as immediate reconstruction needs recede and the government takes a greater share of the burden. The Afghan government's development strategy anticipates that donor assistance will fall from \$6,513m in the fiscal year 2008/09 to \$4,814m in 2010/11 and \$3,908m in 2012/13.[15]

Official forecasts remain reasonably upbeat on near-term economic prospects despite the reduction in aid inflows. The Asian Development Bank in 2011 forecast GDP growth of 8–8.5% per year in 2011/12 and 2012/13.[16] The principal focus of concern is the post-2014 period, when some observers expect aid flows to collapse.[17] However, in light of the reductions in aid that are under way or planned for the period to 2015, as well as awareness on the part of foreign governments that Afghanistan will need stabilisation through aid for a lengthy period after 2014, a more likely trajectory for aid inflows is a brisk decline over a period of at least ten years, rather than a dramatic plunge on 1 January 2015. As a result, Afghanistan will face a strong fiscal contraction in the coming years, with construction and services bearing the brunt of the impact.

The state budget

The precarious state of the economy, and its reliance on foreign aid, is reflected in the public finances. Government revenue has increased more than tenfold in eight years, from Af5.9bn or 3.3% of GDP in 2002/03 to Af63.3bn or 9.4% of GDP in 2009/10. It increased by 26% in the fiscal year 2010/11, mainly due to improved customs and tax collection.[18] As a result, tax revenue as a percentage of GDP rose to 11% in 2010/11, from a level of around 7% five years earlier. However, this was still one of the lowest collection rates in the world.

Ordinarily, low revenue would impel a low-income country to strictly limit its government spending. Afghanistan's government, however, was spending around 20% of GDP in 2010/11, with hefty support from foreign donors. The principal beneficiary was the Afghan National Security Forces (ANSF).[19] The 2009/10 budget provided for as many soldiers as teachers, and the wage bill was much larger for the former. The World Bank estimates that spending on the ANSF amounted to $4.7bn in 2008/09, equal to 449% of government revenue. The bank projects that it will be $5.5bn in 2013/14 (270% of government revenue), $7.1bn in 2018/19 (195% of government revenue) and $9.2bn in 2023/24 (154% of government revenue).[20] Thus the ANSF is likely to be an unsustainable burden for at least a decade, even before the Afghan government's other commitments are taken into account.

The mismatch between revenue and spending has focused interest on fiscal sustainability, which in the Afghan context is defined as having been achieved when domestic revenue equals at least 100% of recurrent expenditure. In 2002/03 the figure was just 38%, but steadily improved in the next few years. The government's medium-term fiscal framework (MTFF), released in March 2008, projected that revenue would equal 101% of regular expenditure in the fiscal year 2012/13, but the July 2009 iteration of the MTFF revised down the 2012/13 figure to 73% and projected a level of 83% for 2013/14. The deteriorating outlook was caused by disappointing growth in revenue as well as expenditure exceeding expectations. On the assumption of 7–9% GDP growth and low inflation, the World Bank forecasts that the rate will be 74% in 2014/15 (although if security expenditure is excluded, the rate will rise to 170%).[21]

It is evident that foreign financing of the ANSF will be required for several years to come. The Afghan government's fiscal plans are explicit on this point, counting on foreign donors to cover most of the $14.2bn that it anticipates spending on security in the period 2008–13. Yet it seems certain that significant aid to support the ANSF will be needed for many years after 2014 too. Based on its forecast of a fiscal sustainability rate of 74% in 2014/15, the World Bank calculates that Afghanistan will need $6bn in foreign financing over five years. If GDP growth is 2–3 percentage points higher than in the base case, that financing requirement would fall to $5bn, whereas in a low-growth scenario it would rise to $10bn (that scenario also assumes the ANSF needing 500,000 personnel, not 400,000).[22] In 2011 the IMF noted that it did not expect the country to attain fiscal sustainability until 2023 at the earliest, compared with a previous estimate of 2015.[23]

A further problem for the state budget, in light of the handover by the end of 2014, concerns the question of state capacity. In an effort to speed up aid delivery and to minimise the risk of losses associated with incompetence and corruption, many foreign donors have chosen to spend money in Afghanistan directly rather than to channel it through the central government budget. This created what James K. Boyce terms a 'dual public sector', in which the externally funded budget is larger than the domestic one. Although justified on the basis of maximising aid effectiveness and short-term results, it does not contribute to the vital goal of building local capacity, which (in particular in the revenue-raising sphere) is the key prerequisite for a successful transition from aid dependency.[24] In 2007, just one-third of foreign aid went through the core budget; in most of the preceding years the fraction was smaller. The World Bank has led efforts to ensure some aid flows go through Afghan structures, with the national government having a say in how the funds are spent,[25] and since 2007 the proportion of funds going through the state budget has risen. However, it is doubtful that relatively belated corrective action in this regard will be sufficient to endow the Afghan government with the appropriate level of capacity to manage and disburse funds from 2015 onwards. Cash-flow management was also a problem, to judge by the rising core budget deficit in 2008/09.[26]

Impediments to economic growth

The absence of security and political reconciliation are patently the greatest hurdles to the growth of a licit economy in Afghanistan. Yet a range of other challenges also clouds the picture. Basic services such as water and power have been disrupted by war damage and a lack of maintenance. Approximately 70% of Afghans do not have access to clean water. The situation in the electricity sector is little better, and this is perhaps the main infrastructure constraint on growth. In 2008, an estimated 20% of the population had access to electricity, but supply was not constant across the day or across the year.[27] The lack of affordable, reliable power around the country constitutes a de facto tax on productivity and warps economic development.

Generating capacity doubled between 2002 and 2007, thanks in no small part to investments of $670m by USAID, which delivered large increases in hydro- and diesel-powered generation.[28] However, this was insufficient to meet rising demand: the increase in total supply from 243MW to 652MW was only made possible by a doubling of electricity imports to 167MW.[29]

Further progress in improving generation has been hampered by low tariffs and high arrears,[30] as well as weak security—most notoriously in the case of the Kajaki hydro plant in Helmand. In per capita terms, generating capacity in 2007 was just 40kwh, compared with 2,200kWh in neighbouring Tajikistan.

Transport infrastructure is a further impediment, in particular because it prevents the development of most export-oriented industries (see Strategic Geography p. xii, 'Shoring up infrastructure'). Although nearly 20,000 km of roads were built or repaired between 2003 and 2008, it was estimated that by the end of that period approximately 85% of the country's 130,000km of roads were significantly degraded or impassible (including 43,000km of major roads – national, regional, urban and provincial). Many bridges were reportedly close to collapse.[31] The country therefore remained dependent on the insecure ring road, Highway 1. Railways have begun to encroach on Afghan territory, but these are the work of neighbouring states that operate different gauges. In August 2011, a 1,520mm gauge line running 85km from Termez in Uzbekistan to the northern city of Mazar-e-Sharif via the Friendship Bridge and Hairatan was opened, principally to supply ISAF as part of the Northern Distribution Network. The greater prize for the Afghan economy is a railway line to connect with a sea terminal. Here, Pakistan (and China) is competing with Iran (and India). Pakistan plans to extend to Afghanistan's southern city of Kandahar a 1,676mm gauge railway that will connect Quetta with the port at Gwadar in Baluchistan.[32] The Quetta–Gwadar railway should also give China the ability to send its exports via the Indian Ocean. Iran, meanwhile, has started construction of a 1,435mm line from Torbat-e Heydarieh, a town on its side of the border, to Herat in western Afghanistan. In tandem with India, Iran is building roads to connect Afghanistan with Iran's easternmost seaport, Chabahar, which is just 72km west of Gwadar. Rail infrastructure could follow, yet it is noteworthy that both Chabahar and Gwadar are located in regions of insurgent activity that may not prove conducive to the development of commerce.[33]

Furthermore, the labour force suffers from poor health, little education and a lack of skills. War devastated the healthcare system: hospitals closed, supplies were non-existent, staff were unpaid and untrained. Afghanistan's statistics on maternal, infant and child mortality are among the worst in Asia; so too its rankings on malnutrition and infectious diseases. In 2007, for instance, just 14% of all births were attended by skilled health personnel, compared with 39% in Pakistan and 37% in Tajikistan. Afghanistan also has one of the highest maternal mortality ratios, at 1,400 per 100,000 live births; this is almost three times as high as for Bangladesh, while the rates for Pakistan and Tajikistan are 260 and 64 respectively.[34] The country's ratings with regard to infectious diseases and the proportion of the population with access to an improved source of drinking water are little better.[35] The number of children in schools has risen sharply since 2002, reaching 5.7m in 2007 compared with fewer than 1m in 2002. However, it should be noted that the damage caused by three decades of conflict cannot be eradicated in a few years. In 1979, before the destruction of the education system, an estimated 90% of the population was illiterate.[36] In 2011, just 28% of adults in the country were considered literate, which is one of the very lowest rates anywhere in the world.[37]

Even if the country had better infrastructure and basic services, plus a more healthy and skilled workforce, Afghanistan would struggle to develop a healthy private sector because of a range of shortcomings with regard to the business environment.[38] Afghanistan is the lowest-ranked Asian country in the 2011 Doing Business rankings, coming 162nd in the assessment, below Bhutan (142nd), Nepal (116th) and Pakistan (83rd). Anecdotal evidence from Chinese executives suggests that corruption problems are significantly worse in Afghanistan than Pakistan.[39] Indeed, Transparency International's 2009 Corruption Perceptions Index put Afghanistan in 179th place out of 180 countries, above only Somalia.

Development plans

Faced with these challenges, what development path might Afghanistan's economy take? Neighbouring states offer a variety of models, of varying levels of suitability. The Iranian model seems impossible for Afghanistan to emulate, because it does not have a sizeable oil industry, direct access to the sea and an educated population. Kyrgyzstan is arguably a more suitable model for Afghanistan, because that economy is based principally around a large gold mine that provides the lion's share of government revenue and has encouraged the growth of ancillary activities. Potentially, Afghanistan could adopt an Uzbek model, wherein it develops a range of resource-extractive industries in order to generate high levels of foreign exchange that in turn provide the investment for the development of import-substitution and relatively high levels of state spending. However, it is likely to take several decades for Afghanistan to develop multiple export–income streams of a sufficient size, and in any case the government is committed to low trade barriers that are inimical to the Uzbek model. A final, though unattractive option, is the Pakistan model of dependence on the IMF.

The Afghanistan National Development Strategy (ANDS) of 2008 embraces the need to increase the rate of investment and to raise productivity. The establishment of security in the country is a prerequisite for both.[40] In the ANDS, the Afghan government has answered the question about the appropriate development model for the country by focusing on agriculture and mining. Agriculture will provide most of the jobs in the country, while boosting food security and giving support to the trade and current-account balance. Mining will deliver the tax revenues necessary to support the provision of government services, while also improving the infrastructure, the power sector and the external balance through trade. Minerals are the only realistic medium-term option for sharply increasing Afghanistan's export earnings.

Mining

Afghanistan is a land of huge but stranded mineral resources. The US government announced in 2010 that there was nearly $1,000bn worth of untapped mineral deposits, which have the potential to fundamentally alter the economy. A Pentagon memo went so far as to speculate that Afghanistan could become to the world lithium market what Saudi Arabia is to the world oil market. Yet as Jack Medlin of the US Geological Survey has noted, the country has no 'mining culture' and hence it will take many years to fully exploit the country's mineral wealth.[41]

Official estimates suggest Afghanistan has 1,490m tonnes of iron ore (worth $420bn in 2009), 41m tonnes of copper ($274bn), 3.5m tonnes of niobium ($81.2bn), 600,000 tonnes of cobalt ($51bn), and 724,000 tonnes of molybdenum ($24bn).[42] US Geological surveys show there are 32,000 metric tonnes of hot-spring mercury, which is sufficient to support a local mercury industry; 2,700kg of gold, which would be enough to support local industry and employment; an estimated 1.4m metric tonnes of rare-earth elements; and sizeable bauxite deposits containing 50% alumina and 12% silica.[43] In addition, the country has over 100 varieties of high-quality marble and generates exports of $15m annually. USAID insists the figure could rise to $450m annually with the right investments in production and infrastructure.[44]

For the Afghan authorities, two giant mineral deposits are the priority for development: the Aynak copper deposit and the Hajigak iron ore deposit (see Strategic Geography, p. xvii, 'Rich in resources?'). Each one will require several billion dollars of investment, which will involve the creation of transport infrastructure, coal mining, power generation and ancillary services. These mines will deliver sizeable revenues to the state budget (which, crucially, will be relatively straightforward to collect) and will become the country's principal exports. The key challenge is to develop the right policy framework, legislation, tax, institutions and scientific database. With these in place, the Afghan government believes that the economy could be revolutionised. The ANDS points to the fruits of reform in other countries: mining production in Argentina rose from $340m before reform to $1.3bn afterwards, while over the same period exports increased tenfold to $700m. For Tanzania, reform raised export revenue from $53m to $350m.[45] However, development of the mining sector is not merely a question of adopting the right policy framework: to succeed, the country needs better roads and perhaps a railway; improved security, particularly in the south; better energy and water supplies; and more skilled labour.

Aynak, located 35km south of Kabul in Logar province, is the first major mine project scheduled to begin production. The contract for Aynak was granted in 2008 to the China Metallurgical Group Corporation (MCC). Aynak is a world-class copper resource with reserves conservatively estimated in 2007 to be worth $25bn. It is expected to generate $155m per year in government revenue through royalties and taxes during the construction phase in 2011–15, rising to $365m once the mine becomes fully operational and produces 200,000 tonnes per year.[46] The copper mine is expected to employ 5,000 people, with a further 10,000 jobs in the supporting coal mine and power plant.

The MCC has struggled to meet its development targets at Aynak since beginning construction in 2009. Progress was delayed by the government's failure to relocate villagers, as well as poor security and infrastructure, insufficient supplies and inadequate numbers of skilled workers.[47] At the time of writing, the MCC is yet to start building the promised railway to link Aynak with Termez in Uzbekistan and Torkham in Pakistan, seemingly because it considers road transit to be a more economic option.[48] The company is yet to reach an agreement with the government on selling half of the output from the anticipated 400mw coal-fired power plant to the national grid.

Employment targets have been missed too. The MCC has complained about a critical shortage of skilled workers. It is evident that a large-scale training effort will be needed by the Chinese company in order to meet the local employment targets.

An consortium led by the state-run Steel Authority of India (SAIL) was regarded in October 2011 as the preferred bidder for Afghanistan's other major resource concession, the iron ore deposit at Hajigak in Wardak province (to the east of Aynak).[49] According to the US Geological Survey, Hajigak has 2.1bn metric tonnes of iron ore at 63–69% weight iron. Nearby deposits raise the total resource figure to 2.26bn metric tonnes.[50] The tender called for the development of a coking coal mine, a thermal coal mine, a power plant, ore processing and steel manufacturing. It was hoped that the plant would create 2,000 direct jobs and another 10,000 indirectly in coal mining, steel production and support industries. Once fully operational, with production at 1bn tonnes per year, government receipts from royalties and taxes could reach as high as $1bn annually.[51] Royalties in the development phase would be significantly lower, however, at $155m per year starting in 2013.[52]

Agriculture

The starting conditions for an expansion in agricultural output are not propitious. Few countries in the world experience such a wide degree of variation in temperatures across the year. The soil is thin and average rainfall is just 180mm per year; and the irrigation system has only been partly reconstructed after its complete destruction in the 1990s. Only in exceptional harvest years does the country achieve self-sufficiency in cereals, which account for three-quarters of agricultural output and a similar proportion of the national diet.[53]

The northern regions of Afghanistan are the breadbasket of the country, accounting for 70% of total production. In those areas, there is a heavy dependence on rainfall, because irrigation is not widespread. According to 2011 data from the US Special Inspector General for Afghanistan Reconstruction (SIGAR), 0.7m of the 0.9m hectares of land sown to wheat in the north is rain-fed, while nationally some 60% of the country's wheat-growing areas are reliant on rainfall alone rather than irrigation.[54] Even in areas where irrigation exists, water management is a problem, with distribution marred by corruption. Many farmers lack other inputs, including basic machinery, fertiliser and seeds, although in secure agricultural zones these shortcomings are being addressed.[55]

Even where farmers can grow abundant cereal crops, they face difficulties in taking those goods to market. According to one assessment, 58% of villages lack all-weather, year-round access to towns by road. Nor are road connections alone sufficient: markets must also be open to new entrants. In the case of Mazar-e-Sharif and other population centres, this is not the case: food markets are exclusionary and non-competitive.[56]

As a consequence of these challenges, most farmers engage in subsistence or near-subsistence farming. According to the 2007/08 National Risk and Vulnerability Assessment (NRVA), 44% of rural households rely on agriculture as their primary source of income; and some 54% of these farm for household consumption.[57]

Narcotics

Insecurity in Afghanistan has helped to fuel the rise of opium production, which is probably the country's largest economic activity (see 'The drugs industry and alternatives', Strategic Geography, p. xiv). Globally, opium production has undergone numerous shifts in the past 40 years, including the decline of Turkish output, the rise and fall of Iranian output, the eclipse of Southeast Asia's Golden Triangle by Central Asia's Golden Crescent, and most recently Afghanistan's ascent as the world's leading producer. It is arguable that in Afghanistan, the opium poppy has found its optimal location for production. Favourable cultivation conditions mean that yields are two to four times higher than in Southeast Asia and other producing areas. Opium poppies in Afghanistan also have higher morphine content, so that only 6–7kg of Afghan opium are needed to produce 1kg of heroin, compared with a requirement of 10kg of opium for Southeast Asian heroin. As a result, Afghanistan's share of world production is markedly higher than its share of cultivation. Opium, hashish and cotton are perhaps the three products produced in northern Afghanistan that are internationally competitive.[58]

The opium poppy was scarcely grown in Afghanistan prior to 1979. It became an incidental source of funding for the anti-Soviet forces, so that in 1986 production amounted to an estimated 350 metric tonnes. In the war economy that emerged after the 1989 Soviet withdrawal, opium became a primary

Table 1 **The post-2001 opium surge**

	2001	2002	2003	2004	2005	2006	2007	2008	2009	2010	2011
Cultivated area (ha)	8,000	74,000	80,000	131,000	104,000	165,000	193,000	157,000	123,000	123,000	131,000
Output (metric tonnes)	185	3,400	3,600	4,200	4,100	6,100	8,200	7,700	6,900	3,600	5,800
Yield (kg/ha)	24.3	45.9	45.0	32.1	39.3	37.0	42.5	48.8	56.1	29.2	44.5

Source: United Nations Office on Drugs and Crime

source of income for warlords. Production rose to 1,570 tonnes in 1990 and 2,335 tonnes in 1995, and flourished under the Taliban, who tolerated and taxed the sector (imposing a 10% agricultural tax and a 20% alms tax upon it[59]). In 1999, output reached 4,565 tonnes. A Taliban ban on the cultivation (but not trading) of opium, prior to the US-led foreign military intervention, shut down cultivation in 90% of the country during 2001. Consequently, output collapsed in that year to just 185 tonnes, virtually all of which was produced in the territory controlled by the US-backed Northern Alliance. Thus, it is once since the downfall of the Taliban that Afghanistan has come to dominate the global opium market.

One of the notable aspects of this dramatic increase in output, to a position in 2009 where Afghanistan became the source of over 90% of global supply, is that the years that saw a decrease in the area under cultivation year-on-year (2005, 2008 and 2009) saw a less pronounced fall in output, suggesting that either growers became better at raising yields or that the organisers of opium production were successful in ensuring that output was maintained in the most productive regions. The dramatic fall in output in 2010 was primarily due to drought and fungus that affected the opium poppy, although eradication programmes in some regions and a narrowing of the spread between net revenue from opium and wheat also caused some farmers to switch to cereal production.[60] The 2011 output level of 5,800 tonnes might prove to be a new equilibrium level, as the record crops posted in 2007–09 exceeded global demand and led to traffickers building up huge stocks of opium poppy (UNODC estimated that in 2009 there was 12,400 metric tonnes of opium in storage because of surplus production).[61] The trend of rising yields since 2004–06 certainly does not suggest an industry in decline; moreover, in 2011 three previously poppy-free provinces returned to cultivation. [62]

Cultivation has thrived in regions that are insecure and where the transit and irrigation infrastructure needed for wheat production has been destroyed.[63] There is some debate among experts over whether cultivation in insecure areas is a function of the absence of law enforcement or the application of coercion by insurgent groups. Traders, rather than farmers, seem to decide where opium poppies are grown. As Interior Minister Ali Ahmad Jalili said in 2004, Afghanistan differs from other countries where cultivators create smugglers, because in Afghanistan smugglers create cultivators.[64] In the mid-2000s there were 350,000 households that grew opium, 10,000–15,000 local traders who bought opium from them and in turn sold it on to 500–600 mid-level traders. Further up the pyramid were 200–250 traffickers and just 25–30 key traffickers.[65]

The increasing sophistication and organisation of the sector is apparent in the increase in value-added on Afghan territory and the diversification into adjacent markets. In 1995, an estimated 41% of opium production was processed into heroin within the country; by 2008, that figure had risen as high as 70%. In 2011, approximately 380–400 tonnes of heroin was produced in the country; this is roughly equal to total global consumption, once seizures are taken into account.[66] Diversification has come principally in a switch from opium to hashish/cannabis production, which yields higher net profits per hectare than opium because of lower labour costs. By 2005–06, Afghanistan had become the world's largest cannabis exporter and in 2010 the area under cultivation amounted to between 9,000 and 29,000 hectares.[67]

Although security conditions and the state of infrastructure are important in determining which crop a farmer will grow, individual production decisions are to a significant extent price-sensitive. More opium than wheat is grown in Afghanistan principally because opium attracts a much higher price and offers superior returns, enabling farmers to ensure their food security and provide income to improve standards of living.[68] According to a study published by UNODC, the gross revenue from one hectare of land used for poppy cultivation in 2005 was $5,385, compared with $947 for rice, $575 for irrigated wheat and $282 for rain-fed (non-irrigated) wheat.[69] UNODC said in 2010 that planting opium was six times more profitable than growing wheat, although the ratio had been lower in previous years.[70] Opium is more labour-intensive to harvest than wheat. It takes 350 man hours to harvest one hectare of opium, compared with 200 man hours for one hectare of wheat.[71] However, opium is easier to grow in areas lacking irrigation. Moreover, in contrast to wheat (which must be transported to market), opium is generally bought by local traders at the farm gate; these traders can also be a source of loans and seeds for farmers too.

It should be noted that the bulk of the multi-billion-dollar profits from opium accrue to international traffickers rather than Afghan farmers or traders. According to calculations for 2009 made by UNODC, an Afghan farmer is paid less than $1 for the opium needed to make one gram of heroin, which will retail for $239 in Europe. In the case of Afghan opium going to Europe, over 90% of the profits are made in Turkey and Europe.[72] UNODC calculations suggest that Afghan farmers earned $440m from opium in 2009, whereas traffickers took $2.2bn and the Taliban gained $140m–170m in informal taxes.[73] In 2011 the total farm-gate value of opium rose to $1.4bn, from $605m a year earlier, thanks to higher production and prices: the farm-gate price of fresh opium rose from \$128/kg to \$180/kg, while the farm-gate price for dry opium increased from \$169/kg to \$241/kg.[74]

The macroeconomic impact of the opium trade is not easily or fully discernible in national accounts data, but for Afghans in rural areas it is of vital importance. Opium is the largest source of export earnings, albeit unrecorded, and a major source of rural incomes.[75] The surge in opium production in the first decade of the twenty-first century had positive effects on poverty and food security, while creating employment. A multiplier effect was evident via a rise in household incomes and demand for goods and services.[76] Although some larger-scale farmers save a portion of their opium revenue, the majority spend it on food and non-subsistence goods, and transport and labourers (the latter in turn spend their wages locally). Opium finances a range of legal and illegal imports. Moving further up Afghanistan's opium-trade hierarchy, a portion of the (larger) profits is directed into domestic infrastructure projects, although sizeable sums are sent abroad.

The impact of opium production on the economy is mixed. It provides a discernible boost to the rural economy, lifting more households out of poverty than subsistence wheat cultivation could manage. Because opium is more labour-intensive than cereals, it also stimulates the labour market in rural areas and is supportive of wages. And with that cash circulating through local economies, it supports economic activities beyond infrastructure. Yet at the same time, the existence of a large industry dealing in an internationally proscribed narcotic encourages corruption and the criminalisation of state structures.[77] It has, as Mark Shaw notes, created pyramids of protection and patronage.[78] This is toxic for the investment climate and denies revenue to the state budget. The size and success of the opium industry also puts upward pressure on the exchange rate, rendering alternative tradable activities less viable. The resource curse (of which the 'Dutch Disease' is merely the most-cited aspect) applies not only to licit resources such as oil, but also to opium.

The vested interests that have supported the growth in opium production and processing since 2001 seem likely to rally around the industry once the majority of foreign soldiers leave in 2014. Production has flourished under the protection of a powerful shadow state; many of the warlords from the 1980s and 1990s now hold positions of responsibility from which they offer (for a price) protection to the production and transport of opium and heroin.[79] These powerful figures currently obtain income from other sources linked to the foreign military presence, including reconstruction aid, but particularly the transport of goods to the US military and the provision of security to those convoys. According to a US congressional report, warlords are the main subcontractors for security of the 6,000–8,000 trucks that supply US forces in Afghanistan each month. They also levy a protection tax on convoys passing through their territory, while every governor, police chief and local ANA commander receives bribes. The sums involved are huge: the Host Nation Trucking contract, which delivers 70% of the goods and materiel needed by US forces in Afghanistan, is worth $2.1bn.[80] After the security handover, there will be much less demand for those services. In this case, it is reasonable to assume that the share of opium-related income in the total illicit income of regional strongmen will increase, and with it their determination to support opium production and trafficking.

A vicious spiral, or a virtuous one?

Services and construction will undoubtedly suffer as the international military and civilian presence in the country winds down in the coming years. The IMF sees external grants at 38% of GDP in 2009/10, falling to 24% in 2012/13 and 16% in 2014/15.[81] However, there is little reason to believe that the 50% of the rural population engaged in subsistence agriculture will be greatly affected. Moreover, the resilience and ubiquity of the opium industry will continue to support large numbers of Afghans living in rural areas.

The state budget cannot afford to support a 400,000-strong ANSF but donors recognise this: the security forces are likely to be sustained by foreign funding for perhaps a decade after 2014. Financing of the current-account deficit, which is likely to shrink as foreign troops and civilian contractors go home, will likewise require foreign grants and concessionary loans. The IMF sees the current-account deficit before official transfers at 54% of GDP in 2009/10, 39% in 2012/13 and 31% in 2014/15.[82] For each year, however, the fund expects sizeable official transfers to bring down the reported deficit to 5% of GDP or less.

For the government, the main priority, aside from seeking to promote licit agriculture, will be to ensure that Aynak, Hajigak and other large-scale mining projects come to fruition. If they do, the government's revenue will increase and so, therefore, will its ability to extend services to a steadily greater proportion of the country and population. As the zone of security increases, so too will the territory open to foreign investment. That in turn would lead to further increases in government revenue, allowing a further increase in state spending. The overall effect would be to create a virtuous cycle, albeit one in which progress was slow and started from a low base. Conversely, a lengthy delay or failure of one of the signature projects could risk creating a vicious spiral in which the government lacked the resources to maintain spending and control, and as a result the area of the country available for peaceful, productive enterprise would contract. Even if this outcome can be avoided, Afghanistan is too isolated from major markets and too scarred by 30 years of war to become a fast-growing emerging market.

The government's ability to manage its own finances and the provision of basic services is a major concern. As Arnold Fields, the US Special Inspector General for Afghan Reconstruction, cautioned in mid-2010: 'We have not done enough to build the Afghans' capacity to manage their government and develop their economy.'[83] The economy's fortunes in the run-up to 2015 and beyond will be inextricably linked with the security situation in the country. A 400,000-strong ANSF is a burden that Afghanistan will be unable to bear alone for many years to come. Yet without security, Afghanistan has no prospect of building the licit economy and large army which it needs to ease problems of unemployment in a country with a fast-growing population.

CHAPTER FIVE

The ANSF and the insurgency

Ben Barry

The progress of a complex and non-linear military campaign is often difficult to assess while the war is still being fought. Only from 2010 did the ISAF operation receive the resources it needed to pursue a full counter-insurgency strategy of 'clear, hold and build'. ISAF reached its peak strength of 131,000 by December 2010, by which time its main effort was concentrated on the Taliban's heartland in Helmand and Kandahar provinces. Most reinforcing US forces had been deployed there, as well as increasing numbers of Afghan forces. ISAF also launched more strikes against insurgent leaders by special forces. In 2010, a tripling in the number of ISAF raids resulted in the killing of more than 1,200 insurgents, including some 300 thought to hold leadership roles.

However, in 2010, 711 foreign troops were killed, the highest annual total in the decade-old campaign. UN figures showed it was also the worst year for civilian deaths, with more than 2,700 fatalities.[1] According to ISAF, the number of attacks across the country fell by 8% in the eight months to September 2011, compared with the same period in 2010. The breakdown on the location of the attacks gives an indication of how much territory out of the five ISAF regional commands plus the capital was under the control of the Afghan authorities in the second half of 2011. As of September 2011, just 7% of recorded insurgent attacks took place in Kabul, Regional Command North (covering the northern provinces that border Turkmenistan, Uzbekistan, Tajikistan and China, running east-to-west from Badakhshan to Faryab) and Regional Command West (the provinces of Herat and Farah, both of which border Iran, plus neighbouring Badghis and Ghor). The vast majority of attacks took place in the southern and eastern regions: 33% in Regional Command South-West (Helmand and Nimruz), 21% in Regional Command South (Kandahar, Zabul, Uruzgan and Day Kundi), and 39% in Regional Command East, which includes the provinces bordering northwest Pakistan and those surrounding Kabul.[2] The distribution and declining number of attacks suggest that ISAF and the Afghan National Security Forces (ANSF) were finally gaining an advantage over the Taliban in the south and southwest, as well as being broadly in control of the northern and western regions. Indeed, independent survey data from 2011 show that in nine out of 14 areas of Afghanistan, a majority of respondents said NATO and the ANSF were winning the war, rather than the Taliban.[3]

However, ISAF has made little progress in the eastern regions, where the foreign troop presence has increased dramatically to counter the insurgency (see 'Ten years of NATO operation', Strategic Geography, p. iv). Moreover, there was no reduction in 2011 in the level of attacks involving improvised explosive devices (IEDs) or in civilian casualties. The UN documented 1,462 civilian deaths in the first six months of 2011, an increase of 15% over the same period in 2010, due to greater use of IEDs against civilians, suicide attacks, targeted killings and more civilian deaths from air-strikes.[4] In spite of the fall in the overall number of attacks, it was difficult as the 2011 fighting season drew to a close to reconcile ISAF's cautious optimism with the insurgents' continued resilience, which also saw them carrying out a successful campaign of assassinations of key government figures, as well as a series of spectacular attacks in Kabul. If such attacks continue with sufficient frequency, they are likely to create in Afghanistan and internationally a pervasive impression of un-governability and failure of transition. Furthermore, if the insurgents sustain their rate of assassinations, they may cause significant attrition to politicians and officials needed to run the country.

The state of the insurgency

Afghan insurgent groups have adopted common strategic objectives: the expulsion of ISAF forces, the overthrow of the Karzai government and, for some groups, the restoration of a Salafist Islamic regime. The insurgency draws largely from the ethnic Pashtun population, the majority of which is based in the southwest, south and east of the country. There are also pockets of Pashtuns and limited activity in Kabul and northern and western Afghanistan.

Although there are full-time insurgents, many 'foot soldiers' are young men who take up arms on a part-time basis. Most of these combatants are motivated by local grievances, including the desire to avenge friends and family members killed in earlier fighting with NATO and Afghan government forces. This means, at the tactical level, that it can often be difficult to distinguish insurgent groupings from militias organised by local drug barons. Afghanistan's complex and fluid tribal systems have made it difficult for ISAF to understand the differences between such groups. The insurgents have further added to the social complexity by exploiting and exacerbating grievances between tribal groupings, particularly over land disputes. Against this background, the insurgents' offer to the

Afghan people remains simple, even if it does not appeal to all of them: security and dispute resolution based on a harsh interpretation of Islamic law. In areas where this contrasts starkly with the absence of Afghan government institutions or their profound corruption, it remains a potent recruiting message. In areas controlled by the insurgents, their 'offer' remains more credible than ISAF's or that of the Afghan government. Their radical ideology is one of their greatest weaknesses, since it is unpopular in many areas. Tactically, their main weakness is their inability to contest ISAF's control of the air and the surveillance, tactical mobility and firepower advantages that this confers on ISAF.

The most active and widespread insurgent movement is the Quetta Shura Taliban led by Mullah Omar and based in Quetta, Pakistan. Their operations have spread from southern Afghanistan to Pashtun areas in the west and north of the country. Secondly, the Haqqani network, responsible for many attacks in the east and in Kabul, has sought to counter the Indian presence in Afghanistan. Its leadership and infrastructure are based in North Waziristan, Pakistan. The network collaborates with the Quetta Shura Taliban, but appears to have a high degree of operational autonomy in eastern Afghanistan. The third major Taliban group, Hizb-e-Islami Gulbuddin, also based in Pakistan, is somewhat less capable than the others. Foreign fighters play a role in all these groups, particularly as suicide bombers, but this is not decisive. Al-Qaeda provides support and funding from safe havens in Pakistan.

The insurgency seeks to dominate the Afghan people by controlling populated areas, using them as a source of recruits and income. In the early years of the conflict, insurgent groups often fought conventionally, massing in platoon- or company-size forces, using small arms and rocket-propelled grenades. Although fighting was often heavy, US and NATO ground forces, using attack helicopters and bombers, prevailed over such conventional targets. Since then insurgent tactics have become increasingly asymmetric, with the ever-increasing use of IEDs. These have tended to be simple, easily fabricated, quickly emplaced and, with the decreasing use of metal components, very difficult to counter. This, and the abundance of ordnance left over from the war with the Soviets, means most insurgents do not need an extensive supply network.

Assassination and intimidation have been used to neutralise government institutions and traditional tribal and religious leadership, allowing the imposition of parallel insurgent structures of governance. The insurgents seek to intimidate the population and reinforce the message that their victory is inevitable after 2015. Much of this effort has been focused on Kandahar, where as well as a host of junior and mid-ranking officials, the deputy provincial governor, mayor, provincial police chief and the head of the Kandahar Shura have all been killed. In addition, two influential figures close to President Hamid Karzai, his special adviser Jan Muhammad Khan and his half brother and important Pashtun power-broker Ahmed Wali Karzai, were assassinated. The killing of former President Burhanuddin Rabbani in October 2011, although disavowed by the Taliban, suggests that some key insurgent figures want to derail the Afghan government's efforts at negotiation.

The construction of the ANSF

Until 2009, international efforts to develop the ANSF through mentoring, training and equipping were insufficient to match the deteriorating security situation. A twin-track approach was undertaken to tackle this. Shortly after his arrival as ISAF commander in 2009, General Stanley McChrystal increased emphasis on building the capability of the ANSF, including the concept of 'embedded partnering'. This aimed to combine the two military forces into a single team, exploiting ISAF's combat power and technology and the ANSF's situational awareness. The concept was applied at every level, from government ministries down to patrols and checkpoints.

Afghan National Army (ANA) formations units are supported by integrated NATO Operational Mentoring and Liaison Teams (OMLTs). Typically, an ANA brigade will have OMLTs at brigade, battalion and company headquarters. These not only assist Afghan commanders with operational planning, but also control NATO combat support, including artillery, helicopters and air-strikes.[5]

Away from the front line, US and NATO efforts to build capacity were stepped up dramatically. Funds allocated by NATO to invest in the ANSF in 2010 and 2011 topped $20 billion, which matches the total invested from 2002 to 2009. Basic army and police training have doubled in capacity. Quality has also been considerably improved, with proper passing-out tests introduced for all graduating recruits. Considerable investment has been made in training bases. One sign of progress was that the number of qualified non-commissioned officers (NCOs) rose from 1,950 in November 2009 to 16,000 in March 2011.

A little publicised aspect of the British and American effort has been to assist the Afghan security service, the National Directorate for Security (NDS), with its counter-Taliban intelligence efforts. Meanwhile, the ANA and the Afghan National Police (ANP) in southern Afghanistan are also receiving help in boosting their human-intelligence capabilities.

At the time of writing, ISAF was confident that the ANSF would reach the target size of 305,000 by the end of 2011. There was no shortage of recruits and systems had been put in place to politically vet new soldiers and test them for narcotics abuse. The ANA is composed primarily of infantry, optimised for counter-insurgency. It has six Corps HQs and a Capital division HQ, with a total of 20 infantry brigades. There are also special-operations forces. ANA formations have limited combat support and logistic capabilities, including counter-IED, artillery and tanks, although NATO plans to considerably improve these capabilities by 2015. The ANA Air Corps is almost 5,000 strong, equipped with 59 aircraft: a mixture of Mi-17 support helicopters, Mi-35 attack helicopters and C-27 transport aircraft. In June 2011, an ISAF assessment found that all but one of the ANA's Corps HQ and 17 of its 20 brigades were capable of executing operations and providing security with ISAF assistance. Among the 158 *kandaks* (battalions), two were regarded as being capable of independent operation, 55 were rated as effective with advisers, 56 effective with assistance, and the remainder 'developing'. (Strategic Geography p. xx, illustrates the process of transition to Afghan control). By 2014, the majority need to be either independent or effective with advisers.

During 2010, the Afghan army played an increasing role in military operations. For example, the third phase of *Operation Moshtarak* saw an Afghan corps HQ take the lead in a substantial operation, and later phases of *Operation HamKari* were initiated with set-piece orders by Afghan rather than NATO commanders. The better ANA units and formations proved themselves capable of taking the lead in operations against insurgents. Successful countering of 'spectacular' attacks in Kabul by Afghan forces was a further sign of progress. However, overall performance remained variable and there were indications of weakness throughout the ANSF.[6]

Partly, this is a question of capabilities. The ANA still requires the creation of the full range of combat support, logistics and administration found in fully functioning armies. Management systems, in particular personnel management, are a weakness,

with particular regard to identifying and developing sufficient commanders and leaders. The army remains susceptible
to bribery, nepotism and tribal favouritism. This has allowed
many ANSF officers to evade service in especially violent areas.
There is not yet a properly structured system to rotate Afghan
troops in and out of operational areas, which erodes morale
and has been a major cause of absenteeism and desertion.[7]

Quality of personnel is another concern. In addition to incidents of individual soldiers and police turning their weapons
on their ISAF mentors, resulting in over 30 ISAF deaths, the
ANA is plagued by the high levels of illiteracy that affect
Afghan society: the national literacy rate is just 28%, according to the UNDP.[8] This has been a significant hindrance to the
development of the ANSF, especially its officer corps, NCO
middle management, combat support, logistics and personnel
management. Since 2009, there has been an increased focus on
literacy: all recruits are now educated at least to the level of
an American first grader. This minimum standard has been
achieved for over half the ANSF and further improvements are
planned. The success of the literacy programme has acted as a
recruiting draw and has improved the prestige of the security
forces within society.

Ethnic tensions within the security forces persist. Overall,
the ANA is broadly representative of the country's mixture of
ethnicities. In 2011, Pashtuns made up 45% of the officer corps
and 42% of the army as a whole. The corresponding figures
for Tajiks are 32% and 40%, for Hazaras 10% and 7%, and for
Uzbeks 6% and 4%. This still leaves a problem in the south,
where ANA recruitment is low; an initiative to allow southern Pashtuns to serve close to home seeks to address this.
Desertion and absentee rates remain high, primarily because
some Afghan soldiers go absent without leave to visit their
families and take their pay home. To counter this, ISAF has

established a chartered air service to help soldiers wishing to go on leave and then return to their units.

As with previous transitions in other countries, the effort to generate the ANP lagged way behind that of the army. Before 2010, the ANP was almost as much a part of the security problem as of the solution, with low-level corruption and predatory extortion at checkpoints of particular concern. The Afghan Uniformed Police (AUP) makes up the majority of the force. National efforts to train the AUP have been bolstered by initiatives such as the British-led Helmand Police Training Centre. Meanwhile, the Afghan National Civil Order Police (ANCOP), a paramilitary arm, is judged by ISAF as relatively trustworthy and effective, having accompanied NATO special forces on raids. ISAF is putting considerable effort into mentoring and developing the ANCOP, especially as its use in high-threat environments has meant that casualty rates have been high.

The ANP comprises 96,000 uniformed police who perform the core civil policing, a 12,000-strong civil order force optimised for counter-insurgency and support of the ANA, 25,000 border police and 2,200 police special forces. There are also specialist counter-narcotics and criminal-investigation capabilities, as well as a major-crimes task force. In addition, there are some 4,000 citizens enrolled into the Afghan Local Police programme, which sustains small self-defence forces in villages that have opted to resist the Taliban in areas with little ISAF or ANSF presence. It has exploited successful revolts against the Taliban by some villages, for example in Gizab district in Uruzgan province. Described by General David Petraeus as a 'community watch with AK47s', the programme is seen as a relatively cheap method of checking the insurgency's progress. With support from co-located US and ISAF special forces, it had become operational in 44 out of a planned 77 sites by September 2011.[9]

In spite of the efforts made to improve the ANP, it is understood that considerable work still needed to be done. The requirement for police training and mentoring after 2015 is expected to be much greater than that required for the ANA.

The outlook for transition, 2011–14

The NATO political strategy was set out in a speech by Mark Sedwill, outgoing Senior Civilian Representative, in March 2011. It focused on improving security across the country so that specific districts and provinces could be transferred to Afghan security leadership. This was to be done in conjunction with efforts to seek reconciliation with key insurgent groups. Governance, including the delivery of public services, was to be improved. Plans for long-term sustainable economic development were to be put in place. However, the fact that all these strands of effort were still being stressed, nearly a decade after the international community began to address the country's governance and economy, underlined the major challenges involved. The task facing the Afghan government and its NATO allies was little short of Herculean.

At the Kabul International Conference in July 2010, the Afghan government and NATO endorsed Intequal, a plan for transition under which the government in Kabul would gradually take full responsibility for security, governance and development across the whole country. In March 2011, Karzai announced the beginning of this transition, with three provinces – Bamyan, Panjshir and Kabul (except Surobi district) – and five districts (Herat City in Herat, Lashkar Gah in Helmand, Mazar-e-Sharif in Balkh province and Mehtar Lam in Laghman) handed over to Afghan government control in July. These areas are home to 20–25% of the population, according to ISAF.

The success of Intequal depends on the Afghan security forces' ability to tackle the security challenges in a given area, albeit with some level of continued support from NATO. The transition is conditions-based, not defined by rigid timetables. A combined Afghan–NATO assessment process has been put in place to oversee the transition. Under this assessment, an area cannot be turned over to Afghan control until the population is secure enough to pursue routine daily activities. Local governance has to reach a certain level so that it is no longer a threat to security. Finally, and most crucially, the Afghan security forces must have the capacity to replace NATO troops without leaving a security vacuum. The assessments also consider the ability of the Afghan government to guarantee the rule of law while managing public administration.

NATO has repeatedly emphasised that the transition represents a gradual shift to a supporting role as Afghan capabilities develop. This process is expected to take between 12 and 18 months in each area. After the transition is complete, ISAF is likely to continue to have a presence, including air support and quick-reaction forces. ISAF mentors will continue to be attached to ANA and ANP units, although the number of mentors will be reduced as Afghan forces grow in confidence and capability.

At the time of writing, the military campaign had become a race against the clock for NATO and the Afghan government to improve security, build the ANSF, develop the capacity and integrity of the Afghan state, and try to persuade 'reconcilable' insurgents to lay down their arms. As much of this as possible has to be completed in time to meet the objective of Kabul assuming the lead for security across the country by the end of 2014.

ISAF troop numbers are set to fall following US President Barack Obama's announcement in June 2011 that 10,000 US troops would be withdrawn by the start of 2012 and a further 23,000 by mid-2012. US troop reductions were likely to be at least matched by cuts in the 40,000 non-US troops.

The Netherlands and Canada have withdrawn combat troops, although both have left smaller contingents to train the ANSF. British Prime Minister David Cameron also announced that the 10,000-strong UK force would be reduced by almost 1,000 by the end of 2012 and that any UK troops remaining in 2015 would no longer have a combat role.[10]

Indications were that in 2012 ISAF would seek to consolidate its security gains in southern Afghanistan, continuing to hand over the most secure areas to Afghan control. Admiral Mike Mullen, outgoing chairman of the US Joint Chiefs of Staff, told the Senate Armed Service Committee that US, NATO and Afghan forces would 'increasingly focus on eastern Afghanistan' in 2012, but that he did not expect to see the effects of these operations before the end of that year.[11] US Secretary of Defense Leon Panetta has assessed that in eastern Afghanistan 'the topography, the cultural geography and the continuing presence of safe havens in Pakistan give the insurgents advantages they have lost elsewhere in the country'.[12]

NATO commanders had anticipated a gradual force reduction, as was recommended by Petraeus. They believed that troop reductions would be 'conditions-based'. However, the relatively steeper drawdown announced by Obama – who made no mention of conditions, nor hinted at flexibility – was expected to make it difficult for ISAF to both sustain security gains in southern Afghanistan and contest insurgent-controlled eastern areas. The military view was that this created an opportunity for insurgents to concentrate forces in eastern Afghanistan and threaten Kabul.

Clearly, given the short time remaining, at least some aspects of NATO's ambitious transition plan are unlikely to be achieved. NATO and the ANSF continued to lack 'silver bullets' to end the insurgency, which – as all parties acknowledged – would require far more than a military solution.

To 2015 and beyond

The security situation from 2015 onwards will depend on three factors: the level of military assistance that the US and its allies offer to the Afghan government, the strength of the insurgency after most foreign troops go home, and the capability and cohesion of the ANSF.

NATO and the United States have repeatedly stated that they are committed to supporting and assisting Afghanistan after 2014. US negotiators have begun preparations to secure a strategic partnership agreement as a framework for long-term political, military and development cooperation. Some countries, including Australia and the United Kingdom, have publicly committed to assistance with training the ANSF.

It is far from clear what size, shape or role the international forces in Afghanistan will have after 2015. The nature and effectiveness of any political settlement between the Afghan government and insurgent groups – if such an agreement is possible – would be a major factor, as well as the capability of the ANSF. Arrangements will also be influenced by the degree of confidence of the Afghan government and the ANSF, and the extent to which both exert national sovereignty. The latter influence, if driven forward by popular Afghan nationalism, could lead to the rejection of foreign advice and assistance and an insistence that any foreign troops or personnel remaining in Afghanistan after 2015 operate under the close direction of Afghan authorities.

At the same time, ISAF contributing nations will be attempting to minimise their footprint in Afghanistan, especially in terms of the numbers of troops stationed in the country. If the security situation has improved sufficiently, it may be possible to reduce to a minimum the number of military advisers needed, principally in ANSF training establishments and government ministries. There would, however, be a continuing need for military and civilian intelligence personnel, ensuring cooperation and connectivity between the US, NATO and Afghan intelligence agencies. This in large part would be to counter the danger that Afghanistan or the Pakistan border regions could act as a breeding ground for international terrorists. Counter-terrorism would also benefit if the US were able to operate unmanned aircraft carrying out surveillance and strikes from Afghan bases.

This option is relevant to NATO's ability to support the ANSF with air-strikes. It is intended that by 2015 the ANA Air Corps will have achieved a fixed and rotary wing air transport capability, as well as fielding attack helicopters. However, the ANSF will still be heavily dependent on ISAF to provide offensive air capabilities. Fixed-wing aircraft and special forces would be less effective if based outside Afghanistan, but political realities may make this necessary.

With regard to the second variable, the insurgency post-2014, it is not clear to what extent Taliban fighters will lose motivation with the departure of foreign troops. Insurgent 'foot soldiers' and leaders whose principal motivation is nationalist resistance to foreign forces could be persuaded to pursue a negotiated settlement after the transition process has significantly reduced the foreign troop presence. It is difficult to predict the extent to which transition to Afghan security leadership will provide these people with the motivation to rejoin the political process. On the other hand, ISAF estimates that 90% of all insurgents killed or captured have their homes within 10km of where they fight.[13] The Pentagon's November 2010 'Report on Progress Toward Security and Stability in Afghanistan' argued:

> the Taliban is not a popular movement, but it exploits
> a population frustrated by weak governance. The
> Taliban's strength lies in the Afghan population's

perception that Coalition forces will soon leave, giving credence to the belief that a Taliban victory is inevitable, exploiting many Afghans' belief that insufficient enduring improvement in security and governance will made before NATO leaves. [14]

Concerns about the ANSF after 2014 centre on its cohesion, effectiveness and corruption. There are worries about the financial affordability of the Afghan security forces. Estimates vary, but UK government officials quote an approximate annual cost of the planned ANSF after 2014 as $6–8bn. [15] At the time of writing, over 90% of the costs of the ANA and ANP are met by the US, with the remainder being contributed by other nations. US Defense Secretary Panetta made it clear he expected NATO nations to make a significant financial contribution to the Afghan security forces after 2014. However, it seems highly unlikely that the US and other Western nations will sustain their current level of financial support to the ANSF. If Afghan indigenous revenues do not rise to meet the shortfall created by declining Western funding, the ANSF will face capability reductions unless third parties, such as Gulf states, help to bridge the gap.

Afghanistan seems unlikely to transition to a benign security environment before 2020 at the earliest. Most likely, the eastern region that currently presents the greatest security challenge to ISAF and the ANSF will never be brought under full control. However, given the capabilities of the ANSF and the likelihood of continuing ISAF support beyond 2014, the most likely prospect for transition is either that the ANSF maintains control of the territory that it held in late 2011 in tandem with ISAF, or that the ANSF loses some ground to the insurgency but does not collapse. In either scenario, a full transition to Afghan control will happen. This assessment was shared by the commander of the ISAF Joint Command from 2009–11, US Lieutenant General David Rodriguez, who insisted that only a major increase in terrorist activity emanating from neighbouring states would prevent the ANSF from securing the country's key terrain.[16]

The greatest long-term risk to stability is that efforts to improve Afghan governance will have been insufficient to remove many of the root causes of popular discontent that are the fuel of the insurgency. If governance does not dramatically improve, then an increase in insurgent violence can be expected. But with the US, NATO and other nations having withdrawn most of their forces, the revived insurgency would have to be primarily countered by the ANSF.

Lessons of previous transitions

Security transition is not new. Bosnia-Herzegovina saw a successful security transition after the signing of the Dayton agreement in 1995. A 60,000-strong NATO peace-enforcement force was steadily reduced to a lighter EU military force, which currently has 1,600 troops. Police forces that had harboured hardline extremists were, after six years of international effort to reform and retrain, assessed by the UN as competent to police their country.

In Iraq, the US-led coalition sought to transition the country to Iraqi leadership from the outset, following the 2003 invasion. The initial strategic intent articulated by President George W. Bush that 'as Iraqis stand up we stand down' could not be achieved until after the 'Anbar Awakening' and the 2007 surge had improved security.

The gains of 2008–09 allowed transition to Iraqi security leadership. When provinces transitioned to Iraqi control, the US ground forces moved from a leadership to a supporting role. US brigades were reconfigured to give 'advice and assistance'. These continued to provide embedded mentors and to train Iraqi forces as well as providing quick-reaction forces. It is likely that the US will apply a similar tactical approach in Afghanistan.

These transitions were in societies that were better-off and more developed than Afghanistan. The security threat posed by irreconcilable forces in the Balkans was much less sustained than is the case in Afghanistan. Nevertheless, among the lessons learned was that the assessment of readiness of any area or capability to transition to local leadership must be rigorous and honest. The British experience in Iraq was that political pressures were brought to bear from all quarters for transition to proceed; but without a fundamentally honest understanding of the situation, risk was increased rather than transferred, deferred or decreased. This explained why Basra province was handed to Iraqi security control far too early. This was followed by inadequate British mentoring of the Iraqi security forces and insufficient situational awareness. The apparent inflexibility of the US drawdown timeline for Afghanistan may produce similar effects.

Prospects

Transition is an inherently risky business, and is likely to see steps both forwards and backwards – in spite of ISAF's insistence that it must be 'irreversible'. There is likely to be tension between the desire to achieve an end-state and the political requirement for an end to foreign combat presence. NATO and the Afghan government may have to resist political pressure from troop-contributing governments anxious to declare success as early as possible, in order to withdraw their forces. Whether they will be able to do so is unclear.

Progress will be made at different speeds in different areas, possibly resulting in different outcomes. NATO's plan needs to be robust and flexible enough to take this into consideration. Where necessary, a clear capacity to re-engage or intervene is required. This means reaction forces will be required. The US surge in Iraq can be seen as a strategic re-intervention to create the conditions that then allowed for a successful transition. Use of over-the-horizon forces was a notable part of NATO's approach in Bosnia. However, declining public support for the Afghan war may make strategic re-intervention problematic. This argues for the formation of both ANSF and ISAF tactical and operational reserves inside Afghanistan, able to intervene again across the country. These do not appear to be part of current NATO planning.

As transition progresses, the information-gathering capacity of the intervening force will decrease, so there is an increased requirement for intelligence and surveillance in order to maintain situational awareness. Developing indigenous intelligence and surveillance capability not only improves the effectiveness of the indigenous forces, but also allows the withdrawing external forces to benefit from the situational awareness of Afghan forces – provided that they have a strong intelligence-sharing relationship.

Applying this approach in Afghanistan would maintain ISAF's ability to understand the situation and influence the ANSF. Over time, an increasing proportion of intelligence and surveillance would be provided by the ANSF. By virtue of their Afghan identity, the ANA, ANP and NDS are usually better at collecting human intelligence than ISAF, and this capability is likely to improve. But they are most unlikely to be able to field the full range of sophisticated capabilities currently fielded by ISAF and the US, so continuing to develop the intelligence capabilities of all three organisations will need to continue, as will improving the ANA and ANP special forces. The later stages of the Iraq War showed a tendency by political leaders to employ intelligence agencies and special forces as political tools, rather than in the national interest. NATO will need to guard against similar behaviour in Afghanistan.

ISAF's influence on the Afghan authorities will probably decline as the latter gain in strength and confidence. They will need NATO less, and so will listen less. This may well lead to increasing divergences in policy. For NATO governments, the ways to mitigate this include increased emphasis on building effective relationships with key politicians, officials, intelligence personnel and military and police commanders.

CHAPTER SIX

The international and regional terror threat

Nigel Inkster

It was the threat from al-Qaeda that brought the United States and its allies to Afghanistan, and it is the need to ensure that the country cannot again become a haven for terrorism that is cited as the primary justification for the continuing counter-insurgency (COIN) campaign, with all its attendant costs and political unpopularity. The death of Osama bin Laden, in a March 2011 raid by US special forces in Abbottabad, Pakistan, undoubtedly represents a major milestone in the US's effort to degrade al-Qaeda. But that job is still far from done, and the likelihood is that bin Laden's death will give rise to revenge attacks which may in the short term exacerbate the threat. Nor is the killing of America's most wanted criminal likely to lead to an early reduction of extremist violence in either Afghanistan or Pakistan, where groups sympathetic to al-Qaeda have launched reprisal attacks against the Pakistani state, including a fedayeen assault on 21 May on Pakistan's main naval base in Karachi.[1]

The circumstances of bin Laden's death have also reactivated the debate that took place in the United States prior to the November 2009 military surge. On one side of the argument were those who advocated 'counter-terrorism plus', that is, maintaining just enough of a US military presence to deter al-Qaeda from re-entering Afghanistan while focusing the bulk of US counter-terrorism efforts on al-Qaeda's new bases in Pakistan.[2] On the other were those, predominantly within the US military establishment, who favoured a continuation and expansion of the existing COIN campaign designed to produce an Afghan state that was stable enough to be able to take responsibility for its own security.

Judgements about the most appropriate strategy for dealing both with Afghanistan and with terrorism depend critically on a good understanding of the nature of al-Qaeda and its relationships with an array of jihadist groups. It also requires an ability to distinguish between terrorists and insurgents, which is not always easy in a situation where the two inevitably overlap to some degree. A particular concern is to determine whether an Afghan Taliban in control of at least part of Afghan territory would necessarily welcome or tolerate al-Qaeda attempting to re-establish its pre-2001 bases there. To determine the nature of the threat now posed by al-Qaeda, and the options available to mitigate that threat, it is helpful to examine the emergence of al-Qaeda, its move to Afghanistan, its relationships with other groups and the evolution of its operational strategy and ideology.

The origins of al-Qaeda

The Soviet invasion of Afghanistan in 1979 was one of four events that year which collectively had a profound impact on the Islamic world – the others being the Egypt–Israel Peace Treaty, the overthrow of the shah of Iran and the occupation by a militant group of the Grand Mosque at Mecca. One arguable consequence of this cluster of events was an upsurge in religiosity, driven by a sense of disempowerment and a lack of alternative vehicles for political expression, and fuelled by a massive expansion of Wahhabi proselytisation. The Wahhabi preachers were backed by a newly oil-rich Saudi regime anxious to ingratiate itself with its own *ulema*, or religious leadership, following the use of Western military forces to resolve the occupation of the Grand Mosque and to counter the influence of Iran, whose Shia theocracy sought actively to export its revolutionary ideology. The mujahadeen resistance to the Soviet occupation of Afghanistan offered Saudi Arabia the chance to assert its credentials as the spiritual leader of the Islamic world by providing substantial material assistance in conjunction with the US. According to one estimate, total CIA funding to the Afghan mujahadeen, channelled through Pakistan's Inter-Services Intelligence directorate (ISI), amounted to $9 billion, with Saudi Arabia matching the CIA dollar for dollar.[3] The official Saudi funding was supplemented by donations from wealthy Muslims in Saudi Arabia and the Gulf states.

This material assistance was accompanied by a growing flow of volunteers from around the Islamic world who wanted to take part in the anti-Soviet jihad. The overwhelming majority of these volunteers, estimated at some 10,000 in total, did not in fact set foot in Afghanistan nor take part in combat operations – though many received some form of military training in mujahadeen camps organised in conjunction with the ISI – but rather focused on providing a range of support services centred around the mujahadeen's main rear-echelon bases in and around Peshawar, the capital of Pakistan's Northwest Frontier Province – now Khyber Pakhtunkhwa. Such initially was the case with Saudi national Osama bin Laden. It is unclear exactly when and in what circumstances bin Laden first came to Peshawar, but by the mid-1980s he was well established there as a philanthropist whose activities included building roads to facilitate mujahadeen access to the Afghan borders.

By 1986, however, bin Laden was no longer content to perform only a support role and moved into Afghanistan, setting up a camp in the village of Jaji, near Jalalabad. When eventually this camp was attacked by Soviet forces, bin Laden's Arab fighters put up an unexpectedly stiff resistance and succeeded in driving off their attackers. Though militarily of no great significance, the events at Jaji cemented bin Laden's reputation as a jihadist and significantly influenced his future direction. It also highlighted the differences between an Arab force that fought uncompromisingly and an Afghan mujaha-deen for whom fighting occupied one point on a spectrum that also included negotiation and retreat. Although there is some debate as to when bin Laden founded al-Qaeda, it may have been as early as the year following his victory at Jaji.[4]

A key factor in the evolution of bin Laden's trajectory towards a strategy of global jihad was the influence of jihadists from countries such as Egypt and Libya, who had been engaged in unsuccessful efforts to overthrow rulers whom they deemed 'apostates'. Among these was Ayman al-Zawahiri, a member of Egyptian Islamic Jihad. In the mid-1980s, after being impris-oned and tortured by the Egyptian authorities for his efforts to overthrow the regime, he moved to Peshawar. Zawahiri later accompanied bin Laden to Sudan and, after a brief and unpro-ductive sojourn in Chechnya, rejoined him in Afghanistan following the Taliban takeover. In due course, Zawahiri merged his Egyptian Islamic Jihad organisation with al-Qaeda and became the group's de facto deputy. The collective experi-ence of the jihadist groups he fought alongside during this time led bin Laden to conclude not only that the overthrow of the 'apostate' regimes required a concerted, global approach, but also that there needed first to be a focus on the Western sources of support for these regimes. Thus the 'near enemy' became a secondary target after the 'far enemy', specifically, the US and its Western allies. There was never a clear consensus within al-Qaeda or other jihadists groups regarding this distinction, as will be seen below.

Following the end of the anti-Soviet jihad – which was misleadingly portrayed in the jihadi discourse as the defeat of a superpower by a dedicated force of jihadi fighters – many of the Arab and other Islamic volunteers dispersed back to their own countries or to other conflicts such as Bosnia and Chechnya. Others, who had acquired Afghan or Pakistani wives and families, remained in Pakistan. Bin Laden returned to Saudi Arabia, where he became progressively alienated from the house of Saud. Eventually he relocated to Sudan, where he began to run terrorist training camps, provide funding and facilitation for jihadist groups throughout the Islamic world, and campaign publicly for the overthrow of the house of Saud.[5] Bin Laden's precise role in an emerging global pattern of Sunni extremist violence as manifested by the 1992 attacks on the World Trade Center in New York and abortive efforts in the Philippines to assassinate the Pope and to blow up multiple airliners over the Pacific – collectively referred to as *Operation Bojinka* – is still somewhat nebulous. The perpetrators of these attacks, Khalid Sheikh Mohamed and his nephew Ramzi Youssef, could not at that point be characterised as cadre members of an organisation called al-Qaeda, nor had they sworn *bay'a* – an oath of loyalty – to Osama bin Laden, though Youssef did acknowledge him as an influence. But a realisation of bin Laden's growing importance as a facilitator and financier of terrorist groups led the US government to pressure Sudan to expel him. In 1996 bin Laden moved his operation to Jalalabad in eastern Afghanistan, where he was welcomed by local warlords whom he had known from the anti-Soviet jihad. Shortly thereafter, the Taliban movement, at whose core was a group of young Kandahari madrassa students led by Mullah Omar and enabled by Pakistani and

Saudi military and financial support, succeeded in establishing control over much of the country.

The relationship that evolved between bin Laden and the Taliban between 1996 and 2001 has often been interpreted as amounting to a symbiosis. The reality was, however, more complex and nuanced. The Taliban leadership, madrassa-educated and with no knowledge of or interest in the world outside Afghanistan, were initially suspicious of bin Laden. He was nonetheless able to ingratiate himself gradually in the way he knew best, by deploying his considerable wealth. As Vahid Majdeh, a former official in the Afghan Foreign Ministry put it: 'Osama and his loyalists were of course well aware of how to influence the Taliban ... The purchase of expensive automobiles for (Taliban leader) Mullah Omar and his loyalists was the first step ... Financial support in the war against the Taliban's opposition, in particular buying off the opposing commanders, [also] proved an effective strategy.'[6]

Bin Laden was to go on to make even more extravagant promises of assistance to the Taliban leadership, on many of which he failed to deliver. According to veteran jihadi strategist Mustafa Setmariam Nasar, better known by his *kunya*, or honorific title, of Abu Musab al-Suri, bin Laden held out the prospect of 'urbanisation projects, road-building, economic projects, the provision of mujahadeen to defend Kabul [but] the wind blew them all away'.[7] Notwithstanding the comments of an observer who was clearly *parti pris* (al-Suri had become progressively more disenchanted with bin Laden and came to see 9/11 as an act of catastrophic stupidity), bin Laden did provide some significant military assistance to the Taliban in the form of the 055 Brigade, an elite foreign jihadi force integrated with the Taliban army and used against both the Northern Alliance forces and in pogroms against the Shia Hazara, a Persian-speaking minority from central Afghanistan.

While seducing his hosts with offers of financial and other support, bin Laden quickly began to try their patience through an increasingly overt espousal of global jihad, both by word and deed. Many in the Taliban leadership took exception to this extreme stance, which appeared to violate undertakings they thought they had extracted from him not to address the media without first consulting them and not directly to antagonise the US. They are quoted as warning him: 'if you wish to fight America and your adversaries, then do so without much talk and shouting from our lands as our condition is critical.'[8] Far from heeding his hosts' injunctions, bin Laden proceeded in May 1998 to proclaim the establishment of the International Islamic Front for Jihad Against the Jewsand Crusaders. Three months later came the attacks on the US embassies in Nairobi and Dar-es-Salaam. Although al-Qaeda denied responsibility for these attacks, it subsequently became clear that the perpetrators had been trained and prepared for their missions in al-Qaeda camps in Afghanistan. The attacks led to US retaliation in the form of missile strikes on some known al-Qaeda training camps. The former head of the Saudi General Intelligence Presidency (GIP), Prince Turki bin Faisal, has claimed that shortly before the East Africa bombings, he had been on the brink of persuading the Taliban leadership to render bin Laden to Riyadh.[9] Whether such an agreement had in fact been reached, the US missile strikes hardened the resolve of Mullah Omar not to yield to outside pressure to give up his guest. By late 1999, the Taliban Council of Ministers had formally endorsed its alliance with al-Qaeda.[10]

Al-Qaeda was by no means the only foreign jihadist organisation located in Afghanistan in that period. Citing the writings of Abu Musab al -uri, Brynjar Lia lists 14 foreign jihadist formations in Afghanistan prior to 9/11, among which were:

- Non-Arab groups: these included Uzbeks based in Mazar-e-Sharif, Uighurs and Turks. Both Uzbeks and Uighurs had sworn *bay'a* to Osama bin Laden. In addition to those non-Arab groups listed by Suri should be added significant numbers of Pakistani jihadists from the anti-Shia Sipah-e-Sahaba Pakistan (SSP) organisation, which had provided much assistance to the Taliban in 1996 and had subsequently taken part in anti-Shia pogroms against the Hazara.
- Arab groups, including al-Qaeda itself, based in the complex of camps at Derunta near Jalalabad; the Libyan Islamic Fighting Group (LIFG); Ayman Zawahiri's Egyptian Islamic Jihad; the Islamic Fighting Group in Morocco, the Egyptian Islamic Group; Algerians, Tunisians and a group of Palestinians and Jordanians based at Herat under the command of Abu Musab al-Zarqawi, who would go on to attain notoriety as the head of al-Qaeda in Iraq post-2003.

In addition to these groups defined by nationality, there was a general entry-level camp at Khalden, near Khost, which is estimated to have had a throughput of some 20,000 jihadist students, a camp specialising in explosives run by the Egyptian Abu Khabbab al-Masri, and the Al Ghuraba camp near Kabul, at which Suri worked, which was formally affiliated with the Taliban.[11] There were also small numbers of Indonesians, Malaysians, Filipinos and Bangladeshis, most of whom were attached to al-Qaeda camps. (For the location of these camps, see 'Pre-2001 training camps', Strategic Geography, p. i).

Some of these groups were aligned with bin Laden from the outset and bought into his vision of global jihad and the concept of attacking the far enemy. Others remained focused on the struggles in their homelands and saw Afghanistan as little more than a convenient staging post en route back to these homelands rather than as a base from which to prosecute attacks on the US. The latter resisted efforts by bin Laden to impose himself as leader of all jihadist groups. As veteran jihadist Abu'l Walid al-Masri put it, following the 1998 US missile strikes: 'A number of the Arab jihadist leaders rose in opposition to bin Laden at this time, all of them affirming the primacy of the domestic front against the Arab regimes, convinced that a shift to a global confrontation against the United States was ill-conceived.'[12]

The foreign jihadists also had differing views about their Taliban hosts. For some, foremost among whom was al Suri, Afghanistan should be seen as an emirate from which global jihad should be propagated. This implied recognition of and subordination to Taliban leader Mullah Omar, whose self-proclaimed status as Amir al-Momineen – commander of the faithful – was a necessary pre-requisite for an emirate to exist. Many foreign jihadists, however, had serious reservations. Arab fighters were imbued with a sense of cultural superiority towards the Afghans. In particular, they looked down on long-established Sufist practices such as the veneration of the tombs of holy men – which for strict Salafists amounted to a rejection of *tawhid*, the indivisible nature of God. Moreover, the fact that the Taliban were seeking recognition from the UN, an organisation which in jihadist eyes was *ex hypothesi* illegitimate, put them further beyond the pale. The jihadists' *takfiri* ideology, under which any challenge to their interpretation of Islam is considered heretical, led some to view the Taliban as unbelievers. Even bin Laden himself appears to have hedged his bets by getting a proxy to swear *bay'a* to Mullah Omar on his behalf rather than doing so himself.[13]

The attacks on the World Trade Center and the Pentagon on 11 September 2001, and the US response they elicited, were a realisation of the worst fears of the Taliban government, which appears to have had no foreknowledge of it, and of those jihadists like Suri, who believed al-Qaeda should consolidate its gains in Afghanistan and play a more strategic game rather than engaging in premature adventurism. Bin Laden appears genuinely to have miscalculated the US response; proposals to fly one of the passenger jets into a nuclear power plant had been vetoed for fear that 'things would get out of control'.[14] Despite their reservations about the Taliban, many of the Afghan Arabs and their Uzbek allies put up fierce resistance to a Northern Alliance assault enabled by CIA advisers and US air power in November 2001. Many Pakistani jihadists, most of them veterans of the anti-Soviet jihad, also crossed the border into Afghanistan from the Federally Administered Tribal Areas (FATA) to resist the Northern Alliance. The majority of them lost their lives in US air-strikes.[15] The extent of the rout suffered by the jihadists emerges dramatically in an exchange of messages between Hamza bin Laden and his father Osama:

> HBL: Oh father! Where is the escape and where will we have a home? I see spheres of danger everywhere I look.
> OBL: Oh son! Suffice to say I am full of grief and sighs ... Pardon me, my son, but I can see only a steep path ahead.[16]

Those jihadists able to survive the Northern Alliance and US onslaught, including bin Laden and Zawahiri, made their way into the North and South Waziristan tribal agencies of FATA. A key figure in assisting the fleeing jihadists, by hiring local tribesmen to provide them with safe passage and sanctuary, was the veteran anti-Soviet jihadist, former Taliban minister and long-time ISI collaborator Jalaluddin Haqqani, who was born in the Khost region of Afghanistan bordering the tribal agencies and now headquartered near Miranshah in North Waziristan.[17] Young tribal leaders radicalised during the anti-Soviet jihad, such as Nik Mohamed Wazir and Baitullah Mehsud, who had begun to challenge the influence of the traditional leaders, or *maliks*, also helped secure safe passage out of Afghanistan. The Pakistani military deployed some forces to the Afghan–Pakistan border and into the tribal agencies in support of *Operation Enduring Freedom*, but its contribution was limited and largely failed to prevent the influx of foreign fighters. Those elements of the al-Qaeda leadership, including Abu Zubaydah, Khalid Sheikh Mohamed and Ramzi bin al-Shibh, who sought to relocate to urban areas were, however, quickly picked up by combined CIA/ISI operations, reinforcing the perception that for al-Qaeda the tribal areas were the safest place to be.

The jihadisation of Pakistan

The Pakistan to which bin Laden and his followers fled in 2001 was a country which had been profoundly altered by the anti-Soviet jihad. It was home to more than two million Afghan refugees and a large number of radicalised young Pakistani men.[18] The 1980s had also witnessed a marked shift away from the country's secular origins towards much greater Islamisation driven by then-President General Zia-ul-Haq and fuelled by widespread Wahhabi proselytising. The anti-Soviet jihad had given rise to the emergence of extreme jihadist groups within Pakistan, beginning in 1984 with the Harakat-ul-Jihad Islami (HUJI), founded by Fazlur Rehman Khalil and Qari Saifullah Akhtar, who was subsequently involved in a 1995 plot to overthrow Prime Minister Benazir Bhutto and establish an Islamic dictatorship.[19] The SSP was established the following year by Maulana Haq Nawaz Jhangvi with the primary aim of combating Shia influence. A significant breakaway group with the same agenda, Lashkar-e-Jhangvi, came into being some years later.

But the real growth in Pakistani jihadist groups occurred in the early 1990s, coinciding with an upsurge of political activism in Kashmir, which in turn led to a proxy war between Pakistan and India. This was prosecuted by Pakistan's ISI using groups such as Lashkar-e-Tayiba (LeT), whose confessional origins are to be found in the minority Sunni Ahl-e-Hadith tradition – which supports a literal interpretation of the Koran and the Hadith – and radical Sunni Deobandi groups such as Jaish-e-Mohammed (JeM) and Harakat-ul-Ansar. These groups raided Indian-controlled Kashmir and India itself out of training camps located in Pakistani Azad Kashmir and other locations inside Pakistan, with the ISI reportedly providing funding, training, weapons and a significant level of command and control.[20] The motivating force for these groups was Kashmir, but most of their membership was made up of non-Kashmiris. Though the involvement of the Pakistani state in these operations was widely known, the arrangement offered the Pakistani government a degree of plausible deniability up until the spring of 1999, when it became apparent that a Pakistani force overrunning strategically important Indian positions in Kargil on the Line of Control, which had been temporarily vacated for the winter, included significant elements of Pakistan's Northern Light Infantry. International pressure forced Pakistani Prime Minister Nawaz Sharif, who claimed to have been unsighted on his own military's plans, to order a withdrawal. This set him on a collision course with his army chief, General Pervez Musharraf, the architect of the Kargil operation, leading to a Musharraf's takeover in October 1999.

In the immediate aftermath of 9/11, the US government demanded the unconditional support of Pakistan for its global

'War on Terror'. In these circumstances it was particularly unfortunate that in December 2001 an attack took place on the Indian parliament by members of LeT and JeM, leading to a military stand-off between Pakistan and India which threatened to escalate into a nuclear exchange. Although it took until the middle of 2002 for India and Pakistan, with much intermediation from the international community, to agree to withdraw forces from each other's borders, on 12 January 2002 President Musharraf made an address to the nation declaring war on extremism and proscribing various extremist groups, including those involved in the attacks on the Indian parliament.[21] This announcement marked a shift away from Pakistan's policy of state-sponsored insurgency in Kashmir, with levels of infiltration declining substantially in the ensuing years – though never entirely ending. Many Kashmiri jihadists, disillusioned and embittered by the change of policy, relocated to the FATA, where their training camps were used both by aspirant jihadists seeking to fight in Afghanistan and by a slowly resurgent al-Qaeda. The ISI continued to liaise with and monitor the Kashmiri jihadist groups, but the fact that they were no longer providing funding deprived them of a significant measure of control.[22]

Musharraf's conversion to the cause of counter-terrorism was by no means as complete as the US might have hoped. It soon became clear to the US and its allies that although the ISI was content to participate in operations against al-Qaeda, especially after a fatwa issued against Musharraf by al-Qaeda in 2003 led to various attempts on his life, the agency's support for the US agenda was far from unconditional. Following Musharraf's 2002 address, some 3,000 militants were arrested, but many were quickly released without charge.[23] Banned groups were encouraged to reconstitute themselves with changes of names; LeT was reinvented as Jamaat-ud-Dawa. As Ahmed Rashid observed: 'The army and the ISI, still obsessed with enemy India, were to resurrect the Islamists from defeat and demoralisation.'[24] The Afghan Taliban, viewed by the military and the ISI as a key strategic asset whose return to power represented the best insurance against an Indian-dominated Afghanistan, were given protection, with their leadership, including Mullah Omar, establishing themselves in Quetta, the provincial capital of Baluchistan. There is some evidence that elements of what became the Quetta Shura were initially interested in exploring the prospects for engagement and reconciliation with the newly formed Karzai government.[25] Whether that was ever a realistic option remains unclear. But by 2003 the Quetta Shura had put in place plans to begin an insurgency against the Karzai government and NATO/ISAF. Until mid-2006 this insurgency was relatively low-intensity, but it increased dramatically following *Operation Herrick*, when a UK battle group was inserted into Helmand province, followed by the insertion of Canadian troops into Kandahar and the Dutch in Uruzgan.

The FATA initially proved a permissive environment for al-Qaeda and related groups. Since the era of the British Raj, no effort had been made to introduce modern forms of governance to the tribal areas, which had been ruled according to the traditional code of Pakhtunwali and the Frontier Crimes Regulations, the latter a blunt instrument which inter alia provided for collective punishments. The Pakistani state was represented only by political agents who sought to exercise influence through the tribal maliks, and by a locally raised gendarmerie, the Frontier Corps. Levels of economic development, literacy and life expectancy were – and have remained – at the bottom of Pakistan's performance indicators; according to a Global Security Organisation report dated May 2009, per capita income in the tribal areas was $250 per year and overall literacy rate at 17%.[26]

Al-Qaeda was able to establish a stronghold in South Waziristan. There, radical young leaders such as Nik Mohamed Wazir and Baitullah Mehsud, with significant forces at their disposal – Mehsud, for example, controlled an army of 5,000– 10,000 men, equipped with heavy weaponry including artillery pieces – were increasingly challenging the established order and were sympathetic to the newcomers. Al-Qaeda fighters began attacking US forces in western Afghanistan from South Waziristan; the group's media operation al-Sahab resumed operations with regular audio and video broadcasts by bin Laden and Zawahiri; and plans were launched to use aspirant jihadis who made their way to training camps, such as that operated by LeT at Malakand, as a means of launching attacks in Western countries. Among those attending such camps and accepting tasking from al-Qaeda to undertake terrorist attacks in their own countries were Omar Khayam, ringleader of the 2004 *Crevice* plot; Dhiren Barot, aka Issa al-Hindi, who had been planning a range of terror attacks in the UK; the perpetrators of the 2005 London bombings; and those involved in the 2006 plot to blow up transatlantic flights using liquid explosives. Over time the Islamic Jihad Union (IJU), an offshoot of the larger Islamic Movement of Uzbekistan (IMU), began targeting northern Europe, exploiting links to the large Turkish diaspora in Germany. And similar operations have been conducted against the US, a case in point being that of Najibullah Zazi, a US resident of Afghan extraction who in February 2010 pleaded guilty to plotting a bomb attack on the New York subway.[27]

In response to evidence that al-Qaeda and other foreign fighters were consolidating their presence in the tribal areas and using them as a base from which to launch attacks on the West and on NATO forces in Afghanistan, the US began to pressure Pakistan to deploy military force against them. Though not entirely unsuccessful, these operations gave rise to unsustainable levels of Pakistani military casualties and to some humiliating surrenders, which led to agreements being signed in 2004 and 2006 with tribal leaders. The import of these deals was that, in return for the Pakistani army withdrawing to its barracks, the tribal leaders would keep the peace and either expel or guarantee the behaviour of foreign fighters.[28] These agreements quickly broke down and simply served to reinforce the status of South and North Waziristan and, to a lesser extent, Bajaur as militant and terrorist safe havens. A lot of the activity ascribed to tribal militant groups, and the resulting tension with Pakistani authorities, was in fact driven as much by local factors such as control of highly lucrative smuggling routes, as by ideology. But the upsurge of fighting in Afghanistan that followed the NATO/ISAF surge into Afghanistan's southern provinces, together with a perception that, in cracking down on militancy, the government of President Musharraf was fighting the US's war, led to a significant increase in ideologically motivated militancy that was not confined to the FATA.

A key event contributing to a general upsurge in militancy within Pakistan was the assault in July 2007 by the Pakistani army on the Lal Masjid and Jamia Hafsa madrassa complex in Islamabad, where a large number of armed militants calling for the overthrow of the Musharraf government had taken refuge.[29] Over the course of the next few months, a spate of bomb attacks occurred throughout Pakistan as militant groups in the FATA repudiated the 2006 truce with the government. In December 2007 Baitullah Mehsud announced the formation of the Tehrik-e-Taliban Pakistan (TTP) or Pakistani Taliban, an umbrella grouping linking some 40 tribal leaders. The declared aim of the grouping was 'to enforce sharia, unite against NATO operations in Afghanistan and perform defensive jihad against the Pakistani army'.[30]

One of the organisations allied to the TTP, the Tehrik-e-Nafaz-e-Shariat-Mohamedi (TNSM), had in 2006 taken over large areas of the Swat valley and imposed sharia law. Attempts by the Pakistani army to dislodge the militants led to a series of ineffectual peace agreements. These served to embolden the militants to the point where, in 2009, they occupied Buner in the 'settled areas', just 100km from Islamabad. The Pakistani army launched a full-scale military operation to clear out the militants and followed up, in June 2009, with *Operation Rah-e-Nijat*, which aimed to drive the TTP out of South Waziristan. These operations, conducted with the consent of a population wearied by the brutality and extremism of the militants, were broadly successful in their objectives, albeit at the cost of major destruction of civilian infrastructure and the temporary displacement of close to 1m people. They were also undertaken against a backdrop of high levels of terrorist violence by Deobandi and sectarian groups within Pakistan itself, much of it directed against the Pakistani security forces. There have been at least 35,000 terrorist-related deaths in Pakistan between 2003 and 2011 of which, more than 30,000 were civilians and more than 5,000 were Pakistani security forces.[31]

The future of al-Qaeda: disaggregating the jihadi nexus

The period of respite and recovery enjoyed by al-Qaeda in its FATA sanctuaries proved to be of relatively short duration. By 2007 drone attacks begun three years previously were beginning to inflict significant attrition on the senior al-Qaeda leadership and their TTP and Haqqani allies. At the time of writing, a total of 234 such attacks had taken place.[32] Neither the total number of casualties arising from these strikes nor the ratio of militant to civilian casualties can be determined with confidence, though one recent study has put the latter at two-thirds militants to one-third civilians.[33] Notwithstanding frequent

Pakistani government complaints about the counter-productive nature of such attacks, the fact that the drones take off from Pakistani air bases to attack targets illuminated by fused intelligence packages containing ISI inputs has long been evident. Indeed, in a rare departure from the official Pakistani government line, Major-General Ghayur Mahmood, commander of the Pakistani army's 7th Division based in North Waziristan, told *Dawn* newspaper in March 2011: 'myths and rumours about US Predator strikes and casualty figures are many, but it is a reality that many of those killed in these strikes are hardcore elements, a sizeable number of them foreigners'.[34]

Funding has for some time been a problem for al-Qaeda, with aspirant foreign jihadists now being required not only to pay for their own training, but also to commit to raising funds for the movement. Al-Qaeda's top leaders have struggled to maintain a convincing media profile. It was several weeks before Zawahiri released a statement on the events leading to the overthrow of the Mubarak regime in Egypt. More broadly, al-Qaeda has struggled to situate the 2011 popular uprisings in the Middle East within its own narrative. It is looking more and more like a parasite organisation, its top leaders dependent for their security on the support and patronage of a few key figures such as Jalaluddin Haqqani, and the organisation as a whole dependent on tactical collaboration with a range of different groups and actors to deliver any kind of kinetic effect. There are thought to be as few as 100 al-Qaeda operatives in Afghanistan, most of them providing specialist support for the Afghan Taliban and the Haqqani network. Officials in US Central Command have spoken of the emergence in Afghanistan of an entity known as Lashkar al-Zil, 'the Shadow Army' – comprising al-Qaeda, the Afghan Taliban, the TTP and the Haqqani network under the command of veteran Pakistani jihadist Ilyas Kashmiri – as amounting to an al-Qaeda military resurgence.[35] Western civilian intelligence officers are, however, sceptical that Lashkar al-Zil is anything more than a term of convenience to connote the sum total of tactical collaborations that have taken place between these groups, and question whether it has any deeper institutional significance.[36] In Pakistan, al-Qaeda has developed similar links, both to groups such as LeT (which remains loyal to the Pakistani state) and to the TTP and other Deobandi and sectarian groups which have, to a greater or lesser degree, turned their guns against the Pakistani state.

If al-Qaeda is indeed a parasite, can it survive independent of its host organisms? And can these host organisms be persuaded to part company with al-Qaeda? In the case of the Afghan Taliban, there have been some intriguing recent statements, including Mullah Omar's September 2010 Eid-ul-Fitr message: 'we want to frame our foreign policy on the principle that we will not harm others nor allow others to harm us. Our upcoming system of government will participate in all regional and global efforts aimed at establishing peace and stability.'[37] One Kandahar-based researcher who has studied the Taliban in some depth judges that 'in the last three years, the Taliban have taken considerable care in their public statements to implicitly distance themselves from al-Qaeda while offering clear indications of their disaffection with the foreign militants in private.'[38] Relations have also been strained between the leadership of the Afghan Taliban in exile – the Quetta Shura – and the TTP. The Quetta Shura have long been uneasy about some of the techniques pioneered by the TTP, especially the use of suicide bombers, the majority of which come from Pakistan's tribal areas, though this has not prevented them from deploying this capability inside Afghanistan. And given their dependence on the support of the Pakistani state, they are unsurprisingly uncomfortable about having to make common cause with an organisation that has declared war on the Pakistani state. This discomfort is epitomised by the case of a retired ISI official known by his operational pseudonym of Colonel Imam. Imam had been kidnapped by the TTP in the tribal areas while on a mission, the purpose of which is not entirely clear. In January 2011 he was killed by TTP leader Hakimullah Mehsud despite pleas for clemency from both the Quetta Shura and the Haqqani network, who were interceding on behalf of the Pakistani state. This event is seen by some experts as constituting a potential tipping-point in relations between the TTP on the one hand and the Quetta Shura and the Haqqani network on the other.[39] But it is perhaps better seen as emblematic of the complex and shifting matrix of relationships between jihadist groups, which also involves a significant degree of compartmentalisation. Hence the Quetta Shura and the Haqqani network are prepared to work with both the TTP and al-Qaeda against NATO/ISAF in Afghanistan, while disassociating themselves from activities undertaken by the TTP, al-Qaeda and some Pakistani Deobandi groups against the Pakistani state.

It remains uncertain whether the conditions exist for reconciliation talks with the Afghan Taliban or indeed who might conduct them. During 2010, a ferocious tempo of decapitation operations targeted against Taliban field commanders in Afghanistan led to the emergence of a new generation of younger, less experienced but more radical commanders who have weaker ties to the older generation of the Quetta Shura. It may be that the undoubted tactical success of the NATO/ISAF campaign has had the strategic effect of fragmenting the Taliban leadership beyond the point where there is a coherent movement with which to negotiate. The situation is further clouded by the Pakistani government's attempts to ensure that it can drive any reconciliation agenda and protect its perceived interests. For example, in 2010 it carried out a spate of arrests of Quetta Shura leaders such as Mullah Abdul Ghani Baradar, who were suspected of entering into talks with the Afghan government behind Pakistan's back.[40]

Key to any process of disaggregation is the position of the Haqqani network, which is often presented as a subdivision of the Afghan Taliban but which is in practice an independent entity. The Haqqani network controls the strategically vital eastern approaches to Kabul. Jalaluddin Haqqani is, as has already been mentioned, al-Qaeda's main patron. Following the 2009 Pakistani army assault on former TTP and other jihadi strongholds in South Waziristan, jihadis were forced to switch their headquarters to North Waziristan, which is Haqqani's fiefdom. David Headley (aka Daoud Gilani) describes the bazaars of its capital, Miranshah, as 'bustling with Chechens, Uzbeks, Tajiks, Russians, Bosnians, some from EU countries and of course our Arab brothers'. He adds: 'Any Waziri or Mehsud I spoke to seemed grateful to God for the privilege of being able to host the "Foreign Mujahadeen"'.[41] The Haqqani network has been responsible, in conjunction with al-Qaeda and the TTP, for most of the major terrorist attacks which have taken place in Kabul, including two attacks on the Indian embassy and the Serena Hotel. Their ability to seek refuge in safe bases inside Pakistan following battles with NATO/ISAF forces has been a constant source of frustration (see 'Militant groups in 2011', Strategic Geography, p. iii).

There is little evidence to indicate what Haqqani wants to achieve and what, if anything, the group might regard as an acceptable resolution of the current conflict short of all-out victory. The group appears to be showing signs of factionalisation, as control of the organisation is in transition from Jalaluddin Haqqani to his seemingly more radical son Sirajuddin. Jalaluddin appears supportive of the al-Qaeda agenda, but his followers have, as already noted, been conspicuous by their absence from al-Qaeda-sponsored terrorist operations outside Afghanistan. For Pakistan, the Haqqani network represents a 'strategic national interest', to which the state turns to promote Pakistani concerns in any future Afghan administration.[42] In June 2010 there was speculation that the Pakistani military and ISI were seeking to promote reconciliation talks between the Haqqani network and the Karzai government, but there is as yet no sign that this initiative has prospered, raising questions about the extent to which Pakistan is able to control the organisation.[43] Meanwhile the Pakistani army has continued to resist US pressure to undertake a repetition of the 2009 *Rah-e-Nijat* operation in North Waziristan, citing resource constraints and the need for a period of recovery following the 2009 campaign. While the factors cited are undoubtedly valid, any military intervention in North Waziristan would, unless carefully choreographed, be tantamount to declaring war on the Haqqani network.

Conclusion

US counter-terrorism strategies are situated within a complex and constantly shifting kaleidoscope, often with more than one actor attempting to move the pieces. The conditions that underpinned the 2009 debate about the nature of the US response have shifted accordingly. Since it was reinforced at the end of 2009, General Petraeus's COIN strategy has significantly altered the dynamic both in Afghanistan and in Pakistan. During the same period the Pakistani army has become engaged in a war with the TTP and other militant groups challenging the Pakistani state, while continuing to support and protect other militant groups that are fighting NATO/ISAF and are linked to al-Qaeda. US drone strikes conducted with tacit Pakistani collusion have, during this period, diminished al-Qaeda's strength in Pakistan.

Interested parties have begun positioning themselves for some sort of end-game in Afghanistan, which will probably involve some kind of accommodation between the Karzai government and significant components of the insurgency. Both Pakistan and India are starting to show tantalising signs of moving away from long-held positions. Pakistan now talks in terms of not wishing to repeat the mistakes of the 1990s – a reference to its role in promoting a Taliban takeover of the country; and India's Research and Analysis Wing appears to be reducing its presence in Afghanistan and reducing operational collaboration with the Afghan National Directorate of Security directed against Pakistan, including withdrawing financial and other support for Baluch separatist groups and the TTP.[44] India's focus has shifted towards emphasising the predominantly economic nature of its interests in Afghanistan, apparently to reassure Pakistan. However, whether these moves can avoid foundering on the rock of Kashmir, as has been the case with a succession of previous peace initiatives, remains at best uncertain. Moreover, it would be unrealistic to expect that the Pakistani state might, as part of this process, be willing – or indeed able – to adopt an undifferentiated approach to indigenous extremist groups whose *raison d'être* has been hostility towards India.

Irrespective of the nature of any political settlement in Afghanistan, extremist groups will remain a threat to the security of the region and beyond. Many of those engaged in militancy in Afghanistan and Pakistan fall into the category of what David Kilcullen has termed 'accidental guerrillas', fighting because the fight has arrived on their doorstep.[45] Such fighters may be susceptible to reconciliation and reintegration, provided this process is adequately staffed and resourced. But so-called foreign fighters seem likely to be impervious to any such process and, having nowhere else to go, can be expected to carry on the fight by whatever means they can. Moreover, the Pakistani army's suppression of militancy in the tribal areas of Pakistan, a region characterised by a culture of revenge, may well produce a chain of continuing violence which will prove hard to break. The same may be true of the US drone strikes.

There is a contradiction at the heart of current US counter-terrorism strategies. A heavy US military presence in Afghanistan creates opportunities to develop a detailed and granular intelligence picture of insurgents and terrorists. This would simply not be possible with a lower level of engagement. At the same time, however, the US presence is a both a *raison d'être* and a rallying-point for groups and individuals who, left to themselves, might be more inclined to accentuate their differences and restrict their violence to their own theatres of operations. Irrespective of how fast the US military drawdown happens, the expectation is that the US will retain sufficient forces in Afghanistan to be able to continue intelligence-led operations against terrorist groups located in the region. But while Pakistan does not wish to precipitate US withdrawal from the region, neither is it likely to want Afghanistan to become a launch-pad for US drone and special-forces operations which might be directed against Pakistani interests. It is not beyond the bounds of possibility that Pakistani pressure, combined with shifts in internal Afghan politics, may translate into a withdrawal of basing rights similar to what happened in Iraq in 2007, under which circumstances the COIN-plus option would prove much harder to sustain.

The US is over time likely to find itself facing a situation of continued militancy in South Asia, but with less direct scope for intervention than it currently has and a greater reliance on collaboration with regional allies to mitigate the threat such continuing militancy poses to US interests. Over time, a reduced US presence – whether military in Afghanistan or CIA in Pakistan – represents the best option for lowering the temperature and creating circumstances in which the countries of the region can best address the threats they face from militancy. But transitioning to that end-point requires US policymakers to assume a different calculus of risk in respect of terrorism, and to accept that whatever the degree of US presence in the region, some residual threat to the security of the US homeland and to US interests will continue to emanate from Afghanistan and Pakistan for the foreseeable future. In the highly partisan environment in Washington, such an acceptance will not be easy to achieve.

Strategic Geography

Pre-2001 training camps

More than 120 training camps reportedly operated in Taliban-controlled Afghanistan and the remote tribal areas of Pakistan before the September 2001 attacks and subsequent Western invasion of Afghanistan. Al-Qaeda was one of many foreign jihadist organisations using the region as a safe haven. Others ranged from Algerians to Uzbeks.

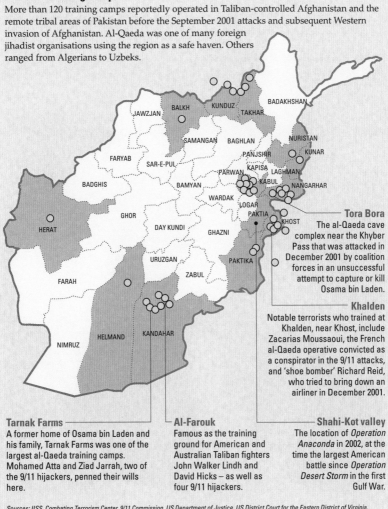

Tora Bora
The al-Qaeda cave complex near the Khyber Pass that was attacked in December 2001 by coalition forces in an unsuccessful attempt to capture or kill Osama bin Laden.

Khalden
Notable terrorists who trained at Khalden, near Khost, include Zacarias Moussaoui, the French al-Qaeda operative convicted as a conspirator in the 9/11 attacks, and 'shoe bomber' Richard Reid, who tried to bring down an airliner in December 2001.

Tarnak Farms
A former home of Osama bin Laden and his family, Tarnak Farms was one of the largest al-Qaeda training camps. Mohamed Atta and Ziad Jarrah, two of the 9/11 hijackers, penned their wills here.

Al-Farouk
Famous as the training ground for American and Australian Taliban fighters John Walker Lindh and David Hicks – as well as four 9/11 hijackers.

Shahi-Kot valley
The location of *Operation Anaconda* in 2002, at the time the largest American battle since *Operation Desert Storm* in the first Gulf War.

Sources: IISS, Combating Terrorism Center, 9/11 Commission, US Department of Justice, US District Court for the Eastern District of Virginia, CNN, Daily Telegraph, MSNBC, Time

© IISS

The Taliban strikes back

In 2002, hundreds of Taliban and al-Qaeda fighters were killed in *Operation Anaconda* in the Shahi-Kot valley, but many others escaped to the lawless Afghanistan–Pakistan border region. Using this base, insurgents were again presenting a menace a few years later. While assessments by the non-governmental organisation ICOS are bleak, a leaked document in 2009 showed even the Afghan government admitting loss of control in certain regions.

Operation Anaconda

👤👤👤👤👤👤👤👤👤👤👤👤👤👤👤👤👤👤👤👤👤 2,000 US troops deployed

👤👤👤👤👤👤👤👤 500–800 militants killed

In *Operation Anaconda*, US and Afghan forces moved in for a three-day light combat operation to clear an al-Qaeda and Taliban base in the Shahi-Kot Valley, but found themselves embroiled in a brutal 17-day battle because of an initial underestimation of enemy strength. Afghan forces were meant to act as a 'hammer' pushing a retreating enemy into the 'anvil' of US forces at the valley's exits, but they unilaterally withdrew. Eight US troops died and 50 were wounded. Former al-Qaeda leader Osama bin Laden is thought to have been among the militants who escaped.

Taliban/insurgent activity (as assessed by ICOS)

■ Heavy
▨ Substantial
□ Light

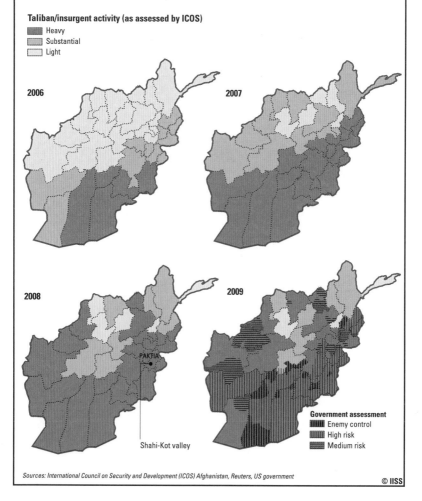

Government assessment
▦ Enemy control
▨ High risk
■ Medium risk

Sources: International Council on Security and Development (ICOS) Afghanistan, Reuters, US government

© IISS

Militant groups in 2011

Although al-Qaeda and the Taliban get most of the headlines, there are dozens of militant groups operating in Afghanistan and Pakistan's remote tribal regions – including the major players below.

■ Afghan Taliban
Leader: Mullah Mohammad Omar
Established: Kandahar, Afghanistan; mid-1980s
Est. strength: 30,000
Notable attacks: Major attack on town of Mosa Qala, Helmand, May 2006; numerous attacks on NATO supply convoys and NATO bases

■ Hizb-e-Islami Gulbuddin (HiG)
Leader: Gulbuddin Hekmatyr
Established: Eastern Afghanistan; 1977
Est. strength: 5,000–7,000
Notable attacks: Attack on US forces in Khost, Afghanistan, February 2009; murder of a foreign medical team in Badakhshan, August 2010

○ Al-Qaeda
Leader: Ayman al-Zawahiri
Established: Peshawar, Pakistan; 1988
Est. strength: 500–1,000
Notable attacks: World Trade Centre bombing, February 1993; 09/11/2001 attacks in New York, Washington DC, and Pennsylvania

■ Tehrik-e-Taliban Pakistan (TTP)
Leader: Hakimullah Mehsud
Established: Northwest Pakistan; 2007
Est. strength: 20,000–25,000
Notable attacks: Suicide attacks on mosque in Lahore, killing 80, May 2010; suspected in the assassination of Pakistani presidential candidate Benazir Bhutto, December 2007

■ Lashkar-e-Tayiba
Leader: Hafiz Mohammed Saifullah Saeed (under house arrest in Pakistan)
Established: Muridke, near Lahore, Pakistan; 1989
Est. strength: 300–1,000
Notable attacks: Mumbai attacks, India, November 2008; Lahore attack on Pakistan cricket team, March 2009

■ Islamic Movement of Uzbekistan
Leader: Abu Usman Adil
Established: 1998
Est. strength: 2,000–4,000
Notable attacks: Several attacks on the new NATO supply route from Tajikistan through the provinces of Kunduz and Baghlan

■ Haqqani Network
Leader: Sirajuddin Haqqani
Established: Khost, Afghanistan; 1980s
Est. strength: 5,000–7,000
Notable attacks: Assassination attempt on President Hamid Karzai, April 2008; various suicide attacks in Kabul (on 5-star hotel Serena, January 2008; on Indian Embassy, July 2008, on UN guesthouse, October 2009)

■ Tehrik-e-Nafaz-e-Shariat-Mohamedi (TNSM)
Leader: Sufi Mohammad
Established: Pakistan; 1989
Est. strength: 5,000–6,000
Notable attacks: Suicide attack on an army convoy in Mingora, Swat, Pakistan, December 2007

Sources: IISS, ISAF, Long War Journal, Radio Free Europe/Radio Liberty, Small Wars Journal, UNHCR, UNODC, Washington Times   © IISS

Ten years of NATO operations

After the battle for the Tora Bora, US operations in Afghanistan concentrated narrowly on counter-terrorism in country's east, as Washington's focus turned to Iraq. ISAF also remained primarily in Kabul, expanding gradually into the north and west until a resurgent Taliban started turning its attention to a strife-torn south in 2006.

Number of coalition battalions (as of January each year)

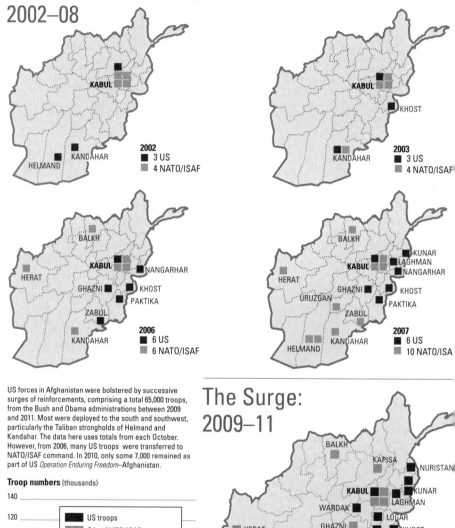

2002–08

2002
- 3 US
- 4 NATO/ISAF

2003
- 3 US
- 4 NATO/ISAF

2006
- 6 US
- 6 NATO/ISAF

2007
- 6 US
- 10 NATO/ISAF

US forces in Afghanistan were bolstered by successive surges of reinforcements, comprising a total 65,000 troops, from the Bush and Obama administrations between 2009 and 2011. Most were deployed to the south and southwest, particularly the Taliban strongholds of Helmand and Kandahar. The data here uses totals from each October. However, from 2006, many US troops were transferred to NATO/ISAF command. In 2010, only some 7,000 remained as part of US *Operation Enduring Freedom*–Afghanistan.

Troop numbers (thousands)

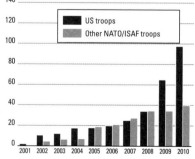

The Surge: 2009–11

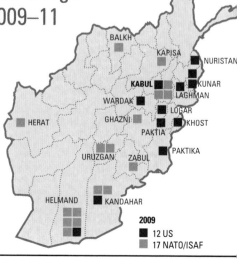

2009
- 12 US
- 17 NATO/ISAF

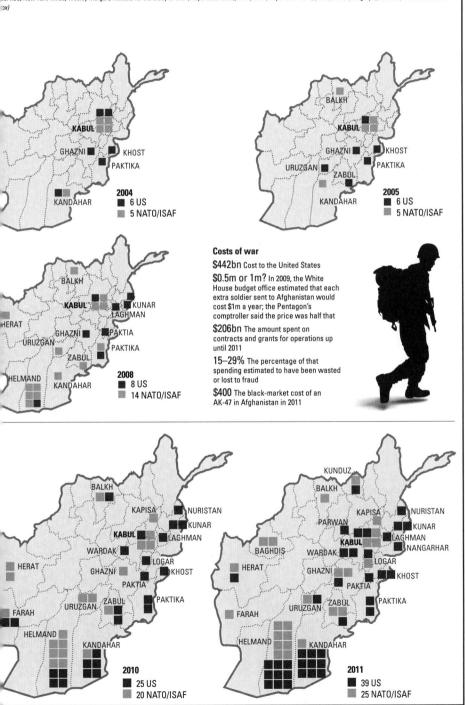

Sources: IISS, New York Times, Wesley Morgan, Institute for the Study of War (Maps 2002–2008); ISAF, IISS (Maps 2009–2011) ; ISAF/NATO (bar graph); Reuters, Cost of War.com (box)

2004
■ 6 US
▨ 5 NATO/ISAF

2005
■ 6 US
▨ 5 NATO/ISAF

2008
■ 8 US
▨ 14 NATO/ISAF

Costs of war

$442bn Cost to the United States

$0.5m or 1m? In 2009, the White House budget office estimated that each extra soldier sent to Afghanistan would cost $1m a year; the Pentagon's comptroller said the price was half that

$206bn The amount spent on contracts and grants for operations up until 2011

15–29% The percentage of that spending estimated to have been wasted or lost to fraud

$400 The black-market cost of an AK-47 in Afghanistan in 2011

2010
■ 25 US
▨ 20 NATO/ISAF

2011
■ 39 US
▨ 25 NATO/ISAF

Coalition and civilian casualties

Public support for the decade-long war has been undermined in many troop-contributing countries by growing military casualties. Civilian deaths are a long-standing source of tension between NATO and the Afghan government.

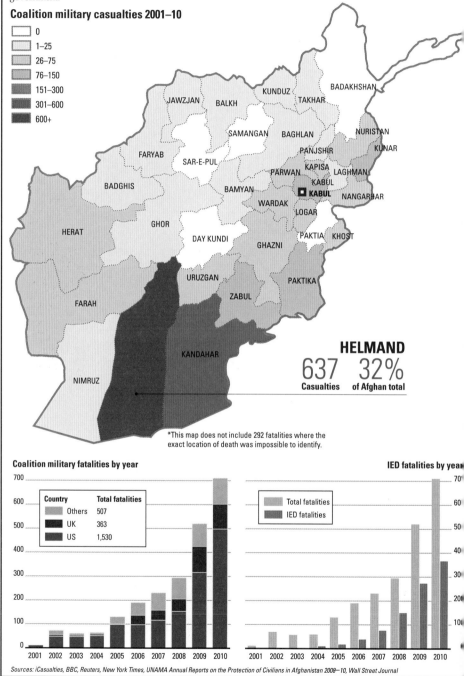

Coalition military casualties 2001–10

- ☐ 0
- 1–25
- 26–75
- 76–150
- 151–300
- 301–600
- 600+

HELMAND

637 **32%**

Casualties **of Afghan total**

*This map does not include 292 fatalities where the exact location of death was impossible to identify.

Coalition military fatalities by year

Country	Total fatalities
Others	507
UK	363
US	1,530

700
600
500
400
300
200
100
0

2001 2002 2003 2004 2005 2006 2007 2008 2009 2010

IED fatalities by year

Total fatalities
IED fatalities

70
60
50
40
30
20
10

2001 2002 2003 2004 2005 2006 2007 2008 2009 2010

Sources: iCasualties, BBC, Reuters, New York Times, UNAMA Annual Reports on the Protection of Civilians in Afghanistan 2008–10, Wall Street Journal

‎ilian casualties 2007–10

‎organisation has counted civilian deaths since 2001. Early on, various reports from academics, human-rights groups and ‎ss agencies made estimates – often more than 1,000 civilian deaths a year – before UNAMA began a systematic tally in 2008. ‎han President Hamid Karzai has long called the level of civilian casualties unacceptable, reacting angrily to the use of aerial ‎cks, 'excessive' force, and 'arbitrary decisions to search people's houses'. In 2009 and 2010, US and NATO commander ‎eral Stanley McChrystal restricted offensive air strikes to try to limit civilian deaths. Although his successor General David ‎raeus reversed this policy, those killed via coalition action was down in 2010.

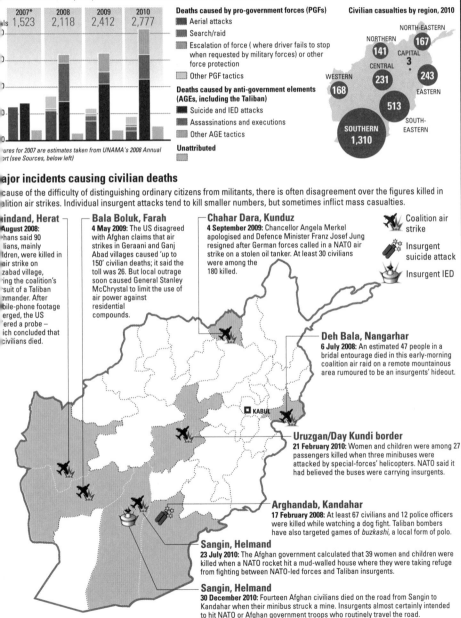

	2007*	2008	2009	2010
‎ls	1,523	2,118	2,412	2,777

Deaths caused by pro-government forces (PGFs)
- Aerial attacks
- Search/raid
- Escalation of force (where driver fails to stop when requested by military forces) or other force protection
- Other PGF tactics

Deaths caused by anti-government elements (AGEs, including the Taliban)
- Suicide and IED attacks
- Assassinations and executions
- Other AGE tactics

Unattributed

‎ures for 2007 are estimates taken from UNAMA's 2008 Annual ‎ort (see Sources, below left)

Civilian casualties by region, 2010

- NORTH-EASTERN **167**
- NORTHERN **141**
- CAPITAL **3**
- CENTRAL **231**
- WESTERN **168**
- EASTERN **243**
- SOUTH-EASTERN **513**
- SOUTHERN **1,310**

‎ajor incidents causing civilian deaths

‎cause of the difficulty of distinguishing ordinary citizens from militants, there is often disagreement over the figures killed in ‎alition air strikes. Individual insurgent attacks tend to kill smaller numbers, but sometimes inflict mass casualties.

‎indand, Herat
‎ August 2008: ‎hans said 90 ‎lians, mainly ‎ldren, were killed in ‎air strike on ‎zabad village, ‎‎ing the coalition's ‎‎suit of a Taliban ‎nmander. After ‎bile-phone footage ‎‎erged, the US ‎‎ered a probe – ‎ich concluded that ‎civilians died.

Bala Boluk, Farah
4 May 2009: The US disagreed with Afghan claims that air strikes in Geraani and Ganj Abad villages caused 'up to 150' civilian deaths; it said the toll was 26. But local outrage soon caused General Stanley McChrystal to limit the use of air power against residential compounds.

Chahar Dara, Kunduz
4 September 2009: Chancellor Angela Merkel apologised and Defence Minister Franz Josef Jung resigned after German forces called in a NATO air strike on a stolen oil tanker. At least 30 civilians were among the 180 killed.

Coalition air strike

Insurgent suicide attack

Insurgent IED

Deh Bala, Nangarhar
6 July 2008: An estimated 47 people in a bridal entourage died in this early-morning coalition air raid on a remote mountainous area rumoured to be an insurgents' hideout.

Uruzgan/Day Kundi border
21 February 2010: Women and children were among 27 passengers killed when three minibuses were attacked by special-forces' helicopters. NATO said it had believed the buses were carrying insurgents.

Arghandab, Kandahar
17 February 2008: At least 67 civilians and 12 police officers were killed while watching a dog fight. Taliban bombers have also targeted games of *buzkashi*, a local form of polo.

Sangin, Helmand
23 July 2010: The Afghan government calculated that 39 women and children were killed when a NATO rocket hit a mud-walled house where they were taking refuge from fighting between NATO-led forces and Taliban insurgents.

Sangin, Helmand
30 December 2010: Fourteen Afghan civilians died on the road from Sangin to Kandahar when their minibus struck a mine. Insurgents almost certainly intended to hit NATO or Afghan government troops who routinely travel the road.

KABUL

© IISS

Supply routes into Afghanistan

Supporting coalition troops in Afghanistan has involved one of the most complex military supply chains in history. As routes through Pakistan have become increasingly dangerous and politically contentious in recent years, ISAF has transported proportionally more consignments through Russia and Central Asia.

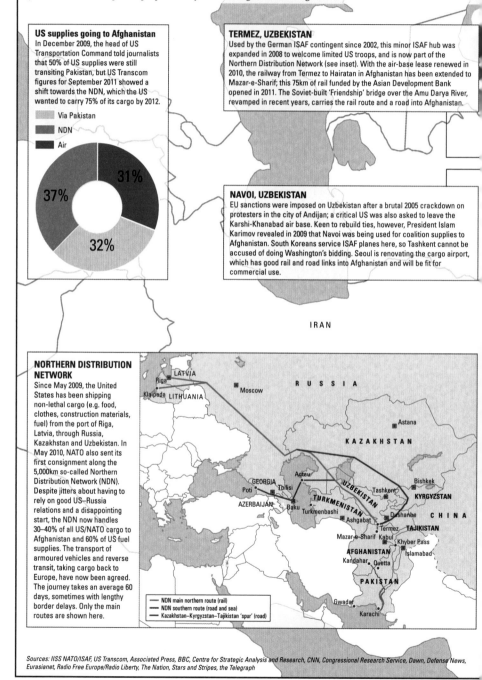

US supplies going to Afghanistan
In December 2009, the head of US Transportation Command told journalists that 50% of US supplies were still transiting Pakistan, but US Transcom figures for September 2011 showed a shift towards the NDN, which the US wanted to carry 75% of its cargo by 2012.

- Via Pakistan
- NDN
- Air

31%
37%
32%

TERMEZ, UZBEKISTAN
Used by the German ISAF contingent since 2002, this minor ISAF hub was expanded in 2008 to welcome limited US troops, and is now part of the Northern Distribution Network (see inset). With the air-base lease renewed in 2010, the railway from Termez to Hairatan in Afghanistan has been extended to Mazar-e-Sharif; this 75km of rail funded by the Asian Development Bank opened in 2011. The Soviet-built 'Friendship' bridge over the Amu Darya River, revamped in recent years, carries the rail route and a road into Afghanistan.

NAVOI, UZBEKISTAN
EU sanctions were imposed on Uzbekistan after a brutal 2005 crackdown on protesters in the city of Andijan; a critical US was also asked to leave the Karshi-Khanabad air base. Keen to rebuild ties, however, President Islam Karimov revealed in 2009 that Navoi was being used for coalition supplies to Afghanistan. South Koreans service ISAF planes here, so Tashkent cannot be accused of doing Washington's bidding. Seoul is renovating the cargo airport, which has good rail and road links into Afghanistan and will be fit for commercial use.

IRAN

NORTHERN DISTRIBUTION NETWORK
Since May 2009, the United States has been shipping non-lethal cargo (e.g. food, clothes, construction materials, fuel) from the port of Riga, Latvia, through Russia, Kazakhstan and Uzbekistan. In May 2010, NATO also sent its first consignment along the 5,000km so-called Northern Distribution Network (NDN). Despite jitters about having to rely on good US–Russia relations and a disappointing start, the NDN now handles 30–40% of all US/NATO cargo to Afghanistan and 60% of US fuel supplies. The transport of armoured vehicles and reverse transit, taking cargo back to Europe, have now been agreed. The journey takes an average 60 days, sometimes with lengthy border delays. Only the main routes are shown here.

LATVIA
Riga
Klaipeda LITHUANIA
Moscow
RUSSIA
Astana
KAZAKHSTAN
Aqtau
GEORGIA
Poti
Tbilisi
UZBEKISTAN
Tashkent
Bishkek
KYRGYZSTAN
AZERBAIJAN
Baku
TURKMENISTAN
Turkmenbashi
Ashgabat
Dushanbe
CHINA
Termez TAJIKISTAN
Mazar-e-Sharif
Kabul
AFGHANISTAN
Khyber Pass
Kandahar
Quetta
Islamabad
PAKISTAN
Gwadar
Karachi

— NDN main northern route (rail)
— NDN southern route (road and sea)
— Kazakhstan–Kyrgyzstan–Tajikistan 'spur' (road)

Sources: IISS NATO/ISAF, US Transcom, Associated Press, BBC, Centre for Strategic Analysis and Research, CNN, Congressional Research Service, Dawn, Defense News, Eurasianet, Radio Free Europe/Radio Liberty, The Nation, Stars and Stripes, the Telegraph

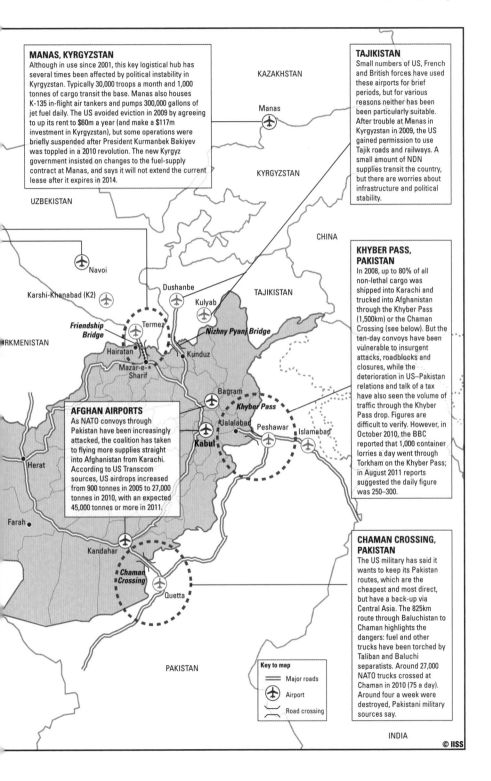

MANAS, KYRGYZSTAN
Although in use since 2001, this key logistical hub has several times been affected by political instability in Kyrgyzstan. Typically 30,000 troops a month and 1,000 tonnes of cargo transit the base. Manas also houses K-135 in-flight air tankers and pumps 300,000 gallons of jet fuel daily. The US avoided eviction in 2009 by agreeing to up its rent to $60m a year (and make a $117m investment in Kyrgyzstan), but some operations were briefly suspended after President Kurmanbek Bakiyev was toppled in a 2010 revolution. The new Kyrgyz government insisted on changes to the fuel-supply contract at Manas, and says it will not extend the current lease after it expires in 2014.

TAJIKISTAN
Small numbers of US, French and British forces have used these airports for brief periods, but for various reasons neither has been particularly suitable. After trouble at Manas in Kyrgyzstan in 2009, the US gained permission to use Tajik roads and railways. A small amount of NDN supplies transit the country, but there are worries about infrastructure and political stability.

KHYBER PASS, PAKISTAN
In 2008, up to 80% of all non-lethal cargo was shipped into Karachi and trucked into Afghanistan through the Khyber Pass (1,500km) or the Chaman Crossing (see below). But the ten-day convoys have been vulnerable to insurgent attacks, roadblocks and closures, while the deterioration in US–Pakistan relations and talk of a tax have also seen the volume of traffic through the Khyber Pass drop. Figures are difficult to verify. However, in October 2010, the BBC reported that 1,000 container lorries a day went through Torkham on the Khyber Pass; in August 2011 reports suggested the daily figure was 250–300.

AFGHAN AIRPORTS
As NATO convoys through Pakistan have been increasingly attacked, the coalition has taken to flying more supplies straight into Afghanistan from Karachi. According to US Transcom sources, US airdrops increased from 900 tonnes in 2005 to 27,000 tonnes in 2010, with an expected 45,000 tonnes or more in 2011.

CHAMAN CROSSING, PAKISTAN
The US military has said it wants to keep its Pakistan routes, which are the cheapest and most direct, but have a back-up via Central Asia. The 825km route through Baluchistan to Chaman highlights the dangers: fuel and other trucks have been torched by Taliban and Baluchi separatists. Around 27,000 NATO trucks crossed at Chaman in 2010 (75 a day). Around four a week were destroyed, Pakistani military sources say.

KAZAKHSTAN

Manas

KYRGYZSTAN

UZBEKISTAN

CHINA

Navoi

Dushanbe

Karshi-Khanabad (K2)

Kulyab

TAJIKISTAN

Friendship Bridge

Termez

Nizhny Pyanj Bridge

RKMENISTAN

Hairatan

Kunduz

Mazar-e-Sharif

Bagram

Khyber Pass

Jalalabad

Peshawar

Islamabad

Kabul

Herat

Farah

Kandahar

Chaman Crossing

Quetta

PAKISTAN

INDIA

Key to map
═══ Major roads
✈ Airport
⌄ Road crossing

© IISS

Afghan ethnicities

Afghanistan's 2004 constitution lists 14 ethnic groups and recognises that others exist. To complicate the picture, many of these categories can be broken down into sub-groups and tribes. Some Afghans' habit of disguising their religion to escape persecution and incomplete data from the last census – begun in 1979 but interrupted by the 1980 Soviet invasion – also make Afghan demography an inexact science.

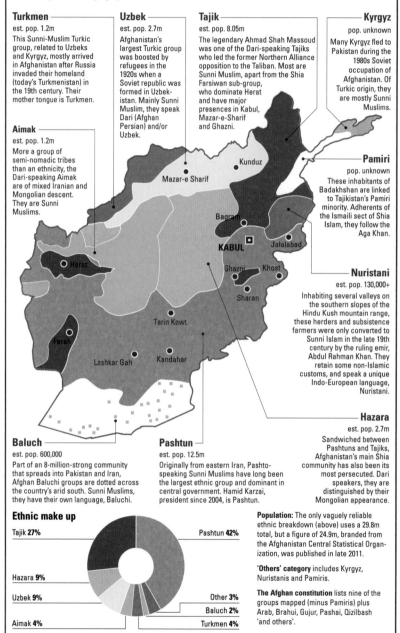

Turkmen

est. pop. 1.2m

This Sunni-Muslim Turkic group, related to Uzbeks and Kyrgyz, mostly arrived in Afghanistan after Russia invaded their homeland (today's Turkmenistan) in the 19th century. Their mother tongue is Turkmen.

Aimak

est. pop. 1.2m

More a group of semi-nomadic tribes than an ethnicity, the Dari-speaking Aimak are of mixed Iranian and Mongolian descent. They are Sunni Muslims.

Uzbek

est. pop. 2.7m

Afghanistan's largest Turkic group was boosted by refugees in the 1920s when a Soviet republic was formed in Uzbek-istan. Mainly Sunni Muslim, they speak Dari (Afghan Persian) and/or Uzbek.

Tajik

est. pop. 8.05m

The legendary Ahmad Shah Massoud was one of the Dari-speaking Tajiks who led the former Northern Alliance opposition to the Taliban. Most are Sunni Muslim, apart from the Shia Farsiwan sub-group, who dominate Herat and have major presences in Kabul, Mazar-e-Sharif and Ghazni.

Kyrgyz

pop. unknown

Many Kyrgyz fled to Pakistan during the 1980s Soviet occupation of Afghanistan. Of Turkic origin, they are mostly Sunni Muslims.

Pamiri

pop. unknown

These inhabitants of Badakhshan are linked to Tajikistan's Pamiri minority. Adherents of the Ismaili sect of Shia Islam, they follow the Aga Khan.

Nuristani

est. pop. 130,000+

Inhabiting several valleys on the southern slopes of the Hindu Kush mountain range, these herders and subsistence farmers were only converted to Sunni Islam in the late 19th century by the ruling emir, Abdul Rahman Khan. They retain some non-Islamic customs, and speak a unique Indo-European language, Nuristani.

Hazara

est. pop. 2.7m

Sandwiched between Pashtuns and Tajiks, Afghanistan's main Shia community has also been its most persecuted. Dari speakers, they are distinguished by their Mongolian appearance.

Baluch

est. pop. 600,000

Part of an 8-million-strong community that spreads into Pakistan and Iran, Afghan Baluchi groups are dotted across the country's arid south. Sunni Muslims, they have their own language, Baluchi.

Pashtun

est. pop. 12.5m

Originally from eastern Iran, Pashto-speaking Sunni Muslims have long been the largest ethnic group and dominant in central government. Hamid Karzai, president since 2004, is Pashtun.

Map labels: Kunduz, Mazar-e Sharif, Bagram, KABUL, Jalalabad, Ghazni, Khost, Sharan, Herat, Tarin Kowt, Farah, Lashkar Gah, Kandahar

Ethnic make up

Tajik **27%**

Hazara **9%**

Uzbek **9%**

Aimak **4%**

Pashtun **42%**

Other **3%**

Baluch **2%**

Turkmen **4%**

Population: The only vaguely reliable ethnic breakdown (above) uses a 29.8m total, but a figure of 24.9m, branded from the Afghanistan Central Statistical Organization, was published in late 2011.

'Others' category includes Kyrgyz, Nuristanis and Pamiris.

The Afghan constitution lists nine of the groups mapped (minus Pamiris) plus Arab, Brahui, Gujur, Pashai, Qizilbash 'and others'.

Sources: Afghan National Area-Based Development Programme, Afghan Central Statistics Organization/National Energy Information Center BBC, CIA Factbook, Congressional Research Service, Minority Rights Group International, National Geographic, PBS, US Library of Congress © IISS

Who wields power?

The Afghan National Assembly consists of a 249-seat lower house, the Wolesi Jirga, and a 102-seat upper house, the Meshrano Jirga. However, ethnic and regional identities, clan loyalties and personality politics also play important roles in the country's government.

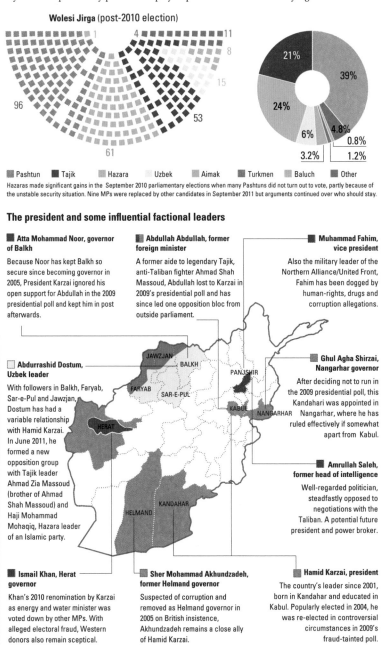

Wolesi Jirga (post-2010 election)

1 4 11 8 15 96 53 61

39% 21% 24% 6% 4.8% 0.8% 3.2% 1.2%

■ Pashtun ■ Tajik ■ Hazara ■ Uzbek ■ Aimak ■ Turkmen ■ Baluch ■ Other

Hazaras made significant gains in the September 2010 parliamentary elections when many Pashtuns did not turn out to vote, partly because of the unstable security situation. Nine MPs were replaced by other candidates in September 2011 but arguments continued over who should stay.

The president and some influential factional leaders

■ Atta Mohammad Noor, governor of Balkh

Because Noor has kept Balkh so secure since becoming governor in 2005, President Karzai ignored his open support for Abdullah in the 2009 presidential poll and kept him in post afterwards.

■ Abdullah Abdullah, former foreign minister

A former aide to legendary Tajik, anti-Taliban fighter Ahmad Shah Massoud, Abdullah lost to Karzai in 2009's presidential poll and has since led one opposition bloc from outside parliament.

■ Muhammad Fahim, vice president

Also the military leader of the Northern Alliance/United Front, Fahim has been dogged by human-rights, drugs and corruption allegations.

□ Abdurrashid Dostum, Uzbek leader

With followers in Balkh, Faryab, Sar-e-Pul and Jawzjan, Dostum has had a variable relationship with Hamid Karzai. In June 2011, he formed a new opposition group with Tajik leader Ahmad Zia Massoud (brother of Ahmad Shah Massoud) and Haji Mohammad Mohaqiq, Hazara leader of an Islamic party.

■ Ghul Agha Shirzai, Nangarhar governor

After deciding not to run in the 2009 presidential poll, this Kandahari was appointed in Nangarhar, where he has ruled effectively if somewhat apart from Kabul.

■ Amrullah Saleh, former head of intelligence

Well-regarded politician, steadfastly opposed to negotiations with the Taliban. A potential future president and power broker.

■ Ismail Khan, Herat governor

Khan's 2010 renomination by Karzai as energy and water minister was voted down by other MPs. With alleged electoral fraud, Western donors also remain sceptical.

■ Sher Mohammad Akhundzadeh, former Helmand governor

Suspected of corruption and removed as Helmand governor in 2005 on British insistence, Akhundzadeh remains a close ally of Hamid Karzai.

■ Hamid Karzai, president

The country's leader since 2001, born in Kandahar and educated in Kabul. Popularly elected in 2004, he was re-elected in controversial circumstances in 2009's fraud-tainted poll.

Sources: Kabul Center for Strategic Studies (parliamentary breakdown; note that other sources have slightly different figures); Afghan Analysts' Network, Congressional Research Service, BBC, Huffingtonpost.com, New York Times, Pajhwok Afghan News

© IISS

Shoring up infrastructure

The West's campaign to win hearts and minds in Afghanistan was meant to be based on providing power, water, roads and other basic services. Certainly, after decades of war and under-development, the country's infrastructure pitiful. However, many reconstruction projects have been hit by cost over-runs, mistakes and short-termism. Electricity projects have been particularly fraught, but even road-building has not escaped criticism.

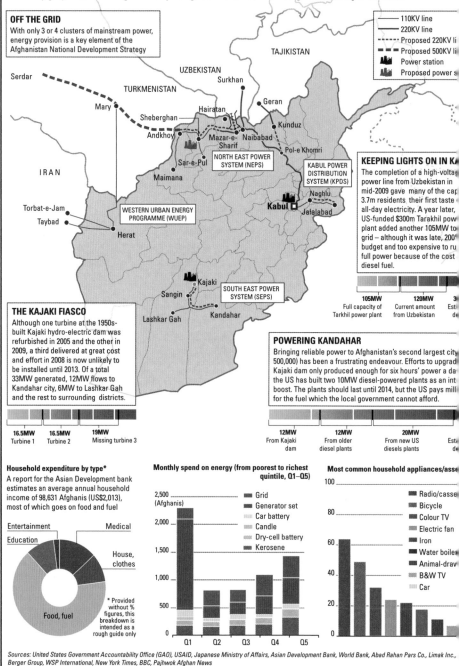

OFF THE GRID
With only 3 or 4 clusters of mainstream power, energy provision is a key element of the Afghanistan National Development Strategy

— 110KV line
— 220KV line
---- Proposed 220KV li
▬▬ Proposed 500KV li
⚒ Power station
⚒ Proposed power s

NORTH EAST POWER SYSTEM (NEPS)

KABUL POWER DISTRIBUTION SYSTEM (KPDS)

WESTERN URBAN ENERGY PROGRAMME (WUEP)

SOUTH EAST POWER SYSTEM (SEPS)

KEEPING LIGHTS ON IN K
The completion of a high-voltag power line from Uzbekistan in mid-2009 gave many of the cap 3.7m residents their first taste all-day electricity. A year later, US-funded $300m Tarakhil pow plant added another 105MW to grid – although it was late, 200 budget and too expensive to ru full power because of the cost diesel fuel.

105MW
Full capacity of Tarkhil power plant

120MW
Current amount from Uzbekistan

3
Esti
d

THE KAJAKI FIASCO
Although one turbine at the 1950s-built Kajaki hydro-electric dam was refurbished in 2005 and the other in 2009, a third delivered at great cost and effort in 2008 is now unlikely to be installed until 2013. Of a total 33MW generated, 12MW flows to Kandahar city, 6MW to Lashkar Gah and the rest to surrounding districts.

POWERING KANDAHAR
Bringing reliable power to Afghanistan's second largest city 500,000) has been a frustrating endeavour. Efforts to upgrad Kajaki dam only produced enough for six hours' power a da the US has built two 10MW diesel-powered plants as an int boost. The plants should last until 2014, but the US pays milli for the fuel which the local government cannot afford.

16.5MW
Turbine 1

16.5MW
Turbine 2

19MW
Missing turbine 3

12MW
From Kajaki dam

12MW
From older diesel plants

20MW
From new US diesels plants

Esti
d

Household expenditure by type*
A report for the Asian Development bank estimates an average annual household income of 98,631 Afghanis (US$2,013), most of which goes on food and fuel

Entertainment
Education
Medical
House, clothes
Food, fuel

* Provided without % figures, this breakdown is intended as a rough guide only

Monthly spend on energy (from poorest to richest quintile, Q1–Q5)

■ Grid
■ Generator set
■ Car battery
■ Candle
■ Dry-cell battery
■ Kerosene

Most common household appliances/asse

■ Radio/casse
■ Bicycle
■ Colour TV
■ Electric fan
■ Iron
■ Water boile
■ Animal-drav
■ B&W TV
■ Car

Sources: United States Government Accountability Office (GAO), USAID, Japanese Ministry of Affairs, Asian Development Bank, World Bank, Abad Rahan Pars Co., Limak Inc., Berger Group, WSP International, New York Times, BBC, Pajhwok Afghan News

Where the road ends, the Taliban begins,' then US Lieutenant-General Karl Eikenberry said in 2005, explaining why asphalt has been a key tool in the effort to stabilise Afghanistan. More than 13,000km of road have been built or rehabilitated, with a focus on the 2,500km ring road between major cities and 800km of international links (see following table). Paved roads make it more difficult to bury IEDs and mines, speed troop movements and help ISAF forces channel traffic along controlled routes. But better roads also make more areas accessible to insurgents and drug traffickers.

Donor	Sector	Funding	Length	Completed
United States	Kabul–Kandahar (Sections B to F)	$311m	389km	2003, 2004
	Kandahar–Herat (Sections 3–5)	$181m	326km	2007
Saudi Arabia (built by US)	Kandahar–Herat (Section 2)	$52m (+$13m)	116km	2007
Japan	Kabul–Kandahar (Section G)	$29m	50km	2006
	Kandahar–Herat (Section 1)	$120m	114km	2009
India	Delaram–Zaranj	$84m	216km	2008/9
Iran	Herat–Islam Qala	$45m	123km	2004
	Herat–Armalik	$25m	60km	2004
European Union[a]	Kabul–Jalalabad	$66m	142km	2004
Pakistan	Jalalabad–Torkham	$50m	74km	2006/7[b]
World Bank	Kabul–Doshi (incl. Selang Tunnel)	$75m	175km	2005
	Pol-e Khomri–Kunduz–Sher Khan Bandar, Kunduz–Taloqan	$30m	232km	2007
Islamic Development Bank	Doshi–Pol-e Khomri	$81m	50km	2010
	Armalik–Leman	$10m	50km	2010
	Andkhoy–Aquina	$20m	37km	2010
Asian Development Bank	Andkhoy–Mazar-e-Sharif	$36m	182km	2008
	Mazar-e-Sharif–Pol-e Khomri	$34m	265km	2009
	Andkhoy–Qaysar	$83m	210km	2010
	Qaysar–Balamurghab–Leman	$340m	233km	Pending
	Kandahar–Spin Boldak (Sector 1)[c]	$25m	61km	2008
Afghanistan	Kandahar–Spin Boldak (Sector 2)	$13m	42km	2009
	Herat–Torghondi	$30m	119km	2009

Notes: [a] The Swedish International Development Agency contributed funds. [b] Some 2011 press reports talking of a small section requiring reconstruction. [c] Japan and Kuwait contributed

Afghanistan has had a ring road since the 1960s, but by 2001 most of it was in dire need of resurfacing and repair, especially the vital link between Kabul and Kandahar. Only half of the northern Andkhoy–Leman sector has ever been sealed, and that only recently. Insurgent attacks, corruption and funding shortfalls have plagued the $2 billion project, while questions remain over the quality of the asphalt surface and who will pay the hefty maintenance costs.

Afghanistan has few railways. Apart from 2km running into Turkmenistan from Torghondi, a 75km, Russian-gauge line from Hairatan to Mazar-e-Sharif was recently built. An international-gauge line to Herat from Iran is under construction. A future Pakistan–Uzbekistan line (via Kabul) is part of the contract with China Metallurgical Group Corporation (MCC) for the Aynak mine, subject to feasibility

— Regional highway
- - - Incomplete highway
++++ Railway
++++ Incomplete railway

© IISS

The drugs industry and alternatives

'Narcotics are like ammunition for the Taliban.' That was how one Afghan police officer described to the BBC the way that drugs production has funded the insurgency. The UN estimates insurgents raise more than $100 milli year from taxing opium production and trade.

2010 opium cultivation and production by region

Opium cultivation, 2010 (hectares)

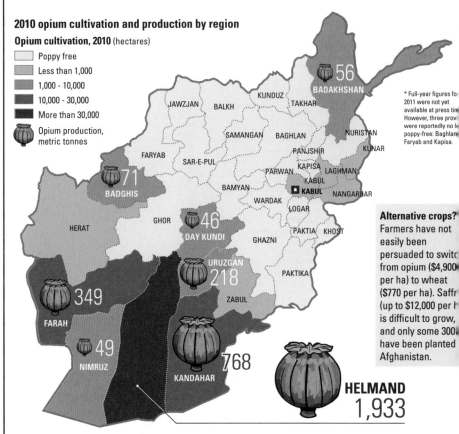

Poppy free

Less than 1,000

1,000 - 10,000

10,000 - 30,000

More than 30,000

Opium production, metric tonnes

* Full-year figures fo 2011 were not yet available at press tin However, three prov were reportedly no l poppy-free: Baghlan Faryab and Kapisa.

BADAKHSHAN 56
KUNDUZ TAKHAR
JAWZJAN BALKH
SAMANGAN BAGHLAN NURISTAN
FARYAB SAR-E-PUL PANJSHIR KUNAR
PARWAN KAPISA LAGHMAN
BADGHIS 71 BAMYAN KABUL KABUL NANGARHAR
WARDAK LOGAR
HERAT GHOR DAY KUNDI 46 PAKTIA KHOST
GHAZNI
URUZGAN 218 PAKTIKA
FARAH 349 ZABUL
NIMRUZ 49
KANDAHAR 768

Alternative crops?
Farmers have not easily been persuaded to switc from opium ($4,900 per ha) to wheat ($770 per ha). Saffr (up to $12,000 per h is difficult to grow, and only some 300 have been planted Afghanistan.

HELMAND
1,933

Crop disease causes 2010 decline

Potential opium production depends on crop yield. The 2001 harvest was close to zero after leader Mullah Omar banned the planting of opium. Military and market forces saw a decline in cultivation 2008–09. Although this stabilised in 2010, bad wea and a widespread fungal disease devastated crops, almost halving opium production. There are worries that the resultant s in price may tempt local farmers to plant more crops, reversing any gains made in recent years.

Opium cultivation in Afghanistan (hectares)

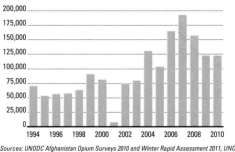

Potential opium production in Afghanistan (metric tonn

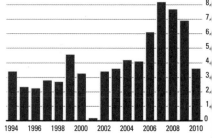

Sources: UNODC Afghanistan Opium Surveys 2010 and Winter Rapid Assessment 2011, UNODC 'Addiction Crime and Insurgency', Government of Afghanistan's Central Statist Office, BBC, Christian Science Monitor, Deutsche Welle, DPA

...adication and seizures

...unter-narcotics strategies have formed a key element of the fight against the Taliban. ...til 2009, ISAF provided funding, intelligence and protection for the Afghan ...ppy-eradication force. That year – following criticism that eradication was proving too ...stly and ineffective, and was angering locals – ISAF switched its focus to interdiction.

...dication of opium cultivation (hectares)

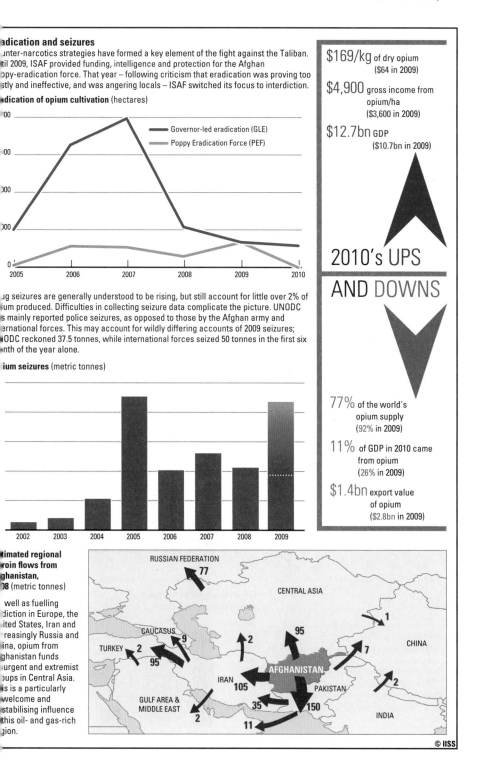

Governor-led eradication (GLE)
Poppy Eradication Force (PEF)

...ug seizures are generally understood to be rising, but still account for little over 2% of ...ium produced. Difficulties in collecting seizure data complicate the picture. UNODC ...s mainly reported police seizures, as opposed to those by the Afghan army and ...ernational forces. This may account for wildly differing accounts of 2009 seizures; ...ODC reckoned 37.5 tonnes, while international forces seized 50 tonnes in the first six ...nth of the year alone.

...ium seizures (metric tonnes)

$169/kg of dry opium
($64 in 2009)

$4,900 gross income from opium/ha
($3,600 in 2009)

$12.7bn GDP
($10.7bn in 2009)

2010's UPS
AND DOWNS

77% of the world's opium supply
(92% in 2009)

11% of GDP in 2010 came from opium
(26% in 2009)

$1.4bn export value of opium
($2.8bn in 2009)

...timated regional ...roin flows from ...ghanistan, ...08 (metric tonnes)

...well as fuelling ...diction in Europe, the ...ited States, Iran and ...reasingly Russia and ...ina, opium from ...ghanistan funds ...urgent and extremist ...oups in Central Asia. ...is is a particularly ...welcome and ...stabilising influence ...this oil- and gas-rich ...gion.

© IISS

The Afghan economy

A reduction in foreign aid in the run-up to 2015 and thereafter will create challenges for the Afghan government. The economy will struggle to offset the impact of lower spending on construction and services. Matching budget revenue to spending will also be tricky: continued progress on tax collection is a must, but reliance on foreign donors will remain.

Population 2010

Urban population % ■
Rural population % ■

Employment by sector 2004

Agriculture % ■
Other % ■

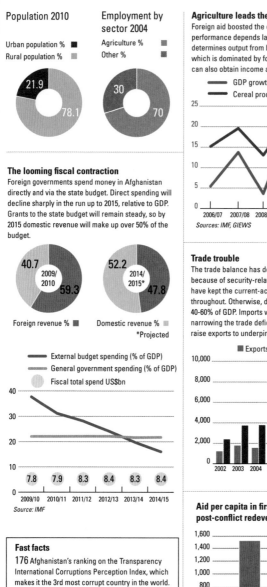

Agriculture leads the way

Foreign aid boosted the economy in 2002-11, but GDP performance depends largely on the harvest. This determines output from both agriculture and industry, which is dominated by food processing. The rural majority can also obtain income and jobs from opium.

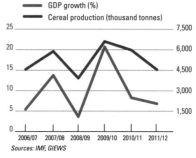

GDP growth (%)
Cereal production (thousand tonnes)

Sources: IMF, GIEWS

The looming fiscal contraction

Foreign governments spend money in Afghanistan directly and via the state budget. Direct spending will decline sharply in the run up to 2015, relative to GDP. Grants to the state budget will remain steady, so by 2015 domestic revenue will make up over 50% of the budget.

Foreign revenue % ■   Domestic revenue % ■
*Projected

External budget spending (% of GDP)
General government spending (% of GDP)
Fiscal total spend US$bn

Source: IMF

Trade trouble

The trade balance has deteriorated since 2002, mostly because of security-related imports. Huge official transfers have kept the current-account deficit to below 5% of GDP throughout. Otherwise, deficits would have ranged between 40-60% of GDP. Imports will fall as ISAF withdraws, narrowing the trade deficit, but Afghanistan will still need to raise exports to underpin macroeconomic stability.

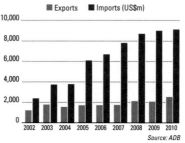

■ Exports ■ Imports (US$m)

Source: ADB

Aid per capita in first five years of post-conflict redevelopment

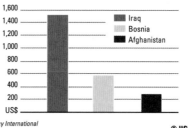

■ Iraq
■ Bosnia
■ Afghanistan

Fast facts

176 Afghanistan's ranking on the Transparency International Corruptions Perception Index, which makes it the 3rd most corrupt country in the world.

154 The country's ranking (out of 183) in the World Bank's 'Ease of doing business' index.

$501 Per capita GDP in 2010/11 according to IMF figures.

Sources: Afghanistan National Development Strategy, BBC, Transparency International

© IISS

Rich in resources

Afghanistan's mineral worth may be worth up to $1 trillion, according to a 2011 Pentagon announcement. That the country is rich in iron, copper and cobalt has been known for decades. However, it has no tradition of mining; and supporting infrastructure – particularly power plants, roads and railways – is grossly inadequate. Insecurity and the legal regime are further hurdles. The government is pinning its hopes on two giant deposits; critics argue it would do better to cast its net much wider.

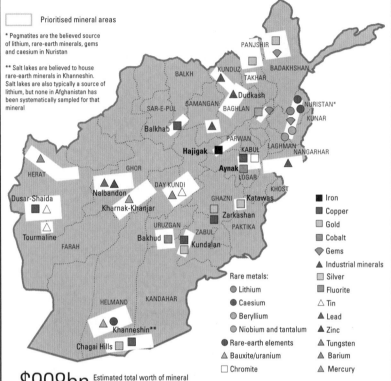

Prioritised mineral areas

* Pegmatites are the believed source of lithium, rare-earth minerals, gems and caesium in Nuristan

** Salt lakes are believed to house rare-earth minerals in Khanneshin. Salt lakes are also typically a source of lithium, but none in Afghanistan has been systematically sampled for that mineral

Rare metals:
- Lithium
- Caesium
- Beryllium
- Niobium and tantalum
- Rare-earth elements
- Bauxite/uranium
- Chromite

- Iron
- Copper
- Gold
- Cobalt
- Gems
- Industrial minerals
- Silver
- Fluorite
- Tin
- Lead
- Zinc
- Tungsten
- Barium
- Mercury

$908bn Estimated total worth of mineral deposits

Major mines

Aynak: China's $3.5bn contract to develop this copper field, promised the biggest foreign direct investment in Afghan history when signed in 2008. The 28 sq km field could contain up to $88bn of ore. But without the infrastructure needed, operators Metallurgical Corporation of China (75% share) and Jiangxi Copper (25%) must build a 400MW power plant and a freight railway from western China through Afghanistan to Pakistan.

Hajigak: Mining firms from India, Iran and Canada were bidding for this 2.1bn-tonne iron-ore project in late 2011.

Gems include emeralds, rubies, sapphires and, perhaps most famously, lapis lazuli from Badakhshan.

Industrial minerals include deposits of brick clay, coal celestite, dolomite, gypsum, limestone and similar materials.

Selected minerals

Mineral	Common uses
Lithium	batteries, especially for electric cars
Caesium	drilling fluids
Beryllium	hardening agent in alloys, radiation shields, aersopace parts, radio-frequency transmitters, high-power transistors
Niobium and tantalum	in superalloys and superconductors (niobium) capacitors, jet-engine parts, surgical equipment, camera lenses (tantalum)
Rare-earth minerals	17 elements (numbers 57–71 of the periodic table, plus scandium and yttrium) with many high-tech uses, including in LED screens, catalytic converters, lasers, fibre optics, cancer medicine and the nuclear industry

Sources: Afghan Ministry of Mines and Industries, US Geological Survey, Bloomberg, CNBC, Eurasianet, New York Times, Reuters

© IISS

Reopening the book on education

The uptake of education in Afghanistan in the past decade has been a rare success story. Despite Taliban attacks schools, more than seven times as many pupils (and 480 times the number of girls) are now enrolled in primary secondary schools. But many do not attend regularly and are forced to drop out early. Overall rates of adult liter are low, and there remains much to do.

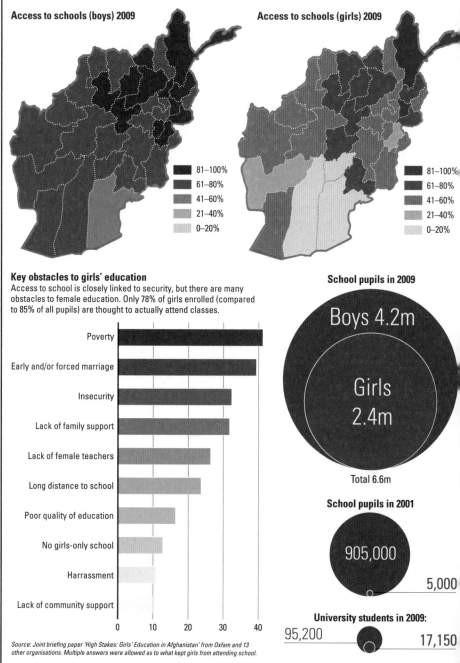

Access to schools (boys) 2009

81–100%
61–80%
41–60%
21–40%
0–20%

Access to schools (girls) 2009

81–100%
61–80%
41–60%
21–40%
0–20%

Key obstacles to girls' education
Access to school is closely linked to security, but there are many obstacles to female education. Only 78% of girls enrolled (compared to 85% of all pupils) are thought to actually attend classes.

Poverty
Early and/or forced marriage
Insecurity
Lack of family support
Lack of female teachers
Long distance to school
Poor quality of education
No girls-only school
Harrassment
Lack of community support

0   10   20   30   40

School pupils in 2009

Boys 4.2m

Girls 2.4m

Total 6.6m

School pupils in 2001

905,000

5,000

University students in 2009:

95,200   17,150

Source: Joint briefing paper 'High Stakes: Girls' Education in Afghanistan' from Oxfam and 13 other organisations. Multiple answers were allowed as to what kept girls from attending school.

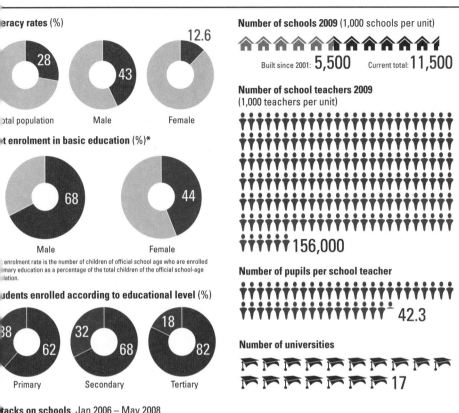

eracy rates (%)

28
43
12.6

total population · Male · Female

t enrolment in basic education (%)*

68
44

Male · Female

enrolment rate is the number of children of official school age who are enrolled
imary education as a percentage of the total children of the official school-age
lation.

udents enrolled according to educational level (%)

38 62
32 68
18 82

Primary · Secondary · Tertiary

Number of schools 2009 (1,000 schools per unit)

Built since 2001: **5,500** Current total: **11,500**

Number of school teachers 2009
(1,000 teachers per unit)

156,000

Number of pupils per school teacher

42.3

Number of universities

17

tacks on schools, Jan 2006 – May 2008

e Back to School campaign launched in 2002 by the Afghan government and the UN is behind many of the past decade's
ucational gains, but growing violence against schools, teachers and pupils since 2006 means continued success is far from
sured. Between January 2006 and December 2008, 1,153 attacks or threats were made towards the education sector (670 of
m in 2008 alone). Attacks continue on schools today.

pe of incidents

Number of attacks per province

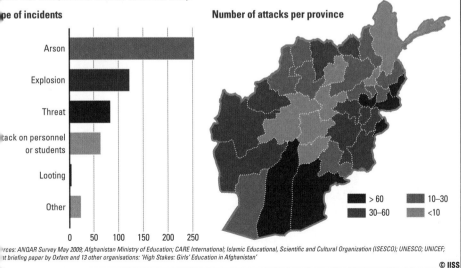

Arson
Explosion
Threat
tack on personnel or students
Looting
Other

0   50   100   150   200   250

> 60   10–30
30–60   <10

rces: ANQAR Survey May 2009; Afghanistan Ministry of Education; CARE International; Islamic Educational, Scientific and Cultural Organization (ISESCO); UNESCO; UNICEF;
nt briefing paper by Oxfam and 13 other organisations: 'High Stakes: Girls' Education in Afghanistan'

Afghans in charge of security

Building effective local forces is fundamental to the eventual departure of international troops by the stated goal of 2014, and the first seven areas made the transition to local security control in 2011. Yet despite increased efforts to recruit and train personnel since 2009, many question whether Afghan security forces can meet an ambitious deadline to step into NATO's role.

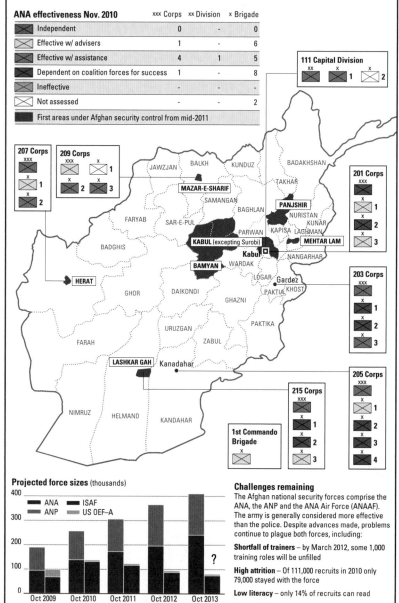

ANA effectiveness Nov. 2010

		xxx Corps	xx Division	x Brigade
	Independent	0	-	0
	Effective w/ advisers	1	-	6
	Effective w/ assistance	4	1	5
	Dependent on coalition forces for success	1	-	8
	Ineffective	-	-	-
	Not assessed	-	-	2
	First areas under Afghan security control from mid-2011			

111 Capital Division
xx | x 1 | x 2

207 Corps — xxx
x 1 | x 2

209 Corps — xxx | x 1
x 2 | x 3

201 Corps — xxx
x 1 | x 2 | x 3

203 Corps — xxx
x 1 | x 2 | x 3

205 Corps — xxx
x 1 | x 2 | x 3 | x 4

215 Corps — xxx
x 1 | x 2 | x 3

1st Commando Brigade — x

Projected force sizes (thousands)

Legend: ANA, ISAF, ANP, US OEF–A

Oct 2009 · Oct 2010 · Oct 2011 · Oct 2012 · Oct 2013
All figures beyond June 2011 are provisional

ANA = Afghan National Army; ANP = Afghan National Police; ISAF = International Security Assistance Force; US OEF-A = US *Operation Enduring Freedom*–Afghanistan

Challenges remaining

The Afghan national security forces comprise the ANA, the ANP and the ANA Air Force (ANAAF). The army is generally considered more effective than the police. Despite advances made, problems continue to plague both forces, including:

Shortfall of trainers – by March 2012, some 1,000 training roles will be unfilled

High attrition – Of 111,000 recruits in 2010 only 79,000 stayed with the force

Low literacy – only 14% of recruits can read

Lack of leadership skills – 26% of NCO positions unfilled

Drug abuse – 30% of applicants rejected because of this

Sources: CENTCOM, CSIS, IISS, ISAF/NATO, Reuters, SIGAR

© IISS

CHAPTER SEVEN

Pakistan

Rahul Roy-Chaudhury

Pakistan has strong and deep interests in Afghanistan, with which it shares a common religion, culture, tradition and history. Yet one point of commonality is also a source of friction: the border is contested and porous, and straddled by sizeable ethnic Pashtun and Baluch communities. Although the violence and instability in Afghanistan adversely impacts Pakistan's domestic politics and security, Pakistan's interventionist policies towards Afghanistan for the past 32 years have decisively influenced the volatile security environment in Afghanistan.

Since the end of Taliban rule in 2001, Islamabad has attempted to build relations with Kabul despite a formidable trust deficit. Pakistan is Afghanistan's principal route to foreign markets and its largest trading partner. It exports some $1.5 billion worth of goods to and imports $111.5 million worth of goods from Afghanistan.[1] Some 60,000 Pakistani expatriates work there. But, even as Pakistan has waged a massive counter-insurgency campaign against al-Qaeda and the local Taliban (Tehrik-e-Taliban Pakistan (TTP)) on its side of the border, it is also widely held to have provided sanctuary and support to Afghan insurgents (including the leadership council of the Afghan Taliban and the Haqqani terror group), which mount attacks on ISAF forces and the government and civilians in Afghanistan from their bases in Pakistan.

The drawdown of ISAF forces creates opportunities and threats for Pakistan. For the Afghan government of President Hamid Karzai, the withdrawal of foreign troops puts added impetus on seeking a political settlement with parts of the Taliban, which is likely to increase Islamabad's influence over the shape of any future peace process or future Afghan government and limit arch-adversary India's presence and influence in Afghanistan. Yet, without a settlement in post-ISAF Afghanistan, there is a risk of civil war or a resurgence of Pashtun separatism, which would gravely threaten Pakistan's security.

Policy evolution

Relations have never been easy. From the earliest days of independence in 1947, Kabul contested the Durand Line, the de facto border between the two countries, and made irredentist claims over the ethnic Pashtuns living in Pakistan. As a result, Afghanistan was the only country to vote against Pakistan's entry into the United Nations in September 1947.[2] In the 1950s, antagonistic bilateral relations between the two often led to Pakistan's closure of transit and trade facilities to Afghanistan. While relations improved in the 1960s, the seizure of the Afghan presidency by Mohammed Daud Khan in 1973 prompted the revival of irredentist Afghan claims as well as a swell of support for Baluchi separatism in Pakistan.[3] Pakistan responded with its 'forward policy' to support disparate Islamic groups against the secular Daud regime. Pakistan president Zulfikar Ali Bhutto and the inspector general of the Frontier Corps, Naseerullah Babar, opened training camps in North and South Waziristan for Afghan Islamists run by the Frontier Corps in conjunction with the Inter-Services Intelligence (ISI) directorate and the Special Services Group (SSG) of the Pakistan army. Some 5,000 Islamic fighters were reportedly trained in Pakistan in 1973–77.[4] From July until August 1975, Pakistani-trained Afghan Islamists, led by Gulbuddin Hekmatyar from Paktia province and Ahmad Shah Massoud from the Panjshir valley, staged an unsuccessful coup against the Daud regime.[5] Undeterred by this setback, Pakistan continued to strive to gain leverage over Afghanistan politics.[6]

The Soviet invasion of Afghanistan in December 1979 and Pakistan's subsequent deep cross-border involvement substantively changed the nature of the bilateral relationship, which has also had an adverse impact on Pakistan's domestic politics and security. Motivated by Cold War rivalry, the US was keen to resist Soviet expansion. For Pakistan, concerns over Soviet ingress into the South Asian region were compounded by fear of Soviet-ally India's growing influence on its western border.[7] This convergence of interests led the US and Pakistan to collaborate in support of an Islamic jihad against the Soviets in Afghanistan. Pakistan encouraged and facilitated some 25,000–30,000 jihadis from Afghanistan, Pakistan and the Arab and Muslim worlds into various armed groups, collectively known as the Afghan mujahadeen ('Islamic fighters'). Saudi Arabia and other Gulf countries provided the financing, while the US supplied both arms and funding. This was the basis of close ISI–CIA ties. The ensuing war forced three million Afghan refugees to flee to Pakistan.

After the defeat and withdrawal of the Soviets from Afghanistan nine years later, the US disengaged from the region. The eviction of the Soviets created an exaggerated sense among the Pakistani military and security establishment of having 'defeated' a superpower, which subsequently inspired efforts to emulate the apparent success with Islamist militants against India. However, Pakistan did not reap the expected political dividends in Afghanistan. The mujahadeen government that emerged was predominantly non-Pashtun, under the leadership of the ethnic Tajiks Burhanuddin Rabbani and Massoud. Fearing the loss of control over Kabul, Pakistani interior minister Naseerullah Babar, who oversaw the opening of training camps for Afghan Islamists in the mid-1970s, acted with the ISI to help establish the Pashtun-dominated Taliban movement to overthrow the Rabbani government. With ISI advice, funds, ex-service personnel, trainers and arms, the Taliban captured Kabul in September 1996. Pakistan became the first of three countries to diplomatically recognise the Taliban government shortly thereafter.

After the 11 September attacks, the US once again turned its sights on Afghanistan, enlisting Pakistan's help in planning and executing an invasion to locate Osama bin Laden and unseat his Taliban protectors. Pakistan's military-backed president Pervez Musharraf granted the US and coalition forces overflight and landing rights for their 'war on terror', which succeeded in forcing out the Taliban government in just one month.

Islamabad then became suspicious of new Afghan president Hamid Karzai, due to the perceived under-representation of Pashtuns in his cabinet and the Afghan National Army (ANA). Those Pashtuns who were given offices in the interim administration were not Pakistan's preferred candidates; the Northern Alliance representatives also attracted Pakistani suspicion because of their links with India. Bilateral relations, generally poor under the Musharraf government, reached a nadir in mid-2008, when Karzai threatened to send troops across the border into Pakistan to fight the Afghan Taliban. Ties improved with Pakistan's return to an elected civilian government under

President Asif Ali Zardari, who took office in September 2008. Karzai attended his inauguration and said that the two countries were like 'conjoined twins',[8] a comment he repeated during a March 2010 visit to Islamabad, when he also stated he would not allow Afghan territory to be used against Pakistan.[9] In November 2003 Pakistan set up two new consulates in Mazar-e-Sharif and Herat, expanding its existing diplomatic network beyond its embassy in Kabul and its consulates in Jalalabad and Kandahar.

Interests and policy

In addition to providing critical transit access to the sea and bilateral trade, Pakistan has pledged an estimated $330m for the reconstruction of Afghanistan, including infrastructure, education and health projects. These include the new Torkham–Jalalabad road (yet to be completed), the Nishtar Kidney Centre in Jalalabad, a 200-bed Jinnah Hospital complex in Kabul (under construction) and educational faculties in various universities across Afghanistan. Another half a dozen large projects, including two eye hospitals, a limb centre at Badakhshan and two nuclear medical centres in Kabul and Jalalabad, are in the pipeline.[10] The two states have also made a provisional commitment to the TAPI gas pipeline project. Pakistan has offered 1,000 scholarships, subsequently doubled in March 2010, to Afghan students; 60% of all Afghan students who study abroad attend educational institutions in Pakistan. More than 1.7m Afghan refugees continue to live in Pakistan.[11]

Yet despite its economic and reconstruction activities, Pakistan is not popular in Afghanistan. This is due primarily to its interventionist policies, its past support for Taliban rule, and the widespread perception that, in pursuit of its current interests, it continues to support Afghan insurgents. In a June 2009 Gallup poll of Afghan perceptions, Pakistan's role in the country was viewed more negatively than India's, the UN's, NATO's and Iran's. Moreover, 33% of Afghans said Pakistan's role in Afghanistan was supporting the Taliban leadership, compared with the 30% who said its current role was reconstruction.[12] In a survey conducted in December 2009 for major Western television networks, Pakistan also came last among the select list of countries viewed 'very favourably' by the Afghans. Furthermore, only 9% of those polled perceived Pakistan as playing a 'positive' role, while an overwhelming 73% felt it was playing a 'negative' role in Afghanistan.[13]

The Durand Line and 'Pashtunistan'

Established in 1893 to counter a potential Russian threat to British India, the Durand Line traverses an area inhabited by a large Pashtun population.[14] Pakistan maintains that the agreement that created this de facto border was essentially formalised by the peace treaty of the Third Anglo-Afghan War (1919) and by a subsequent 1921 treaty.[15] But Afghanistan refused to formalise the Durand Line due to the presence of a large number of Pashtuns on the Pakistani side. Later, the Taliban regime in Kabul refused to recognise the line as an international border.

The rise of Pashtun nationalism in the tribal areas and the Northwest Frontier Province (NWFP) began in the late 1920s, before Pakistan gained independence. The July 1947 referendum offered no option to the Pashtuns of NWFP other than to become part of either Pakistan or India.[16] With Afghanistan seeking a separate 'Pashtunistan', Islamabad attempted to ensure that its own Pashtuns looked towards Peshawar or Islamabad for direction and leadership, not Kabul. The most recent initiative was the symbolic renaming of the NWFP as Khyber Pakhtunkhwa in April 2010. An estimated 42m Pashtuns now live in both countries.

The quest for strategic depth

Pakistan was created out of the partition of British India in August 1947 on the contested basis of a 'two-nation' theory, which held that Hindus and Muslims of the Indian subcontinent could not live together, and therefore Pakistan should serve as a separate homeland for the Muslims. A significant Muslim minority continued to live in India. Three wars with India followed over the sovereignty of the Hindu-ruled but Muslim-majority princely state of Jammu and Kashmir. However, Pakistan itself faced break-up when East Pakistan (now Bangladesh) declared independence following Pakistan's defeat in the 1971 Indo-Pakistani War. Several military crises with India have also taken place, including the 2001–02 military confrontation, leading to fears of nuclear escalation. For Pakistan, India remains the principal existential threat to its security, greater than any of its 'home-grown' domestic security concerns. The Pakistani military is obsessed with the threat from India, following its public humiliation in the 1971 war.

The principal strategic interest for Pakistan's involvement in Afghanistan has been the quest for 'strategic depth', in light of the power asymmetry with its arch-rival, India. Pakistan–India relations have been strained for most of the nearly six and a half decades of independence; the Kashmir dispute is a principal, although not the only, cause of friction.

Fear of the Indian threat, fuelled by the Soviet withdrawal from Afghanistan in 1989, prompted the ISI to clandestinely support and direct jihadi fighters against Indian-controlled Kashmir and the rest of India. This includes support to the al-Qaeda-linked Lashkar-e-Tayiba (LeT) terror group, responsible for the 2008 Mumbai terror attacks, and the Jaish-e-Mohammed (JeM), responsible, along with the LeT, for the 2001 attack against the Indian parliament (although Pakistan has strongly denied this). The scope of LeT's jihad has expanded since 9/11 to include the West.[17]

Afghanistan is the solution to Pakistan's desire for 'strategic depth' because it can add political weight to Pakistan. Therefore it is vital for Pakistan to ensure that its neighbour is responsive, because of the deep hostility that exists in relations with India to the east. Zero-sum thinking is also part of the picture, because if India exerts decisive influence over Afghanistan, then Pakistan faces a threat on two fronts.

Pakistan perceives India's presence and influence in Afghanistan as a deliberate attempt to 'encircle' it and to deny its 'legitimate' pre-eminence in Afghanistan.[18] India's embassy in Kabul and its four consulates are often accused by the Pakistan government of carrying out clandestine operations against Pakistan in the restive province of Baluchistan and the tribal areas. India is alleged to have provided training, arms and funds to Baluchi rebels,[19] as well as funds, arms, ammunition, medical equipment and medicines to the TTP in the tribal areas.[20] Both claims are strongly rejected by India. Additionally, Pakistan is suspicious of India's aid programme and reconstruction activities in Afghanistan (especially in rural Pashtun areas) along with its outreach to the Pashtun community, while resenting the goodwill Afghans generally display towards Indians.

Both India and Pakistan have high stakes in the stability and security of Afghanistan. However, their mutual suspicions over each other's activities in the country, exacerbated by bilateral tensions, have led to conflicting priorities and competition for influence there. The country has become an arena for India–Pakistan rivalry and zero-sum thinking. In December 2010, Prime Minister Yusuf Raza Gilani told US Senator John Kerry that to gain Pakistan's trust India would have to 'decrease its footprint in Afghanistan'.[21]

While Islamabad still perceives India to be the main threat to Pakistan, its perception of 'strategic depth' may be changing. In February 2010, Pakistan's army chief, General Ashfaq Pervez Kayani, said his country wanted a 'peaceful, stable and friendly' Afghanistan that would automatically provide it 'strategic depth'. Significantly, he stated that strategic depth in Afghanistan did not imply controlling Afghanistan.[22] Subsequently, in December 2010 Kayani handed over to US President Barack Obama a paper on the Pakistan army's view of the war in Afghanistan. This paper reportedly defined Pakistan's long-term interests in Afghanistan as 'achieving enduring peace based on a stable environment', significantly omitting the traditional reference to a 'friendly Afghanistan'.[23] This has been interpreted as an attempt by Islamabad to convey the view that Pakistan needs Afghanistan to be 'peaceful' not just vis-à-vis India, but for its own domestic stability and security. Islamabad also made no official comment on India's May 2011 decision to bolster its economic package for Afghanistan, and played down the India–Afghan strategic partnership agreement in October 2011,[24] even though the latter action agitated its strategic community.

Relations between the Taliban and their Pakistani supporters are underscored by tension, as the former regards the latter as manipulative. Despite accepting Pakistani assistance in its rise to power, the Taliban regime previously refused to recognise a key Pakistani security concern, the Durand Line. If the Taliban were to return to power in Afghanistan, it would encourage and offer a blueprint for the TTP in its effort to overthrow the Pakistani government. Significantly, Kayani said: 'we can't have Talibanization. We want to remain modern and progressive ... we cannot wish for Afghanistan what we don't wish for Pakistan.'[25]

These factors may well imply that Pakistan could be shifting its position towards accepting a continued, albeit restricted,

Indian presence in Afghanistan.[26] Pakistan withdrew its opposition to India's participation in the Istanbul conference on Afghanistan in November 2011, having vetoed its participation in the previous year's conference.[27] Significantly, Pakistan withdrew six divisions from its border with India in 2009 to carry out counter-insurgency operations against al-Qaeda and the TTP in its tribal areas.[28]

Counter-insurgency in the border zone

As the only 'frontline' state fighting the Soviet occupation of Afghanistan in the 1980s, Pakistan suffered greatly. After the Soviet withdrawal, a large number of mujahadeen were directed by the Pakistani security forces towards operations in Indian-controlled Kashmir, and subsequently became 'foot soldiers' for terror groups linked to al-Qaeda, such as the TTP and the sectarian militant group the Lashkar-e-Jhangvi (LeJ), which fight against the Pakistani state. There have also been severe law and order problems associated with this: a surge in the narcotics trade and a proliferation of small arms resulting in a 'Kalashnikov culture' in Pakistan, along with a refugee population. At the same time, the number of madrassas (religious schools) in Pakistan is estimated to have increased from 900 in 1971 to 8,000 registered and 25,000 unregistered by 1988,[29] with some becoming the base for the radicalisation of extremists and terrorists.

These costs have escalated since 2001, with the further radicalisation of Pakistani Pashtuns and Punjabis in the wake of the US military intervention in Afghanistan and CIA drone attacks against Pakistan's tribal areas and the NWFP. According to Kayani, by early 2010, Pakistan was suffering even more terror attacks than Afghanistan.[30] The siege of the Red Mosque (Lal Masjid) in the heart of Islamabad in July 2007 and the growing public opposition to Pakistan's support of ISAF forces in

Afghanistan led to an unprecedented rise in extremism and terrorism. More than 8,500 IED attacks have taken place.[31] Suicide bombings rose from two in 2002 to 59 in 2008 and 84 in 2009, before dropping to 53 in 2010, they still accounted for the largest number of people killed (1,271) that year.[32] Some 5,000 security forces have been killed, more than the combined death toll among the coalition forces in Afghanistan, along with more than 30,000 civilian victims.[33]

The largest number of attacks has taken place in the Pashtun belt in Khyber Pakhtunkhwa and the tribal areas. But, significant attacks also include the destruction of the Marriott Hotel in Islamabad on 22 September 2008, the attack on the Sri Lankan cricket team in Lahore on 3 March 2009, and the attack on the Mehran naval air station in Karachi on 22 May 2011. As a result, it is estimated that the Pakistan economy has suffered a loss of some $40bn.[34]

There have been high-profile attacks on politicians. Former premier Benazir Bhutto was assassinated in Rawalpindi on 22 December 2007. Punjab Governor Salman Taseer was assassinated on 4 January 2011 and the Christian Minister for Minority Affairs Shahbaz Bhatti was shot dead on 2 March 2011 for apparently seeking to amend Pakistan's harsh blasphemy law. Most clerics refused to condemn Taseer's murder or perform his funeral rites; and his killer, bodyguard Mumtaz Qadri, became a national religious hero showered with rose petals when he appeared in court for the first time. The government eventually shelved any change to the blasphemy law, thereby emboldening the extremists and demonstrating a lack of decisive leadership.

As a result of US pressure and two failed assassination attempts against President Musharraf, the Pakistan army entered the 'lawless' tribal areas for the first time in February 2004 to conduct limited forays against al-Qaeda and select affiliated militants in South Waziristan.[35] At the same time, however, acting on its anxiety that this action could upset local Pashtuns, Islamabad offered Pashtun leaders in these areas 'peace deals'. This allowed Pashtun militants to assert control over and administer parts of the tribal areas and provide a safe haven for al-Qaeda and the Afghan Taliban,[36] ensuring the latter's resurgence from late 2005.[37] With support from these lawless areas, Taliban fighters launched attacks against ISAF forces across the border in southern and eastern Afghanistan, inflicting an ever higher toll on Western troops there. In 2005, 66 US troops were killed in combat in Afghanistan, more than in the previous four years combined.[38]

In view of the growing defiance from local Pashtun militants, Pakistan sharply increased the number of troops deployed in the border area to 140,000 by mid-2011, up from 80,000 in 2004. These operations helped to fuel a surge in terrorist violence led by the TTP. One consequence was a dramatic rise in suicide bombings against the Pakistan government and the army, including the ISI's main and provincial headquarters. By early 2009 the militants had exerted influence over the Swat valley, which just one year earlier had been a holiday destination. In April 2009 they extended their control over parts of nearby Buner, some 100km northwest of the capital.[39] This finally led to a change of policy in Islamabad. On 8 May 2009, Pakistani troops began a major push against the TTP in the Malakand division, beginning with Lower Dir district and then Buner and Swat. Combat aircraft were used in the NWFP for the first time, along with helicopter gunships and artillery. The action resulted in some 3m internally displaced persons (IDPs). Within two months, the offensive was declared a success. In August, TTP leader Baitullah Mehsud was killed in a CIA drone attack. On 17 October 2009 the army re-launched its operations against South Waziristan. By mid-2011, the Pakistan army was predominantly engaged in counter-insurgency operations with deployments in six of the seven tribal areas and Khyber Pakhtunkhwa.

These operations have inflicted a major blow on al-Qaeda and Pakistan's home-grown terrorist threat. Defence officials claimed that 1,451 'hardcore militants' had been killed (including al-Qaeda's Marwan al-Suri) and 'over 901 al-Qaeda operatives' had been apprehended, including Abu Zubaydah in March 2002, Ramzi bin al-Shibh in September 2002, Khalid Sheikh Mohamed in March 2003, and Abu Faraj al-Libbi in May 2005.[40] The December 2010 US White House review to Congress noted that Pakistan had no long-term strategy to cope with militants across the country but stated that

> there has been significant progress in disrupting and dismantling the Pakistan-based leadership and cadre of al-Qaeda over the past year. Al-Qaeda's senior leadership has been depleted, the group's safe haven is smaller and less secure, and its ability to prepare and conduct terrorist operations has been degraded in important ways.[41]

Hedging and the Taliban

Pakistani intelligence and security forces have had considerable success against al-Qaeda and the TTP in the tribal areas and Khyber Pakhtunkhwa. However, it has taken little or no action against elements of the Afghan Taliban (including the Quetta Shura leadership body), the Haqqani network, or powerful Afghan warlord Gulbuddin Hekmatyr's Hizb-e-Islami Gulbuddin (HiG) group, all operating within its borders. Despite Pakistan's support for the 'War on Terror', it is widely believed that the ISI and the military have maintained secret links to Afghan insurgents after the 11 September attacks.

In a diplomatic cable in September 2009 ISAF Commander General Stanley McChrystal said: 'Afghanistan's insurgency is clearly supported from Pakistan. Senior leaders of the major Afghan insurgent groups are based in Pakistan, are linked with al-Qaeda and other violent extremist groups, and are reportedly aided by some elements of Pakistan's ISI.'[42]

The key question is whether this policy is 'passive' – one of non-aggression and contact, along with occasional support, for insurgents focused on Afghanistan but not Pakistan – or 'active', that is, amounting to a systematic provision of sanctuary and logistical support, including arms and training, to enable cross-border attacks in Afghanistan. A British report in June 2010 alleged that support to the Afghan insurgency was official ISI policy, noting that 'the ISI orchestrates, sustains, and strongly influences the [Taliban] movement' and provides military and logistical support.[43] Attribution is difficult because, as an IISS assessment noted, the ISI department responsible for relations with jihadist groups and for operations outside Pakistan, the 'S Wing', is known to consist solely of retired military officers. This allows the government to deny responsibility for ISI actions.[44]

But some Taliban-linked groups such as the Haqqani terror group, run by Jalaluddin Haqqani and his son Sirajuddin, are believed to be closer than the Afghan Taliban to the ISI. In September 2011, Admiral Mike Mullen, the outgoing chairman of the US Joint Chiefs of Staff, accused the Haqqani network of being 'a veritable arm of the ISI', and asserted ISI's complicity in recent attacks by the group against the US embassy and other targets in Kabul.[45]

The Pakistani government and security establishment have strongly denied these charges. While the military leadership acknowledged that the ISI had contacts with the Haqqani network, it denied support or endorsement of it.[46]

Prime Minister Gilani also rejected Mullen's assertion of ISI complicity in the 2011 Kabul attacks.[47] The Pakistani security establishment also argues that it does not distinguish in terms of its approach to countering militant groups on an ideological basis, but rather because it lacks resources for prioritising and sequencing operations, and is under operational constraints given the risk that an offensive in North Waziristan (head-quarters of the Haqqani network in Pakistan) would further aggravate the situation among Pakistan's Pashtun community. The devastating floods of summer 2010 also impacted military operations.

For some, therefore, Pakistan is playing a 'double game'[48] by extending assistance to ISAF and the Afghan government while also giving succour to Afghan insurgents. In a sharp indictment, British Prime Minister David Cameron, on a visit to India on 28 July 2010, said 'we cannot tolerate in any sense the idea that this country is allowed to look both ways and is able in any way to promote the export of terror, whether to India or whether to Afghanistan, or anywhere else in the world'.[49] Others see Pakistan's approach as a hedging strategy in light of the eventual withdrawal of the US military from Afghanistan and the possibility of the Taliban shaping any future peace process and gaining influence in a new Afghan government. Also, Pakistan demonstrably has some capacity to act as spoiler: in February 2010 it arrested the former Afghan Taliban military commander Mullah Baradar, reportedly because he had defied the ISI by reaching out to the Afghan government.[50] The prospects for stability in Afghanistan are under more immediate pressures, however, in the form of the enduring links between Pakistan-based insurgents, especially the Afghan Taliban and the Haqqani network, and the Pakistani security establishment. In December 2010 Admiral Mullen reiterated ISAF's long-standing position that it could not succeed in Afghanistan without first shutting down safe havens in Pakistan.[51] This was also underlined in a 2010 British parliamentary report, which concluded that 'the continuing existence of Pakistani safe havens for Afghan insurgents makes it extremely difficult, if not impossible, for ISAF's counter-insurgency campaign to succeed'.[52]

Pakistan's Relations with the US

Despite committing $15bn in aid, primarily for security, since 2001, the US has been unable to pressure Pakistan into shutting down the 'safe havens' and ending support to the Afghan Taliban and the Haqqani network. In a leaked diplomatic cable, US Ambassador to Pakistan Anne Patterson was quoted in September 2009 as saying that 'no amount of money' could effect this change.[53] Limits to US influence were also partly due to NATO's dependence on Pakistan for supply routes to carry its goods, arms and ammunition to Afghanistan, over-flights and human intelligence. But, Pakistan's leverage may be diminishing in this respect thanks to the opening of the Northern Distribution Network. Routes through Pakistan carry half as much as they used to as of July 2011, although the proportion is still significant, at 35% of all supplies to Afghanistan.[54]

By far the most significant factor in the deterioration of relations between Islamabad and Washington was the May 2011 killing by US Navy SEALs of Osama bin Laden in Pakistan. US officials did not brief their Pakistani counterparts before the operation for fear of a leak by extremist sympathisers within the military and intelligence establishment. In the wake of the raid, US attention focused on whether Pakistani officials had helped bin Laden to evade US intelligence – he had been living in Pakistan for at least five years – or whether they had simply failed to locate him. The Obama administration stopped short of accusing Pakistan's civilian and military leadership of collusion,[55] but it did increase the pressure to provide* intelligence on several terrorists, including bin Laden's deputy, Ayman al-Zawahiri, Afghan Taliban commander Mullah Omar, Sirajuddin Haqqani, operational commander of the Haqqani network, and Ilyas Kashmiri, an al-Qaeda leader (subsequently reported to have been killed by a drone attack). The US put further strain on relations with Pakistan by maintaining a relatively high tempo of CIA drone strikes on extremist targets in the tribal areas, while suspending some $800m in military aid to Pakistan, amounting to over one-third of its total annual commitment.

The Pakistani army was angry and humiliated by its inability to prevent a violation of Pakistani sovereignty and respond to a US military raid deep inside its territory. This led to unprecedented public criticism of the army in the local media and on the streets, with questions raised about the army's priorities and preparedness. There was increasing pressure on Kayani, who was already attempting to quell growing anti-American sentiment within the military. It also prompted the Pakistani government to draw closer to China, which hosted a delegation headed by Gilani within a fortnight of the bin Laden killing. Earlier, Gilani had reportedly told Karzai that China would be a better partner than the US in striking a peace deal with the Taliban and rebuilding the Afghan economy.[56]

Policy after 2014

Pakistan's relationship with Afghan insurgents, and the underrepresentation of pro-Pakistan Pashtuns within Afghanistan's government, has created a significant deficit of trust between the two countries. This was apparent in an exchange of fire across the border in summer 2011. Defence cooperation is also minimal, due largely to the low proportion of Pashtuns in the ANA[57] and the reluctance of non-Pashtuns to train in Pakistan.

Despite this difficult context, from 2010 the Afghan government showed greater interest in obtaining Pakistan's assistance to obtain a political settlement with the Taliban. Thereafter trade relations improved[58] and the Afghanistan–Pakistan Joint Commission for Peace was formed to address the issue of talks with the Taliban.[59] The inaugural meeting at the level of heads of government was held on 11 June 2011 in Islamabad, with the first meeting of the working level, headed by Foreign Ministry officials but including military and intelligence representatives from both sides, held in June in Kabul. But the killing on 20 September 2011 of former Afghan president Burhanuddin Rabbani, chairman of the Afghan High Peace Council (responsible for steering the reconciliation talks with the Taliban), with alleged official Pakistani complicity, was a major setback to relations.[60]

Crucially, US policy has become more favourable to a settlement involving the Afghan Taliban. Pakistan too has an interest in seeing Afghanistan stabilise, to prevent further negative fallout on its own territory and to reduce US demands upon it that have stirred up such strong anti-American sentiment in the Pakistani army. Drone attacks against the tribal areas and Khyber Pakhtunkhwa incense the local Pakistani population, regardless of whether the leadership has reconciled to it. At the same time, the continued presence of ISAF forces in Afghanistan could bolster terror attacks in Pakistan. Any attempt to coerce the Pakistan army by putting US special forces on the ground in Pakistan – in a repeat of the raid that killed bin Laden – would meet resistance from the Pakistan army or create a schism between troops and their officers. A civil war in Afghanistan would be deeply destabilising for Pakistan, bringing fresh waves of refugees across the border together with arms and militants, and result in the 'Talibanisation' of Pakistan. It could also raise the spectre of Pashtun separatism.

The point is often made by the Pakistan strategic community that were it not for the 'overspill' of the Afghan insurgency, Pakistan would not have the extremist and terror challenges it confronts today. Pakistanis argue that the Afghan government therefore should address the issues of Pashtun political representation, governance, narcotics and corruption before blaming Pakistan for providing sanctuary and support to the Afghan insurgents. Border posts are another problem from Islamabad's perspective, with Pakistan establishing 821 border posts in contrast to Afghanistan's 120.[61] Moreover, Pakistani analysts argue that the twin objectives of helping reconcile Taliban leaders while attempting to eliminate them at the same time are inherently incompatible, while seeking a mutual reduction in violence to offer space for serious negotiations, including with the Haqqani network.[62]

Islamabad's policy options before and after 2014 therefore appear to be to strive towards facilitating a political settlement between the Afghan government and the insurgents (including the Haqqani network), while ensuring that Indian influence is reduced and the worst-case outcomes of a civil war or Pashtun irredentism are pre-empted. This could also enable the Afghan insurgents resident in Pakistan to return to Afghanistan.

CHAPTER EIGHT

Iran

Emile Hokayem

As an immediate neighbour sharing a long border and deep historical, linguistic and societal ties, Afghanistan occupies a central place in the statecraft of the Islamic Republic of Iran. The security of Iran is, to an extent, directly dependent on the situation in Afghanistan. Indeed, as a chronically weak if not failed country prone to foreign interference by Iran's regional and global rivals, Afghanistan presents profound challenges to Iran's external as well as internal stability.

Iranian foreign policy is the product of a dual identity: a quasi-imperial nation pursuing political hegemony and an anti-status quo Islamic revolutionary power. It is also the product of profound geopolitical insecurity stemming from fears of encirclement, foreign meddling and perceived breaches of its sovereignty, all of which have historical resonance. In this regard, Iran's neighbourhood has undergone profound change in the first decade of the new century.

To its west, Iran's regional posture has been enhanced by the US-induced demise of the country's most reviled enemy, Saddam Hussein of Iraq, and his replacement with a friendly regime in Baghdad. Its reach into the Arab world has increased thanks to its senior membership in a resistance front that opposes US and Israeli designs in the Middle East, which includes Arab actors like Syria, Hizbullah, Hamas and Iraqi factions. Its advocacy of Arab causes has also attenuated the stigma of being a Persian Shia power in an otherwise Sunni-dominated Arab region, and has alienated Arab governments that resent and fear Iranian interference in Arab affairs. In particular, a cold war which pits Iran against the Arab Gulf states, most notably Saudi Arabia, has taken on a more sectarian character and geopolitical significance.

To its east, Iran's relations with Pakistan are characterised by ambivalence. The latter has at times been a partner, especially in helping Iran break its isolation. Pakistan imports energy from its neighbour and awaits the completion, despite US opposition, of a $7.5 billion pipeline that would provide Pakistan with 7.8bn cubic meters of gas a year from Iran's South Pars gas field; the two countries plan to increase bilateral trade from a meagre $1bn in 2011 to $5bn in 2015;[1] railway and infrastructure projects are also being discussed. While Pakistan is reluctant to clash with Iran, Islamabad's strong ties to Saudi Arabia, Iran's avowed rival in the Arab world, are meanwhile the source of considerable friction and mistrust. Indeed, because of that relationship, Iran perceives Pakistan as a potential state threat, particularly due to the Saudi monarchy's history of sponsoring radical Sunni factions with Pakistani facilitation, including in Baluchistan and Afghanistan. In recent years, however, the prospect that a nuclear-armed Pakistan would turn into a failed state where Sunni Islamist militants would thrive has also preoccupied Iranian policymakers.

Interests and policy

In trying to prevent Afghanistan's ills from spreading, however, Tehran must make do with limited reach due to the difficulty of navigating the complex Afghan political, ethnic and sectarian terrain. Accordingly, while Iran attempts to project power in the Arab world through ideological and emotional appeals to a largely sympathetic audience that sees Iran as a champion of Arab causes, its approach to Afghanistan has been characterised by a pragmatic, cautious and largely opportunistic assessment of its reach and prospects there.

Iran has no territorial claims over Afghanistan. Rather, Iranian behaviour in Afghanistan is largely the function of Tehran's calculation of the threat posed by Afghan developments to its own stability, but it is also driven by concerns about the intentions and role, real or imagined, of external players operating on Afghan soil.

Iran has an interest in preventing the Taliban from returning to power, whether through war or through a reconciliation process that disregards Iranian concerns. Iran has a contentious history with the ethnically Pashtun, Saudi- and Pakistani-backed Taliban. It cultivated close relations with Afghanistan's non-Pashtun (anti-Taliban) factions which, following the fall of Kabul to the Taliban in 1996, formed the Northern Alliance, to which Iran provided significant military, material and political backing. Iran also withheld diplomatic recognition from the new regime.

Tensions between Iran and the Taliban quickly escalated. One aspect of the Taliban campaign was systematic repression of the Shia Hazara minority, culminating in a massacre after the capture of the opposition stronghold of Mazar-e-Sharif in 1998. The plight of Afghan Shi'ites naturally attracted sympathy and outrage in Iran, but it was a direct Taliban affront that drove the two countries to the brink of war. During the seizure of the city, ten diplomats assigned to Iran's consulate and one Iranian journalist were among those killed by Taliban forces. In response, Iran deployed 70,000 troops to its border, while a

top official promised 'we will get revenge for their blood'.[2] A
UN mediation averted war, but the stand-off only exacerbated
hostility. Tehran's support for the Northern Alliance increased,
but it was not enough to defeat the Taliban.

Equally bad from Iran's perspective, civil war and Taliban
excesses drove refugees into Iran. In 1996, the year the Taliban
took power, the figure stood at 1.4 million. After the fall of the
regime in 2001, a marked decline in the population of refugees was recorded, with 377,000 returning to Afghanistan.[3]
Repatriations have continued, with or without UN assistance;
Iran has sought to voluntarily repatriate the majority of refugees, though there have been reports that some legal refugees
have been deported. The 1m who remained as of June 2010[4]
face arduous working conditions in the Iranian informal
agriculture and construction sectors and state policies that
increasingly regard them as a burden.[5] A 2006 joint statement
by the Iranian government, the Afghan government and the
UN's High Commission for Refugees, apparently affirmed the
countries' commitment to observing international laws governing the status and protection of refugees, while 'welcoming the
voluntary repatriation to Afghanistan of over 1.3m Afghan
refugees and displaced persons since the start of the voluntary
return operation in April 2002'. Of this number, the statement
added, 840,000 have repatriated voluntarily under the joint
Iran–Afghanistan–UNHCR programme, and 530,000 'repatriated spontaneously'.[6]

Similarities in language and culture, cemented by transnational social networks, also make Iran an attractive option for
migrants. According to a research study on Afghan deportees
from Iran, growing numbers of single Afghan men are migrat-
ing to Iran, where wages can be up to four times higher than
in Afghanistan. It is estimated that remittances from these
migrant workers make up 6% of Afghan GDP. Nearly half of

the men who go are the sole breadwinners in their families, making for a precarious existence should they be discovered and deported. Almost 80% cross the border with the help of a smuggler, to whom they pay half of what it would cost for a visa to enter the country, where they make up just 2% of the workforce.[7]

In addition to the refugee problem and that of economic migration, Iran is worried about the trafficking of Afghan opium: huge volumes cross the country en route to Western markets, but Iran also has a sizeable drugs problem of its own. The UNODC estimated in 2009 that Iran had 1m opium addicts and accounted for 42% (450 metric tonnes) of global consumption.[8] Iran's interest in Afghan stability is therefore paramount. The direct and indirect costs of hosting refugees and Iranian consumption of narcotics include massive border-control measures, as well as rising criminality and social upheaval that exacerbate Iran's existing problems.

Compounding this is the vital importance for Iran of containing regional rivals, most importantly Pakistan and Saudi Arabia. Already squeezed between these geopolitical allies – one populous, militarily strong and nuclear armed, the other wealthy and proselytising a form of Sunni Islam hostile to Shi'ism – Iranian power would be further checked were they to command overriding influence in Afghanistan. The two Sunni powers have worked in tandem in Afghanistan since the 1980s, with Saudi money and Pakistani intelligence propping up the fractious resistance against the Soviet occupation. In the 1990s, they threw their decisive support behind the Taliban and helped unify various Pashtun factions. Saudi Arabia even overcame its displeasure at the Taliban's hosting of Osama bin Laden's al-Qaeda. In the eyes of Tehran, they effectively conducted a proxy war against Iran on Afghan soil.

After the defeat of the Taliban in 2001, privileged relations between Iran and many former members of the Northern Alliance thrived. To be sure, Iran supported the transitional process that brought Hamid Karzai to power and has since been a vocal backer of the Afghan central government, distinguishing itself from Pakistan's ambivalent, at times hostile approach. This has also taken the form of direct cash payments amounting to millions of dollars to Karzai and other Iranian officials. The *New York Times* revealed that Iran had given €700,000 to Karzai, who publicly admitted this in October 2010, saying: 'They do give us bags of money — yes, yes, it is done. We are grateful to the Iranians for this.'[9] He also stated that Iranian help in ending the violence in his country would have a stabilising effect on Iran: 'We are very hopeful that our brother nation of Iran will work with us in bringing peace and security to Afghanistan so that both our countries will be secure.'[10]

Still, besides its support for Karzai and its contribution to the country's reconstruction and economic development, Iran has hedged by maintaining and sometimes strengthening relations with the myriad warlords it has supported since the 1980s, while also forging relations with new political players and even some Taliban-affiliated groups. This reflects continued Iranian unease at Karzai's reliance on NATO forces to extend the reach of his government, build up his security forces and secure the country's borders. In late 2010 Iran banned the export of fuel to Afghanistan, a move that hurt Afghanistan's economy and society. There was speculation that it was meant as retaliation against US pressure on Iran to freeze its nuclear programme, though others explained it as a reflection of Iran's own energy problems or as a show of its displeasure with Afghanistan's support for the routing of the proposed Turkmenistan–Afghanistan–Pakistan–India (TAPI) gas pipeline that bypasses Iran.[11] Around that time, Karzai distanced himself from US support and made thunderous calls for the withdrawal of NATO forces, angering the US but pleasing Tehran. Despite this, Iran remains restive with Karzai's so-far unsuccessful attempts to reach out to Pashtun groups, and with his stated desire for a conditional reconciliation with the Taliban. It also views with great suspicion the recent rapprochement between Karzai and Pakistan. Therefore, Iran's investment in Afghan allies and proxies also amounts to an insurance policy, should Afghanistan relapse into civil war.

Iran's involvement in Afghanistan is not immune to the factionalism in Tehran. The Supreme National Security Council, the Revolutionary Guard – through the Quds Force – the Ministry of Intelligence and the office of the president all operate on Afghan territory, working sometimes at cross purposes and often with little coordination, including on cultivating Afghan allies.[12] Corruption in Iran's police and border guards also renders the Iranian–Afghan border very porous.

Iran is keen to prevent the use of Afghan territory by the United States to pressure or coerce Tehran, but in a way that avoids any kind of overt or direct confrontation with Washington. After a short honeymoon in 2001 when the US relied on the then-Iranian-backed Northern Alliance to oust the Taliban and install a new government in Kabul, the underlying US–Iranian animosity overcame their objective convergence of interests. Iran has become a strident critic of the US and NATO presence in Afghanistan, blaming it for the continued instability in the country. This criticism has allegedly extended to providing Taliban factions with weaponry. A US diplomatic cable released by WikiLeaks in 2010 alleges that 'Iran is engaged in an extensive covert campaign to arm, finance, train and equip Taliban insurgents, Afghan warlords allied to al-Qaeda and suicide bombers fighting to eject British and Western forces from Afghanistan'.[13]

In September 2007, NATO forces in western Afghanistan seized an arms shipment that was blamed on Iran,[14] and another was interdicted in Kandahar in March 2010. In August 2010, the US government issued an Executive Order against two Quds officers for supporting the Taliban. In March 2011, another weapons batch was intercepted by ISAF in Nimruz, with the UK foreign secretary asserting that 'detailed technical analysis, together with the circumstances of the seizure, leave us in no doubt that the weaponry recovered came from Iran'.[15] Such accusations do not originate only from NATO; in July 2009, the Afghan governor of Nimruz announced the arrests of five Afghans who had trained as suicide bombers in Iran. According to WikiLeaks cables, a main recipient of Iranian entreaties is Gulbuddin Hekmatyr, a Pashtun warlord who was briefly prime minister of Afghanistan prior to the Taliban takeover.[16] Yet the former Afghan prime minister maintains a conflictual relationship with Iran, which hosted him in exile in 1997 but expelled him in 2002 over his opposition to the Karzai government and the US presence. The alleged destination of Iranian arms shipments, for example Kandahar, suggests that Iran maintains relations with Taliban factions as well.

The US presence in Afghanistan exposes it to the threat of Iran-orchestrated attacks and retaliation by Iranian proxies to deter any US attack on its territory while maintaining deniability and flexibility in its response. Just as in Iraq, Iran has cultivated Afghan allies and proxies that would make it costly for the United States to embark on a military campaign.

Iran's strategic vision of its role in Afghanistan goes beyond security concerns, however. Iran seeks to become an essential player with regard to regional integration. This means consolidating its political and economic prominence in the region of Herat, previously a province of Iran. Herat serves as Iran's entry point into Afghanistan but also as a security buffer. It has been the main recipient of Iranian religious, economic, educational and infrastructure programmes. Iran has tried to cement its position in Afghanistan by contributing significantly to its reconstruction. It is building roads, railroad, electrical and water plants, opening religious schools and universities, providing finance and advice for agricultural projects. Annual bilateral trade is estimated at \$1.5bn.[17]

Ultimately, Iran's vision also involves leveraging its position in Afghanistan to join any major project linking Central Asia to the Persian Gulf. Railroad, road and pipeline projects, ongoing or under discussion, would boost trade, industry, energy and transportation and cement Iran's eastern orientation. Indeed, Afghanistan's economic future matters greatly to Tehran. An improvement of Afghan economic conditions would encourage the return of Afghan refugees, ensure the viability and reach of the central authorities and counter the rise of the Taliban. But Iran has an interest in constraining the country's development if it proceeds outside the context of Iranian–Afghan relations. This is best evidenced by Iran's concerns over transit infrastructure. The TAPI pipeline project stands to reduce Iran's prospects to export gas to South Asian markets for a decade or more. The development of highways and railways in Afghanistan could allow for trade routes linking Central Asia to the Indian Ocean that circumvent Iran's Chabahar port to the benefit of Pakistan's Gwadar port. US and multilateral sanctions on Iran and the availability of alternative trade and transportation links would encourage traders to bypass Iran altogether. Consequently, Tehran has an interest in ensuring that it is not excluded from Afghanistan's development plans. In this regard it enjoys support from India, which may be sufficiently strong to sway Afghan authorities away from Pakistan-centric infrastructure planning.

Policy after 2014

Iran is carefully watching US and NATO plans in Afghanistan. Iran upholds the principle that any foreign presence anywhere is fundamentally disruptive, even more so on its borders.

This applies principally to the United States, whose deployment in Afghanistan to destroy al-Qaeda and defeat the Taliban Iran cautiously welcomed at first. As tensions between the two countries escalated over the US occupation of Iraq, Iran's controversial nuclear programme and other issues, Tehran became more hostile towards US operations in Afghanistan. From Iran's perspective, the United States harbours aggressive intentions and encircles Iran with bases in Central Asia, Iraq, the Gulf and Turkey.

Without strong ISAF backing for the Afghan government, however, there will be concern in Iran about whether Afghanistan's fragmented, largely unreliable army and police forces will be able to defeat or contain the Taliban, or even to avoid infiltration by it. This would require greater Iranian intelligence efforts to cultivate relationships within the military and police. In parallel, Iran would have to consolidate its ties to various warlords in case of a renewal of civil war.

If the security situation in Afghanistan deteriorates markedly after 2014, Iran would be compelled to deepen its involvement. Its reach there may be similar to that which it had in Iraq, but it will probably face greater geopolitical and ideological pushback. It would also have to expend more energy, capital and resources to preserve its existing relations. The upside for Tehran would be a greater sense of security with the departure of US troops.

For Iran, the risk resides in the possibility of a Saudi- and Pakistani-brokered reconciliation process in Afghanistan that purposely excludes Iran, with or without US approval. Pakistan and Saudi Arabia are eager to contain Iranian influence in Afghanistan and to mobilise and direct Sunni extremist elements there, including anti-regime Baluchi militants. Indeed, a weak government in Kabul would pose a threat insofar as large swaths of Afghan territory would remain under the control of forces likely to espouse a fundamentalist Sunni outlook that could be manipulated or leveraged by Iran's enemies. Given their close intelligence, financial, political and religious ties with the Pashtun community, Saudi Arabia and Pakistan could position themselves as the pivotal players able to facilitate a political settlement that delivers the Taliban and other allied groups like the Haqqani network.

One way for Iran to counter Saudi and Pakistani attempts to displace it is to cultivate good relations with as many Afghan factions as possible, including the central government. Hazara, Tajik and Uzbek minorities are suspicious of Saudi and Pakistani intentions, so they are likely allies of Iran. Yet, Iran's early strategy of containing the Pashtun plurality and backing minority factions, including the Hazara co-religionists, failed, most notably in 1996 when the Taliban captured Kabul from their hands. Iran's rapprochement with Karzai, a Pashtun himself, reflects its preference for a government that reflects the country's diversity while cultivating allies to be at once part of Afghanistan's political and economic future and pre-position proxies for contingencies. A smaller US military footprint in Afghanistan that removes the threat of a US attack from the east could lead Tehran to support more wholeheartedly the central government after 2014. Given Karzai's travails, however, the perceived strength and viability of that government will matter just as much.

To preserve its interests in Afghanistan, Iran would first need to ensure that any post-NATO-drawdown regional dialogue is inclusive. This has so far proven complicated, since US–Iranian tensions have precluded a direct engagement on the issue, even though US officials have repeatedly admitted that a regional solution would require Iranian participation. In any case, orchestrating such a regional dialogue has proven difficult for the United States because of other rivalries in the region. A NATO drawdown could motivate neighbours to meet and agree on a managed competition out of fear that a vacuum or a weak government in Kabul could draw them in at great cost. That scenario is more probable, owing to the rise of tensions elsewhere in the region. Given its lack of resources to check Saudi Arabia and Pakistan, Iran would then want to reinforce its political coordination with Central Asian states and most importantly India, countries that share its concerns about Pakistani encroachment.

CHAPTER NINE

The Central Asian states and Russia

Oksana Antonenko

Afghanistan's northern neighbours – the five post-Soviet Central Asian states and Russia – receive scant attention in most regional analyses. Yet Afghanistan's northern neighbourhood is vital in assuring stability in the post-ISAF period. Three Central Asian states share a border with Afghanistan: Tajikistan, Uzbekistan and Turkmenistan. Kyrgyzstan is host to the Manas air base, the largest US and ISAF base in Central Asia; and Kazakhstan has sought to play a diplomatic role by promoting the involvement of the Organisation for Security and Cooperation in Europe. In addition to this, ISAF forces rely heavily on the Northern Distribution Network (NDN), a web of transit routes that traverse Kazakhstan and Russia and bring supplies to NATO troops (see Strategic Geography 'Supply routes to Afghanistan', p. viii). As a former imperial power and potential trading partner, but also as a prime destination for illegal opium exports, Russia too has vital interests in finding solutions to Afghanistan security problems.

Russia's engagement in the region generally, and in Afghanistan particularly, dates from the nineteenth century, during a period of geopolitical rivalry with the British Empire known as 'the Great Game'. But it was a more recent episode that set the tone for Moscow's dealings with Afghanistan: the Soviet Union's intervention against the mujahadeen from 1979 to 1988 left a troubled legacy with which both countries are still grappling today. The conflict gave way to decades of under-development and severe poverty, for which Afghans hold the USSR responsible; memories of the war and its toll on the people of Russia as well as Central Asia have created insur-mountable barriers to a future Russian intervention, regardless of whether it is mandated by a UN resolution. On the posi-tive side, personal ties remain between many military leaders now serving in the Afghan National Security Force, and their former Soviet instructors, to whom they can turn for knowl-edge and understanding. Some former Soviet specialists have returned to Afghanistan to rebuild the economic infrastructure which they originally helped to establish. Many of the lessons from the Soviet period, including that of the Soviet withdrawal from Afghanistan, are relevant to the contemporary challenges faced both by the Afghans themselves and by ISAF as it moves towards the exit.

The people and elites of former Soviet Central Asia have co-existed with Afghans for centuries; indeed, Tajiks and Uzbeks are the second- and third-largest ethnic groups in Afghanistan. These two groups, plus the Hazara Shia and the Turkmen people, have ties with Central Asian states and Russia. While the Sovietisation of Central Asia interrupted traditional inter-ethnic ties between Tajiks and Uzbeks living on both sides of the border, links were re-established by the thousands of Central Asians who served in the Soviet Army in Afghanistan from 1979 onwards. In the 1990s, Russia and the Central Asian states became the principal external supporters of Ahmad Shah Massoud, the military leader of the anti-Taliban Northern Alliance. Massoud was the principal buffer between the Central Asians and the Taliban. The additional assistance provided to anti-Taliban forces following Massoud's death in September 2001 helped to drive the regime out of Afghanistan by the end of that year.

Russia and Central Asian states have three key security concerns arising from the war in Afghanistan: the threat of insurgency and terrorism; political radicalisation of their people; and the spread of drugs and organised crime. Russia and China are concerned about the presence of US and NATO forces in the region, whereas the Central Asian states have welcomed this because it has increased their bargaining power with Moscow and Beijing.

Interests and policy

Tajikistan and Uzbekistan have lived under the shadow of a threat from Afghanistan since they became independent in 1992. The collapse of the Soviet Union left them with poorly protected borders and weak internal security structures. While Afghanistan was under the control of the Taliban, it pursued an expansionist regional agenda, offering support to Islamist opposition movements in Central Asia.

Among the Central Asian states, Tajikistan has the deepest ties to Afghanistan. The main anti-government force in the 1992–97 Tajik civil war, the United Tajik Opposition (UTO), which included Islamists as well as anti-Soviet democrats, operated from and found refuge in Afghanistan. In September 2010 there was a notable increase in deadly clashes in Tajikistan between the authorities and insurgents, which raised fears of a new internal conflict emanating from Afghanistan. In one of these incidents, a group linked to al-Qaeda claimed responsibility for an ambush that killed at least 28 Tajik soldiers near the country's frontier with Afghanistan.[1] It followed another incident on the border in which Tajik security forces claimed they killed 20 Taliban fighters who were trying to enter the country from Afghanistan; around the same time, police announced they had recaptured four Islamist militants who were among a group of 25 escaped prisoners.[2] The men had been jailed for fomenting unrest and plotting to overthrow the government. Islamists were also blamed for two bombings in September 2010: one in a Dushanbe nightclub in which five people were injured, and a suicide car bombing which killed two policemen and injured 25 in the northern city of Khujand.[3]

Uzbekistan is also directly exposed to the threat from insurgent groups that operate with impunity from Afghan territory. One of these groups, the Islamic Movement of Uzbekistan (IMU), which has roots in the Fergana valley (an area associated with al-Qaeda) and seeks to establish a caliphate across Central Asia, was ejected from Uzbekistan in the late 1990s. The IMU took refuge in Afghanistan and from there staged two major attacks: on the Batken gorge in the Fergana valley in 1999, and near Tashkent in 2000. As an ally of the Taliban, the IMU suffered major losses in Afghanistan in the wake of the US-led invasion, but it reconstituted itself, drawing in other nationalities, establishing training camps in North Waziristan, Pakistan, and forging links to other groups such as the Haqqani network. Since 2008, perhaps in anticipation of ISAF's departure, the IMU has consolidated its presence in northern Afghanistan in order to mount a fresh challenge to Uzbekistan's president, Islam Karimov. Afghan and coalition security forces have engaged IMU militants in Balkh, Kunduz, Takhar and Baghlan.[4] While the Uzbek government fears that the NDN could bring the war to Afghanistan's neighbours, it has also reaped benefits from its participation. Tashkent has been able to use its cooperation over the supply route as a bargaining chip, increasing transit fees twice in 2010 and again in 2011, and lobbying the US for a relaxation of sanctions banning the provision of military assistance. General Stanley McChrystal noted the potential for the NDN partners to exert increased influence in their dealings with the US as early as 2009, saying: 'ISAF's Northern Distribution Network and logistical hubs are dependent upon support from Russian and Central Asian states, giving them the potential to act as either spoilers or positive influences'.[5]

In addition to concerns about insurgency and terrorism originating from and/or sustained through bases and safe heavens in Afghanistan, the Central Asian states are concerned about the risk posed to their societies by radicalisation from Afghan elements. Governments in all five Central Asian countries are committed to preserving secular states and are anxious about the threat of Islamist movements. This has led them to oppose efforts at reconciliation in Afghanistan for fear that it will result in the state becoming more Islamic in character.

The final major security concern shared by the Central Asian states and Russia is the high volume of drug trafficking from Afghanistan to the north. According to the UN's Office on Drugs and Crime, in 2008 Afghanistan produced an estimated 380 metric tonnes of heroin, just 5 metric tonnes of which were consumed in-country. Some 95 metric tonnes were exported via Central Asia, while an estimated 70 metric tonnes went to Russia, which has over 160,000 heroin users.[6] This boosts organised crime in Russia as well as putting a further strain on public health. The perceived failure of ISAF to tackle opium production in Afghanistan has been a major source of friction between the coalition and Russia.

Economic interests
Beyond the security threats, there are economic possibilities for the CIS states in Afghanistan. Due to their geographic situation, the five land-locked post-Soviet Central Asian states rely on overland routes to deliver their principal exports of oil, gas,

uranium, cotton and aluminium. Soviet planning distorted the economic geography of Central Asia. Most of the roads, railways and pipelines from the region run north to Russia and other parts of the former Soviet Union, providing the infrastructure for a single economic system. The states of Central Asia now aspire to much broader commercial relationships, looking to China, India, Southeast Asia and the markets of Europe and North America, but the infrastructure to facilitate these ties is, for the most part, lacking. The shortest distance from Central Asia to the ocean is south through Afghanistan, to Pakistan or Iran. Such a route would offer increased access for the region's raw materials to other large markets, thus bolstering Central Asian states' independence and bargaining power vis-à-vis its two large neighbours, Russia and China.

Realisation of these ambitions depends to a large extent on securing and developing Afghanistan as a transit state. Thus the Central Asian states have a considerable economic stake in Afghanistan's future, an interest that is fully consonant with that of Afghanistan. Economic partnership could stretch well beyond transit: Tajikistan has the potential to supply electricity, generated by hydropower plants, to northern Afghanistan; along with Uzbekistan, it also has the wherewithal to lead a variety of infrastructure projects in Afghanistan, from construction to irrigation. Russia's state-run power utility Inter RAO, which owns generating companies in Kyrgyzstan and Tajikistan, is seeking partners with which to build the Central Asia South Asia Electricity Transmission and Trade Project (CASA-1000), a power line that will connect Central Asia with Pakistan.[7] Preliminary agreements were signed in 2010 to build a Turkmenistan–Afghanistan–Pakistan–India (TAPI) gas pipeline to deliver gas to the energy-hungry Indian subcontinent, although the four countries have not yet finalised agreements governing gas sale and purchase and the pipeline framework.[8] There are potential points of friction, linked with the shortage of water in Central Asia, which may hinder cooperation on other projects. If, for example, Afghanistan were to develop its agricultural sector in the north, this would put a strain on scarce water resources on which the water-intensive agricultural sectors of Uzbekistan and Turkmenistan rely.[9] Moreover, as long as security problems, including drugs, persist in Afghanistan, the Central Asian states and Russia will be reluctant to relax border controls for small-scale commerce, all of which acts as a brake on efforts to boost the economy of Afghanistan and the wider region.

Attitudes to ISAF

ISAF's presence in Afghanistan has benefited the Central Asian states in several ways. It has drawn the fire of the Taliban and associated groups such as the IMU away from former Soviet Central Asia. By supporting the Karzai government, ISAF has also ensured that the authorities in Afghanistan are largely secular and so do not support political Islam in Afghanistan's neighbours. Without ISAF's work in stabilising Afghanistan, economic projects that are strategically important for Central Asia, such as infrastructure development, would be impossible. Furthermore, ISAF has extended legitimacy and financial support to the governments of former Soviet Central Asia, and from 2010 onwards it began to take more concerted action to shut down opium production and exports from Afghanistan.

All this notwithstanding, there are reservations about the ISAF presence on the part of the Central Asian states and Russia. This is partly because of a perception that the Western military presence has fuelled the insurgency, while it has not directly tackled the IMU or the cultivation of poppy fields that are particular Central Asian and Russian concerns. These countries are also anxious that the NDN could become an avenue for the export of instability into former-Soviet Central Asia.

Uzbekistan was the first country to offer the Bush administration the use of its military facilities, with Kyrgyzstan following soon after by opening the Manas air base to US forces in December 2001. This became a transit hub for ISAF. Russia, meanwhile, offered full support in the early stages of the anti-Taliban operation, but suspicions that the US is seeking to establish a permanent foothold in Central Asia led to a cooling in Russia's attitude. The 2010 'reset' in relations by presidents Dmitry Medvedev and Barack Obama once again put cooperation on Afghanistan at the centre of bilateral relations.

Nevertheless, despite the benefits realised or promised by NATO intervention, it has prompted significant mistrust, mostly in Russia but also in other former Soviet states. Russia was often interpreted as hoping to see the Alliance tied down in Afghanistan for years, and thus unable to intervene in regions of greater importance to Russia. However, once it became apparent the US was contemplating leaving Afghanistan, Russia's approach started to change. ISAF's withdrawal has raised concerns about regional stability, prompting Russia and its neighbours to offer a greater level of support to ISAF and the government of Afghanistan. This found expression most clearly in the establishment of the NDN, which carries between 30% and 40% of non-lethal supplies to US and NATO forces. The importance of the NDN to ISAF grew as the security of its routes to Afghanistan via Pakistan declined. In May 2009, when regular deliveries on the NDN began, the volume of container traffic was just 560 containers per month. By August that year, the figure had risen to 1,000 containers per month, and in January 2010, 1,640 containers were transiting the route every month.[10] Furthermore, the development of the railway line from Hairatan to Mazar-e-Sharif has boosted the operational capacity of the NDN by fixing a logistical bottleneck along the Uzbek–Afghan border.

Russia's contribution to supporting ISAF in Afghanistan has increased considerably since the announcement of the 2014 deadline for handing the country over to Afghan security control. The US and Russia cooperated in the field of counter-narcotics, launching joint operations and stopping illicit financing of Afghan-related terrorism from narcotics trafficking. According to a June 2010 White House press release, Russia's assistance has been significant. Moscow has agreed to waive fees for more than 4,300 official US flights and allow an unlimited number of commercial charter flights carrying supplies. In addition to this, 'Russian companies have provided vital airlift capacity for over 12,000 flights in support of ... operations in Afghanistan and Iraq, 30% of the fuel US military troops use in Afghanistan and over 80 MI-17 helicopters to the Afghan National Army, Afghan National Police, and Afghan Drug Interdiction Forces'.[11] The same document acknowledged ISAF's reliance on the Russian section of the NDN, through which 65% of all NDN traffic passes.

The support of Russia and the Central Asians has come at a price for ISAF. The US has been obliged to re-establish links with authoritarian governments, and to pay more for the use of military facilities in Central Asia. The Kyrgyz government that came to power in 2010, following the country's second revolution in ten years, pushed to re-negotiate supply contracts for the Manas air base. The Uzbek government, which had been shunned by Western states following the killing of hundreds of unarmed protestors at Andijan in 2005, insisted on full engagement in return for making military facilities available to ISAF. It even managed to secure an invitation for President Karimov to NATO's 2008 summit in Romania, as a reward for agreeing to open the northern supply route running through the

Termez–Hairatan border crossing and the Friendship Bridge, by which Soviet forces entered Afghanistan in 1979 and left in 1989. Cooperation with Tajikistan was slowed by rampant corruption and fears about internal instability. Turkmenistan, which follows a policy of neutrality and is less worried than its neighbours about the potential for radicalisation of its population, has also been patchy in its assistance. However, from 2008–09 onwards the Turkmen authorities opened some roads and airfields to ISAF and US forces for the delivery of non-lethal supplies. There have also been reports that clandestine agreements with Turkmenistan have allowed the US to bring lethal supplies into Afghanistan and to transport personnel out.[12]

In addition to the legitimacy that they have derived from deeper US engagement, Central Asian elites have benefited financially. For example, in 2005–09, when Uzbekistan was subject to EU sanctions over Andijan, the German government paid €67.9 million for use of the Termez air base.[13] The leasing of bases – and indeed the threat to revoke basing rights – has been an especially powerful bargaining chip. Former Kyrgyz president Kurmanbek Bakiyev managed to play off Washington against Moscow by using just such a threat in February 2009. On the day he announced the end of the US lease for the strategically important Manas air base, Moscow pledged $2 billion in aid, which had apparently been agreed during an earlier visit to Moscow. At the same time as it was hinting strongly at the closure of the base, however, Bishkek was engaged in haggling with Washington to secure a deal that would allow US troops to stay on at an increased rental cost of over $60m a year, up from $17.4m a year. Under the new terms, which became law in July 2009, the US also reportedly pledged $36.6m to expand the base.[14] Having already disbursed $450m to Kyrgyzstan in Spring 2009, Moscow withheld the remainder of the promised aid, amid allegations that the money paid out was 'not used according to its [agreed] purpose'.[15] There is evidently much to be gained from balancing the interests of the great powers, including the promise of tied development aid: France provided the Tajik government with a low-interest, long-term loan of €20m to build a new airport terminal in Dushanbe; India paid for the reconstruction of the runway and hangars at the Ayni air base near the Tajik capital; and Iran has offered to build roads in Tajikistan that will improve regional connections and bypass existing routes that cross Uzbek territory.

Cooperation strained
Although there is a high degree of congruence among Russia and the five Central Asian states (and China) with regard to Afghanistan, cooperation among them has been hindered by rivalries, principally between resource-rich Kazakhstan and populous Uzbekistan. Both aspire to the status of a regional leader. In addition, there is tension between Uzbekistan on one side, and Kyrgyzstan and Tajikistan on the other, over water management. The upstream states' desire to build dams and hydroelectric power plants is perceived by the Uzbek government as a threat to the sector that supplies most of the country's jobs: cotton production. Tajik–Uzbek relations are further strained by diaspora and border issues, as well as Uzbekistan's regional-power ambitions.

External rivalries also undermine cooperation. Firstly, Russia's role as the region's security guarantor was called into question in July 2010, when several Central Asian states were reluctant to authorise its intervention in crisis-torn Kyrgyzstan. Russia itself had shown little appetite to involve itself at first. While Russia wishes to address all questions surrounding Western military bases in Central Asia through the forum of NATO's dialogue with the Collective Security

Treaty Organisation, the Central Asian states insist that they deal bilaterally with the US or other ISAF contributors.

Secondly, China is providing stiff competition for Russia by investing heavily in the energy sectors of Central Asian countries. It already has a larger stake in the Kazakh energy sector than Russia. As of May 2010, China had a majority stake in 15 Kazakh energy companies, and was said to control 40% of Kazakh oil production;[16] Kazakhstan sent just under a third of its crude oil output (25.6m tonnes) for that year to China.[17] Much of the oil imported from Central Asia is carried by the Kazakhstan–China pipeline, which was completed in 2009.[18] Elsewhere in Central Asia, China is vying with Russia for access to markets in Uzbekistan, where it had reportedly invested $600m in the energy sector by 2005.[19] China was expected to overtake Russia as the main importer of gas from Turkmenistan, if its gas fields prove capable of supplying the agreed 40bn cubic metres of gas per year in return for sizeable investments from Beijing. At the end of 2009, the first branch of a gas pipeline transiting Turkmenistan, Uzbekistan and Kazakhstan came online with a throughput of 13bn cubic metres a year to China. When it reaches full capacity, it will carry 40bn cubic metres per year. According to the Economist Intelligence Unit, China has also taken on the role of the region's main creditor, providing Turkmenistan with $4bn in loans to develop gas reserves in South Yolotan, and handing out $10bn to Kazakhstan as a sweetener for its joint purchase in 2009 of state oil-producer ManistauMunaiGas.[20]

The third factor hindering cooperation is continuing suspicions between Russia and the US. Although both have military bases in Central Asia, there is precious little interaction between their personnel. In Kyrgyzstan the two bases are located just kilometres from each other, yet even when a popular uprising led to the overthrow of the Bakiyev government in spring 2010 they made no contact. The first contact took place in February 2011 when Russian air force personnel visited the US base at Manas. Major efforts will be required before Central Asia and Russia will be able to play a positive, coordinated role in stabilising and developing Afghanistan after 2014.

Finally, Russians and Central Asians have few trusted allies in the current leadership in Afghanistan. President Hamid Karzai made his first official visit to Russia in January 2010, during which he called Russia 'a great political, economic and military power'. Karzai held talks with Dmitry Medvedev on the possibility of contracting equipment and training from Russia for Afghan security forces, and met with business leaders to discuss opportunities in the energy sector.[21] Despite these apparent first steps towards greater regional cooperation, Russia and Central Asian states are still concerned about the diminishing representation of ethnic Tajiks and Uzbeks in important government and state posts in Afghanistan, which they see as an attempt by Karzai to sideline the interests of former Soviet countries in favour of an outreach to Afghanistan's Pashtun communities.

Moreover, there is little confidence in Karzai's political leadership, particularly after ISAF's withdrawal. Governments in Central Asia and Russia are less concerned than Western states about corruption and democratic shortcomings in Afghanistan; for them, the real concern is the patchy exercise of effective government control in more remote areas of the country. They are also concerned about alleged links between senior officials and opium producers and traffickers, which undermine their efforts to promote counter-narcotics campaigns.[22]

Policy after 2014

The drawdown of ISAF forces will inevitably raise concerns over the prospect of an increased militant threat to Central

Asia. Although ISAF was often criticised in Moscow for failing to tackle opium production and Central Asian militants with sufficient rigour, it nevertheless shielded Central Asia from a range of threats. At the same time, a reduction in the presence of US forces in Central Asia will ease the anxieties of Russia and China about US involvement in their backyards, although the extent will depend on how large a footprint the US military retains in Afghanistan. For the Central Asian states, this complicates the challenge of pursuing cooperation with the US while also maintaining cordial relations with the regional powers Russia, China and Iran. Maintaining equilibrium in relations as ISAF winds down will not be easy.

The evolution of Russian and Central Asian policy towards Afghanistan after 2014 will depend on several factors: the security situation in Afghanistan; the political settlement and the role that Afghanistan's Tajiks and Uzbeks have within it; development aid flows for Afghanistan, particularly those with a regional dimension; Afghan opium production; the post-2014 US military presence in Afghanistan; and the stability of the former Soviet Central Asian states themselves.

To preserve their influence within Afghanistan and to check security threats emerging from the country, the Central Asian states will continue to oppose moves to foster a national reconciliation in Afghanistan that would bring the Taliban into government. There is a long-held suspicion that the US is willing to make deals with Pakistan and the Pashtuns, to facilitate its exit, at the expense of the Tajiks, Uzbeks and other northern-based minorities in Afghanistan. These fears are only likely to be assuaged if ISAF brings Russia and the Central Asian states more deeply into discussions about Afghanistan and regional decision-making structures. Transparency and engagement are vital.

A major point of interest for Russia and the Central Asian states is Afghanistan's role as a producer and exporter of opium. There is a widely held perception in these former Soviet states that ISAF has chosen the path of least resistance on opium growing, in order to avoid driving Afghans into the arms of the insurgency, at the cost of fuelling organised crime and drug consumption in Russia and the Central Asian states. For them, it is vital that before 2014 ISAF takes steps to significantly reduce the flow of drugs from Afghanistan, to destroy laboratories, to reduce the volume of precursor chemicals flowing into Afghanistan, and to break down some of the most notorious organised crime groups. If this is not done it is likely that drug traffickers and their clients will entrench their influence in Afghanistan and Central Asian states. In this case the goal of securing borders and fighting corruption and violent crime in Central Asia will never be realised effectively. Likewise, the Central Asian states are eager to see decisive action against the IMU, by disrupting its networks and arresting its leaders and commanders in northern Afghanistan.

Levers of influence

While Afghanistan's northern neighbours have significant interests and stakes in the trajectory of Afghanistan's development after 2014, their influence remains limited. This stems from their reluctance to send armed forces into Afghanistan to mitigate existing and potential threats. Owing to the scars left by its previous intervention, for example, Moscow has been particularly vocal in its resistance to the idea of joining any future deployments. Speaking at the IISS Shangri-La Dialogue in 2010, Deputy Prime Minister Sergei Ivanov stated that, while his country was helping ISAF in various ways, there was a strict limit to its support for operations in Afghanistan. He told the conference: 'a Russian soldier can never again enter

Afghanistan. I think you understand why. It is like asking the US whether they will send troops to Vietnam; it is totally impossible.'[23] The Soviet legacy also limits Afghanistan's readiness to request Russian military assistance in dealing with internal security problems, such as the narcotics trade. President Karzai directly invoked the Soviet legacy when he criticised Russian involvement in a 2010 joint operation with the US against Afghan drug laboratories.[24] This legacy is also the major obstacle to the expansion of Russian military training assistance, which has so far been restricted to training police from the northern provinces.

Reservations about Russia's role are not restricted to Afghanistan. Central Asian states also have concerns about its participation, along with NATO, in training border guards and officials from Central Asian states and Afghanistan to deal with cross-border drug trafficking. Long-standing arrangements to base a Russian mechanised regiment in Tajikistan and to allow Russian border guards to patrol that country's frontier with Afghanistan were reviewed in 2005, when Dushanbe insisted it no longer needed the Russian presence to protect its borders. The withdrawal left only a few hundred advisers, which was further reduced in 2011 to 200.[25] Although Tajikistan has agreed to host a Russian military base for another 49 years,[26] there are serious doubts about the ability of the base to deter threats from Afghanistan, not least because Russian forces have not been operationally deployed from the base since the end of The Tajik civil war. For their part, the Tajik authorities have claimed that they confiscated just as many tonnes of narcotics from traffickers since 2005 as their Russian supervisors did before their withdrawal.[27]

Uncertainties also persist as to the military capabilities of the as-yet untested Collective Rapid Response Forces (CRSF), set up under the Collective Security Treaty Organisation in

2009 to deter and to repel external attack; fight international terrorism, transnational organised crime and drug trafficking; and respond to natural disasters. The non-intervention of these forces in the crisis in Kyrgyzstan in 2010 dealt a severe blow to their credibility as the principal tool for regional states to deal with security threats. Deep divisions between member states have been the key factor preventing the CSRF from fulfilling its role, although it remains the most likely potential means of ensuring regional security.[28]

Another possible source of future tensions is the historic link between tribal warlords and their erstwhile financiers in Russia. Moscow, as well as a number of Central Asian governments, continues to maintain ties with the former Northern Alliance. Should a new civil war break out following the withdrawal of ISAF, or insurgency spread on a much larger scale to the north, the former practice of arming and funding of proxies in Afghanistan could resume. As power is devolved from Kabul to the regions after 2015, Russia and Central Asian states might restore close ties with ethnic Tajik and Uzbek warlords and officials in the north in order to retain influence and to prevent potential Taliban advances towards their borders. This has the potential to destabilise factional Afghan politics yet further.

Politically, Afghanistan's neighbours have limited capacity to develop a closer regional concert of powers which could promote their solutions to Afghanistan's problems. Divisions are legion, with each state intent upon asserting its individual role. Kazakh President Nursultan Nazarbayev set up a Conference on Interaction and Confidence Building Measures in Asia (CICA), to enhance cooperation towards promoting peace, security and stability in Asia. He has urged the organisation to take the leading role in discussing regional strategy for Afghanistan (which is also a member). At the NATO summit in Bucharest in 2008 Uzbek President Islam Karimov proposed to create new 6+3 talks[29] to develop a common long-term strategy for Afghanistan and to address the issue of national reconciliation with international support. In 2011 President Emomali Rahmon of Tajikistan hosted the quadripartite summit with the leaders of Russia, Afghanistan and Pakistan; he also sought to forge closer ties with Iran (including joint projects in hydropower energy and joint military exercises) and with India (which has been invited to modernise one of Tajikistan's main military airfields and military bases at Ayni). Russia, for its part, is pushing the profile of the CSTO – where its influence is undisputed – as the key regional partner for NATO in developing a regional approach towards Afghanistan. These divisions and rivalries are likely to intensify after 2014, when each of the Central Asian states will be seeking to consolidate its regional influence.

The Central Asian states are also limited in their ability to promote economic development in Afghanistan. This input depends to a large extent on Afghanistan's security forces making sufficient progress to assure the viability of major infrastructure projects to connect Central Asia and Russia to South Asia via Afghanistan. Both the CASA-1000 and the TAPI pipelines are unlikely to be implemented in the near future as investors will be put off by the high risk of attacks as well as the complications caused by political tensions between regional states (CASA-1000 is opposed by Uzbekistan).

Central Asian hopes for the creation of new transit corridors across Afghanistan to the Indian Ocean and the markets of South Asia rest on further gains in stability and the availability of finance. To the extent that increased stability will depend on integrating parts of the Taliban into the Afghan government, the realisation of the Central Asians' economic agenda in Afghanistan will come at the cost of their political influence in the country. Greater Pashtun representation in the government will, they fear, diminish the influence of the Uzbeks and Tajiks. The strongest insurance against this loss of influence for Central Asian states, and perhaps the greatest guarantor of stability in Afghanistan, is the formation of a broad regional consensus behind President Karzai. Should his government fail, however, the only recourse would be to the former Northern Alliance figures.

The stability of Central Asian states beyond 2014 remains in doubt. Uzbekistan, Kazakhstan and possibly Tajikistan may be in the throes of leadership transitions. Stability in Kyrgyzstan is also far from assured. There is a chance that IMU elements may increase attacks within Central Asia, exploiting internal tensions and rising Islamist sentiments. Therefore Central Asian leaders are likely to look for guarantees for regime security and specific military solutions against the IMU in Afghanistan in exchange for their support of the US/ISAF-led settlement for Afghanistan after the withdrawal of Western fighting forces. There are many deals that will have to be done to secure the fullest participation of former rivals in building Afghanistan's future. Both Russia and China will be seeking guarantees that the US does not establish a long-term military presence in Central Asia as a prerequisite for their input into the region-led stabilisation programme.

CHAPTER TEN

China

Christian Le Mière, Gary Li and Nigel Inkster

Until relatively recently China's relations with Afghanistan have been extremely limited. As a consequence of negotiations between the United Kingdom and Imperial Russia in the late nineteenth century as part of the 'Great Game', China acquired a land border with Afghanistan in the form of the Wakhan corridor, a narrow strip of land on the northern edge of the Hindu Kush running between Tajikistan and Pakistan. But the border, located in a remote and inhospitable region with a sparse nomadic population, has been closed for the past 100 years and direct communication between Afghanistan and China has been non-existent during that period, as has Chinese interest in Afghanistan. During the anti-Soviet jihad in the 1980s, China took advantage of the situation to sell at inflated prices large quantities of arms including assault rifles, rocket-propelled grenade-launchers and even Type 59 tanks to the Afghan mujahadeen via the CIA station in Beijing. US journalist Steve Coll observed that 'tens of millions of dollars in arms deals annually cemented a growing secret anti-Soviet collaboration between the CIA and Chinese intelligence'[1] which included a chain of US-run signals-intercept stations along China's border with the

Soviet Union. But China never sought direct engagement with the Afghan mujahadeen, preferring always to work through either US or Pakistani proxies. And following the collapse of the Soviet Union, relations between China and the US became both more complex and less collaborative as the strategic glue that bound their interests melted away.

In the chaos following the Soviet departure in 1989, China's main concern in respect of Afghanistan was to minimise the risk of jihadist ideology inflaming the situation among its ethnic Uighur population in Xinjiang. The Uighurs are ethnically, linguistically, culturally and religiously distinct from the Han Chinese population, and have long harboured a sense of separation from the eastern provinces of China, enforced by the geographical impassability of the Gobi Desert. This sense found expression in 1933 and 1944, brief periods of self-proclaimed independence as the East Turkistan Republic, before the region was subsumed by warlordism and Chinese Nationalist and subsequently Communist control. As a result, although Xinjiang has been under Beijing's aegis continuously since 1949, albeit with periods of great autonomy, there remains a strong separatist sentiment both within the Uighur population in Xinjiang and among expatriate or exiled Uighurs.

Beijing fears that this separatism could be enflamed or exacerbated by a militant Islamism incubated in the tribal areas of Pakistan and southeastern Afghanistan. There have indeed been indications in recent years that this may be occurring, albeit on a small scale. Separatist expatriate Uighur militants were previously organised under the banner of the East Turkistan Islamic Movement, formed in 1989. The group changed its name to the Turkistan Islamic Party in 2000, but suffered a serious setback in October 2003 when its leader, Hasan Mahsum, was killed by Pakistani security forces in South Waziristan. It then appeared to have become dormant, although a 2007 raid by Chinese authorities on a suspected insurgent camp in western Xinjiang reportedly ended in 18 Uighur militants being killed and 17 arrested. This was the first indication of the group's re-emergence after a period of consolidation, and was followed a year later by the arrest of ten suspects and the seizure of 18 explosive devices in January 2008.

From then on, the operational tempo of Uighur separatists and the Turkistan Islamic Party (TIP) appeared to increase, possibly to coincide with the hosting of the Olympic Games in Beijing, although due to state secrecy, claimed attacks are notoriously difficult to verify, as are raids carried out by the Chinese authorities. In March 2008, a Uighur woman unsuccessfully attempted to light two soft-drinks cans filled with petrol aboard a flight from Urumqi to Beijing. In July, the TIP released its first online video, with a series of incredible claims of attacks in China.

The first successful attack by Uighur militants for several years occurred in early August 2008 in Kashi (Kashgar), when a truck was driven into a troop of 70 border police officers during their training. During the attack, two attackers dismounted, throwing improvised explosive devices and using bladed weapons. The eventual death toll was 17 police officers (the two attackers were arrested, convicted and executed in April 2009). Less than a week later, a series of co-ordinated attacks by up to 15 Uighur militants targeted 12 government buildings in Kuqa, which was followed by three separate knife attacks in western Xinjiang.[2]

Although it is unclear whether there was a correlation between the attacks in Kashi, Kuqa and Xinjiang and the heightened profile of the TIP (which claimed responsibility for none of these attacks but said it was responsible for other events, the nature of which is impossible to verify), the increased tempo of Uighur militancy is clearly a concern for Beijing. When married with growing separatist sentiment and discontent among the Uighur population, it suggests that an insurgency could take hold in the region despite China's heavy security presence. For this reason, the severe violence that disrupted Urumqi and Kashi in early July 2009, when ethnically targeted rioting killed at least 197 people (by the official count), although unrelated to the resurgence of the TIP, only heightens Beijing's anxiety over the possibility of Islamic militancy crossing the border from Afghanistan.

Since then, a steady drumbeat of small-scale attacks and video releases from the TIP suggest that an insurgency is very slowly gathering momentum. The TIP's leader Abdul Haq al-Turkistani was killed in an air-strike in February 2010, but this did not appear to hamper the campaign. Three attacks in July 2011, including a brazen assault on a police station in Hotan, and the ambushing of a truck and simultaneous bombing and storming of a restaurant in Kashi, demonstrated the continued vigour of the campaign, the dedication of its militants, the co-ordination involved in the attacks and the growing sophistication of the tactics involved. All of the 12 civilian victims in the Kashi attacks were of Han Chinese origin, suggesting a racial targeting. The TIP claimed responsibility for all of the events.[3]

Beijing is now faced with the gathering pace of a seemingly self-perpetuating insurgency, which is capitalising on widespread discontent with China's rule over Xinjiang and transmigration policies that have seen the Uighur population move from being a clear majority in the mid-twentieth century to become a smaller minority than the Han Chinese population in the province today. This consideration dominates Beijing's relations with Central Asia generally, and in particular fuels China's desire to see a stabilised Afghanistan and friendly Pakistan to its west.

China's regional strategy

From a wider strategic perspective, China's policy towards Afghanistan has to be seen in the context of its efforts to construct a regional architecture in Central and East Asia which offers it the most favourable peripheral environment and minimises the risk of strategic encirclement by the US. Securing its land borders, historically the main source of threat to successive Chinese dynasties, has been a major preoccupation. As Aaron Friedberg has observed:

> Even as it begins to build a new regional architecture centered on itself, Beijing has been working hard to lock in the strategic opportunities presented by the dissolution of the Soviet empire. In addition to removing a potentially dangerous adversary from along its continental frontiers, the emergence of independent republics permitted China to expand its influence into Central Asia. Thanks largely to these developments, the view among Chinese strategists is that the 'land environment showed a marked trend towards easing'.[4]

China has massively increased its economic presence and political influence in Central Asia and Russia's Far East, to the point where some Russian policymakers talk uneasily of a possible 'soft' Chinese takeover of Siberia.[5] This influence has been achieved through the energetic pursuit of bilateral relations, but also via the Shanghai Cooperation Organisation (SCO), a mutual security organisation founded in 2001 and comprising China, Russia, Kazakhstan, Kyrgyzstan, Tajikistan and Uzbekistan. (Iran, India and Pakistan have observer status. Turkmenistan is not a member.) The SCO has established a number of joint projects in the fields of energy, transportation and telecommunications and has developed an active programme of joint military and counter-terrorism exercises. For China, the economic aspects of SCO cooperation far outweigh the military and security benefits, in contrast to Russia, where the military component predominates, but overall the SCO offers China a valuable counterweight to the perceived threat from US attempts at strategic encirclement. Afghanistan has voiced its desire to become a member of the SCO, with a contact group formed in November 2005 and an application for observer status made in May 2011.[6]

From that perspective, Afghanistan is a potential cause of concern to China due to the substantial NATO presence there and the concomitant existence of US bases in Kyrgyzstan and Uzbekistan (the Uzbek base was closed down in 2005). Some younger hawks within the People's Liberation Army (PLA) have characterised Afghanistan as a central link in a C-shaped land encirclement of China by the US.[7] It is unclear to what extent these views are representative of official Chinese thinking since junior- and middle-ranking PLA officers often espouse controversial positions in books designed to sell as many copies as possible. But there can be little doubt that China is hoping for a military withdrawal from Afghanistan by NATO and the US military as soon as this can be achieved without giving rise to major instability and without leaving any US military bases in the region. China's position is probably best exemplified by the remarks of a senior Communist Party official involved in foreign-policy issues who observed in October 2009, 'China hopes that the USA will remain in Afghanistan long enough to ensure long-term stability there – and not a day longer.'[8] There is, however, no sign of China being willing to undertake any actions which might actually assist the USA to expedite the achievement of this objective. NATO requests for China to open its border on the Wakhan corridor to create an alternative to the southern supply route through Pakistan – which has been the subject of frequent jihadist attacks and occasional closures by the Pakistani government – appear to have been the subject of serious consideration within China's policy community during 2008 and early 2009. But as of mid-2011 the official Chinese reaction has remained one of polite procrastination.[9] And requests for China to provide more direct security assistance to Afghanistan, such as that made by former UK Prime Minister Gordon Brown in 2008, have been flatly rejected.

A key factor in China's approach to Afghanistan is the question of access to natural resources, seen as a prerequisite for sustaining strong economic growth rates vital to ensuring China's internal stability. During the 1990s China made the transition from being self-sufficient in oil to becoming a net oil importer. The bulk of China's oil imports transit the Malacca Straits, seen as a potential choke-hold vulnerable to a US or even Indian naval blockade and a risk China has long been anxious to mitigate. China has invested heavily in energy pipelines from Central Asia; 200,000 barrels of oil per day are now piped into Xinjiang from Kazakhstan, and a gas pipeline from Turkmenistan via Uzbekistan and Kazakhstan, which opened in December 2009, has the potential to meet half of China's estimated natural gas needs by 2013.[10] Afghanistan's proximity to these pipelines makes it an important factor in China's energy security,[11] even though China shows no inclination to engage directly in efforts to enhance security there.

The one area where China has sought direct engagement with Afghanistan is the exploitation of the mineral resources whose total value the US Geological Survey has put at in excess of US$1 trillion. In 2007 the state-owned China Metallurgical Group Corporation won the contract for a 30-year lease of the Aynak copper mine situated in Logar province to the south of Kabul. First identified by Soviet geologists in 1979, Aynak is thought to contain over 240 million tonnes of high-grade copper ore. The bidding process, in which a number of firms from the US, Canada, Russia and India took part, was criticised for its lack of transparency.[12] The China Metallurgical Group – which put up a bid of $ 3.5 billion, to include the construction of a 400MW power plant and a $6bn railway line to Torkham on Afghanistan's border with Pakistan – was accused of supplying a $30m bribe to the then-Afghan Minster for Mines Mohamed Ibrahim Adel. Though this accusation was never conclusively proven, concerns about the Aynak bidding process led in 2010 to the cancellation and re-issue of a call to tender for the exploitation of the Hajigak iron-ore mine in Bamyan province, in which China Metallurgical Group had also expressed an interest.[13] Meanwhile, it remains unclear whether the security situation in Logar will enable exploitation of the Aynak mine to start as scheduled in 2014, with doubts having been raised about the viability of this and other projects in the current security climate.[14]

China's commercial engagement with Afghanistan has also translated into a substantial Chinese presence centred on Kabul and providing a wide range of goods and services which might otherwise not be readily available. In general this community operates unmolested,[15] but in view of the overall security situation has unsurprisingly suffered some casualties, most notably in 2004 when 11 Chinese workers were killed. The Chinese government has also provided financial aid to the government of Afghanistan since 2002 amounting to $130m, with a further $75m pledged. And it has provided some training to Afghan security forces in mine clearance.[16] A less well-publicised Chinese contribution has been the use of private security contractors to provide police training in Logar province with a view to ensuring the security of Chinese investments, such as the Aynak copper mine. This came to light through a series of blog posts by a former People's Armed Police officer, which were quickly taken down, demonstrating the sensitivity for the Chinese government of such activity, which may well not be confined to Logar province.[17]

The other important factor conditioning China's approach to Afghanistan is that it sees this predominantly through the prism of its relationship with Pakistan. This relationship, which dates back to the 1960s, has been driven by China's desire to find a regional strategic counterweight to India, with which it fought a brief border war in 1962, and by Pakistan's even more pressing need for a powerful protector against an Indian state with which it has fought and lost three wars and come close to fighting a fourth. As Pakistani Ambassador to Washington Husain Haqqani has observed, 'for China, Pakistan is a low-cost secondary deterrent to India and for Pakistan, China is a high-value guarantor of security against India'.[18] China has provided Pakistan with significant military hardware and technology transfers, and this collaboration has not been limited to conventional weaponry. In 1983, China handed Pakistan a complete nuclear-weapons design and helped Pakistani scientists to enrich weapons-grade uranium at the Kahuta facility,[19] and in 1989 and 1991 invited Pakistani scientists to Lop Nor, where the warhead subsequently sold by A.Q. Khan to Libya may have been tested.[20] China has also transferred short and medium-range ballistic missiles (M11 and M9) and the relevant technology to Pakistan. Though there is little evidence of continuing state-sanctioned co-operation in respect of Pakistan's nuclear-weapons programme, China continues to provide assistance to that country's civil nuclear programme, having constructed a 300MW nuclear reactor at Chashma and declared its intention to build another. Over the years there has been significant Chinese investment in Pakistan, as well as a trading relationship currently worth $7bn per year. As of 2010 there were some 10,000 Chinese workers in Pakistan, engaged in a total of 120 engineering and infrastructure projects.[21] These include the construction of a deep-water port in Gwadar on the Makran coast. There is thus far no evidence that China intends to build a naval base at the port, notwithstanding an announcement to that effect made by Pakistani Defence Minister Chaudhury Ahmed Mukhtar following the US operation in Abbottabad that killed Osama bin Laden.[22] Pakistani officials like to contrast what they describe as the 'all-weather friendship' with China with what they perceive as a 'fair-weather friendship' with the United States. In fact China, while always maintaining a public posture of friendship and support for Pakistan, has shown itself ready to adopt a brutally instrumental and hard-headed approach in its dealings as, for example, when it pressured the government of General Pervez Musharraf to take military action to free some Chinese sex workers kidnapped by the occupants of the Red Mosque in Islamabad in November 2007. China has also put behind-the-scenes pressure on Pakistan to take action against Uighur separatists located in Pakistan's tribal areas. When it comes to Afghanistan, however, the indications are that China will not do anything that could be seen by the Pakistani government as contrary to its interests. This may at least partially explain China's continuing refusal to open the Wakhan corridor as a NATO supply route, since this would deprive Pakistan of a significant source of revenue. For the same reason, China is unlikely to support any developments in Afghanistan seen as likely to benefit India, with whom relations have assumed a new edge following India's conclusion of a civil nuclear cooperation agreement with the US.

In the final analysis, China appears to be playing a waiting game with respect to Afghanistan. Like its ally Pakistan, China remains far from convinced that the country can be fully stabilised before 2015 and kept in that condition thereafter. At the same time, any outcome which leads to an entrenched, long-term US military presence in the region will be a cause for concern. While maintaining amicable relations with the Karzai government, China is loath to do anything visibly contrary to the interests of the Taliban and its allies, lest they should subsequently either return to power or become important power-brokers in some future political arrangement. China is essentially caught between the competing interests of its partners in the SCO, all of whom support the Tajiks and Uzbeks who collectively are the bedrock of the Karzai government, and Pakistan, whose interests lie unequivocally with the Pashtuns who feel largely excluded from power. At the same time, China will wish to do nothing which risks exacerbating the threats of separatism, terrorism or extremism in Xinjiang.[23] In that sense, it views Pakistan's support for militant groups with unease.

Circumstances in Afghanistan arguably pose a challenge to China's long-held policy of non-interference in the affairs of other states. An outcome in Afghanistan resulting in a resumption of civil war would undoubtedly jeopardise Chinese economic and security interests, and a more direct engagement designed to prevent such an outcome would certainly be in China's interests. But while China's non-interference policy has undergone some degree of erosion as its global interests have proliferated, there is little likelihood of significant security or military engagement in a country seen by Chinese strategists as a 'graveyard of empires'. It is equally unlikely that China will press Pakistan to curb its support for the Taliban, in order to bring about a stabilisation of Afghanistan that would help to secure the supply of Central Asian raw materials to China and to open Afghanistan for Chinese businesses. By the time NATO operations are scheduled to come to an end in 2014, China will be two years into a government whose leaders will be more collectivist and more cautious even than the current generation, and with correspondingly limited appetite for foreign adventurism. Faced with a deteriorating security environment in Afghanistan, China's instincts will be to do all it can to secure its own borders while seeking to avoid taking sides or unnecessarily antagonising any of the protagonists. An important factor in China's calculations will be that if it cannot exploit Afghanistan's natural resources, no other country is likely to be able to, and that if and when stability returns, China will be well placed to resume its commercial engagement. China is well versed in the exercise of strategic patience and that is the approach it is most likely to adopt with regards to Afghanistan.

CHAPTER ELEVEN

India

Rahul Roy-Chaudhury

India's ties with Afghanistan are civilisational and historical, including the spread of Buddhism in the 3rd century BCE and trade ties through the Silk Road. From the late nineteenth century until 1947, the Durand Line served as the border between Afghanistan and British India. However, Indian independence and the creation of a separate Pakistani state in August 1947 denied India geographical contiguity with Afghanistan, thereby curtailing its policy options. India has enjoyed working relations with the leaders of all major ethnic communities in Afghanistan. Its backing for Afghanistan's communist government in the 1970s and 1980s, and its tacit support for the 1979 Soviet invasion, caused a rift between India and Pashtun leaders that has proved difficult to mend, particularly in the context of Indian–Pakistani strategic competition in Afghanistan. Nevertheless, India's political, cultural and economic power makes it an important external player.

Prior to Indian independence on 15 August 1947, India had maintained close ties with various leaders of Afghanistan's dominant Pashtun tribe. Indian leader Mahatma Gandhi had close links to Sardar Khan Abdul Ghaffar Khan, a prominent

Pakistani Pashtun leader known as the 'Frontier Gandhi'. The Pashtun/Indian affinity was also the subject of the 1956 novel by Indian nobel laureate Rabindranath Tagore, *Kabuliwalah*. However, India's refusal to condemn the Soviet invasion of Afghanistan in December 1979 and its support for the Moscow-backed People's Democratic Party of Afghanistan (PDPA) government drove a wedge between New Delhi and Afghanistan's Pashtun community.

A year after the Soviet withdrawal, India closed its consulates in Kandahar and Jalalabad (set up in the 1950s). It thereafter sought to restore relations with Pashtun tribal leaders and the Afghan government, but closed its embassy in Kabul prior to the 1996 Taliban takeover. That event was a major setback for India, which withdrew from Afghanistan for five years. During this period, the Taliban government tolerated terror camps in Khost that trained militants from Kashmir, Pakistan and other states to fight against Indian rule in Jammu and Kashmir. Until they were destroyed by US missile attacks in 1998, the camps were host to the Hizbul Mujahadeen, the Harkat-ul-Mujahadeen (formerly known as the Harkat-ul-Ansar) and the Markaz Dawa Al Irshad and its militant wing, the Lashkar-e-Tayiba (LeT).[1] However, the nadir for Indian security interests was the December 1999 hijacking of an Indian Airlines flight from Kathmandu to Kandahar, by Pakistani hijackers with the assistance of the Taliban in Kandahar.

After the fall of Kabul in 1996, India continued to recognise the exiled Burhanuddin Rabbani government and to provide support for the predominantly non-Pashtun Northern Alliance, under the ethnic Tajik warlord Ahmad Shah Massoud. This included the provision of a 25-bed hospital at Farkhor airfield in Tajikistan on Afghanistan's northern border, military advisers, equipment and the repair of Soviet attack helicopters.[2] After the Northern Alliance recaptured Kabul in late 2001, with

US backing, India participated in the Bonn conference and helped forge consensus support for Indian university-educated Pashtun leader Hamid Karzai as president. In December 2001 India re-opened its embassy in Kabul, set up two new consulates in Herat in the west and Mazar-e-Sharif in the north in August 2002, and four months later re-opened its consulates in Jalalabad in the east and Kandahar in the south. Its immediate priorities were to rectify the legacy of its previous association with the PDPA government and focus on reconstruction and development activities. In August 2005 Manmohan Singh became the first Indian prime minister to visit Afghanistan in nearly 30 years.

As a proximate neighbour of Afghanistan, India cannot pursue an exit strategy in the manner of Western states, as Singh indicated during a visit to Kabul in May 2011. On that trip, Singh announced a bilateral 'strategic partnership', indicating India's long-term interests in Afghanistan. He backed Afghan President Hamid Karzai's peace efforts with Taliban insurgents and announced an increase in the amount of Indian aid pledged to Afghanistan since 2001 by one-third, to $2 billion.[3]

The possibility of Pakistan engineering a political solution to Afghanistan's conflict, in which Taliban hardliners play a part in any future peace process or enter government, is of concern to India. So is the prospect of a weak Afghan state lacking in external support and ripe for civil war. In either case, Indians fear that Afghanistan could serve as a safe haven for terror attacks and the spread of jihadi violence and suicide terrorism against India.

India's policy options post-2014 will therefore need to focus on whether a sustained Indian presence and role in Afghanistan would be tenable. If it is, how will India's presence and development projects be reshaped? And, if not, what practical measures would India need to undertake to mitigate emergent risks to its domestic stability and security?

Interests and policy

India's interests in Afghanistan are predominantly strategic (to prevent the return of Taliban rule and the establishment of anti-India terror camps) and developmental (to build Afghan capacities in infrastructure and human resource development to strengthen governance),[4] while ensuring the security and safety of its projects and people in Afghanistan. Since 2001 India has committed $2bn for civil reconstruction and development throughout Afghanistan – more than it gives in aid to any other country. The contribution makes India the largest regional and the fifth-largest bilateral donor in Afghanistan.[5] Over a third of India's aid had been spent by late-2011, thanks to the presence of NATO's ISAF forces, which India supports but to which it does not contribute troops.

Among the projects led by India are the construction of the Zaranj–Delaram road, the installation of power transmission lines from northern Afghanistan to Kabul, the building of the Salma Dam, and the construction of the Afghan parliament building in Kabul. The latter two are yet to be completed.[6] India also runs several sanitation projects in Afghanistan. In October 2011, it signed two memorandums of understanding with Afghanistan on mineral exploitation and the development of hydrocarbons, which followed bids by two Indian entities for a multibillion-dollar contract for exploration of the Hajigak iron ore mines in Bamyan province in central Afghanistan.[7]

Bilateral trade is another area in which India is strengthening its ties with Afghanistan. Figures from the Asian Development Bank show that India is Afghanistan's principal export market and the only sizeable country with which Afghanistan enjoys a rough balance in trade, with imports worth $521.8 million in 2010, compared with imports from Pakistan and the US of $1,535m and $2,368m respectively. Afghanistan's exports to India were worth $116.2m, almost a quarter of the total exports for 2010.[8] The full potential of the market in India cannot be realised, however, as long as land-transit routes via Pakistan are obstructed; it is also hampered by persisting security issues. In the mean time, Afghanistan offers some opportunities for employment, although the Indian diaspora is shrinking. By early 2011, 3,500 Indian nationals worked in Afghanistan, and a small Indian diaspora of Sikhs and Hindus were long-term residents. Attacks on Indians in Afghanistan have led to a drop in the number of migrant workers.

India has also sought to project 'soft power' towards Afghanistan. Ambassador to Afghanistan Jayant Prasad has said that India's relations are with the people of Afghanistan as well as with its government.[9] To this end, the Indian government provides nearly 2,000 scholarships annually to educate and train Afghans in India, including 500 Afghan civil servants who are trained in India.[10] More than 50 Indian-supported, Afghan-owned small development projects are being implemented; 50 more are in the pipeline.[11] Indian medical missions in Kabul, Jalalabad, Kandahar, Herat and Mazar-e-Sharif provided free treatment and medicines for over 350,000 Afghans in 2009, mainly women and children.[12] The Indian embassy in Kabul issued over 44,000 visas in 2010 and expected to issue 60,000 in 2011, while the four consulates issued over 5,000 visas in 2010.[13] In that year, medical visas accounted for 40% of all visas provided.[14] There were at least 13 heavily used flights per week between the two countries.[15] Equally important, India's cultural impact is visible in Afghanistan. Indian song and dance sequences of Bollywood films, TV soap operas and classical music are extremely popular in Afghanistan.

These include the 1975 blockbuster *Dharmatma*, filmed in Band-e-Amir, near the Bamyan valley in Afghanistan.

As a consequence of its cultural power and development assistance, India is very popular among ordinary Afghans. In a June 2009 Gallup poll, for instance, Afghans favoured India's role in reconstruction and development efforts over that of the UN, NATO, Iran and Pakistan.[16] In a survey conducted for major Western television channels in December 2009, India topped the list of countries viewed 'very favourably' by Afghans.[17]

Countering Pakistan

Since 2007, New Delhi has been increasingly concerned at what it perceives as Pakistan's efforts to force its withdrawal from Afghanistan. It lays the blame for terrorist attacks against Indian diplomats and nationals in Afghanistan squarely on Pakistan, and particularly on the country's intelligence agency, the Inter-Services Intelligence (ISI). Two car bombings of the Indian embassy in Kabul would appear to be specific attempts to derail India's pursuit of soft power in Afghanistan. The first of these, in July 2008, carried out by the Pakistan-supported Haqqani terror group, killed 54 people, including two senior Indian diplomats and two Indian security personnel. The second, in October 2009, carried out by the LeT, killed 17 Afghan civilians.[18] In the aftermath of the first embassy attack, Indian national security adviser M.K. Narayanan went as far as to call for the destruction of the ISI and was quoted in the Indian media as saying 'we have no doubt that the ISI is behind this'. [19] In February 2010, the Taliban, along with the LeT, is believed to have carried out coordinated suicide bombings and a gun fight in Kabul; Indians staying at a guest house were said to have been the primary target of the attack.[20] In May 2011, a terror plot targeting the Indian consulate in Jalalabad was foiled. Two men arrested by the Afghan security forces reportedly confessed that the ISI had given them money in return for carrying out the plot. The government of India believes that such terror attacks are planned by the ISI, but carried out by its proxies. Since 2001, 20 Indian nationals have been killed in Afghanistan.

Pakistan rejects these charges, but the US government regards them as credible. In leaked US diplomatic cables, ISI and Pakistan military personnel are reported to have exhorted and helped the Haqqani group to launch suicide attacks against the Indian embassy in Kabul.[21] In late September 2011, Admiral Michael Mullen, the outgoing chairman of the US Joint Chiefs of Staff, publicly accused the Haqqani group, which is known to have links to the Afghan Taliban and al-Qaeda, of acting as 'a veritable arm of Pakistan's ISI'. At the same time, he accused the ISI of complicity in the 13 September 2011 attack by the Haqqani group against the US embassy in Kabul; both charges were strongly denied by Pakistan.[22] The Indian government has also blamed the ISI for continuing to nurture and fund the LeT terror group, which targets Indian interests, and for planning and coordinating the devastating November 2008 Mumbai terror attacks.[23] New Delhi is also concerned over Pakistan's provision of access to and support for China in Afghanistan, amid difficulties in Sino-Indian relations.

Meanwhile, Islamabad perceives New Delhi as having deliberately built up a significant presence and influence in Afghanistan post-2001 for the sole purpose of preventing it from attaining 'strategic depth' in the country. Pakistani analysts also complain that India has shown hostile intent towards Pakistan by funding the refurbishment of Ayni air base in Tajikistan, maintaining its links with Afghanistan's Tajiks and Uzbeks (via its erstwhile partners in the Northern Alliance), and through the alleged clandestine activities of the Indian consulate in the Iranian city of Zahedan, on that country's border with Pakistan. Although claims of an India–Pakistan 'proxy' war in Afghanistan are exaggerated,[24] the competition for influence in the country and their fierce rivalry has often been at odds with their stated development goals. A former Indian foreign secretary and special envoy of Prime Minister Singh, for example, noted that Pakistan's search for strategic depth was 'good enough reason for us to deny it to them'.[25]

Defence and security cooperation

India has a very light security footprint in Afghanistan, where its contribution is largely confined to training and the provision of equipment. This role began as early as July 2002, with the training of 250 Afghan police officers and cadets in 12 different courses, with 19 police officers undergoing training in the field of VIP security, and in the identification and handling of explosives.[26] There have been calls in India for sizeable military deployments in order to fight the Afghan Taliban,[27] or alternatively to undertake training of the Afghan army in India on a large scale. One military expert has said India has the capacity to train up to 5,000 Afghan troops at any one time.[28] Until 2010, only a few hundred personnel from India's mountain-trained paramilitary force, the Indo-Tibetan Border Police (ITBP), were deployed in Afghanistan to protect contractors working on construction projects including the Zaranj–Delaram road.[29] After the February 2010 attack in Kabul, another, smaller ITBP contingent was deployed to protect personnel in Indian diplomatic missions and posts. India provides 150 training scholarships to Afghan army personnel in various staff and training facilities in India, and has given 300 vehicles to the Afghan army, including troop carriers, field ambulances and jeeps.[30] Under the terms of the bilateral strategic partnership agreement signed on 4 October 2011, India has agreed to assist, 'as mutually determined', in the training, equipping and capacity-building of the Afghan National Security Forces.[31] The Afghan government also appears interested in Indian cooperation in counter-insurgency training and support, as well as spare parts for its Soviet-era aircraft and tanks.

Curtailed engagement

In view of the growing risks associated with operating in Afghanistan, along with the targeting of Indian nationals by the Taliban and the Haqqani group at the behest of the ISI, the Indian government curtailed its reconstruction activities from 2008 onwards. Although several small Indian projects are still running, there is a growing tendency to employ Afghan engineers and workers on them. Indian businesses and charities are relocating staff to India.[32] Following the February 2010 attacks, New Delhi suspended medical aid and English teaching programmes in the Afghan Military Academy; though these have since been resumed. But Indian government officials are reportedly reluctant to sign on for the next batch of 'mentors' for their Afghan counterparts, notwithstanding high non-taxable salaries.[33]

This 'pullback' coincided with a decline in Indian influence on Afghan affairs. New Delhi was excluded from the Istanbul 2010 conference on Afghanistan, reportedly due to Pakistani pressure. Karzai's sacking of his powerful pro-India intelligence chief Amrullah Saleh in June 2010, reportedly at the behest of the ISI,[34] was another blow to India. The Indian government is anxious that its influence will decline further as the reconciliation process draws Karzai closer to elements of the Taliban, and by extension, to Pakistan. However, the drive for reconciliation suffered a major setback with the assassination in September 2011 of chairman of the Afghan High Peace Council Burhanuddin Rabbani.

Policy after 2014

Beyond 2014, several questions loom for India's government. Will the security situation allow it to continue to operate its embassy and the four consulates, and to undertake new development projects? Can it maintain ties to all of Afghanistan's ethnic communities, or will it be obliged to focus on its long-time allies in the Northern Alliance? Will Afghanistan continue to be an arena of competition with Pakistan? And, can India reach out to the Afghan insurgents?

In the event of a sharp decline in the security situation in Afghanistan, the temptation for India's government would be to desist from efforts to build links with all communities in Afghanistan, and focus instead on the Northern Alliance. Militarily, this could involve an increase in the clandestine provision of financial and logistical support to an anti-Taliban coalition by India's external intelligence agency, the Research and Analysis Wing of the Cabinet Secretariat. This aid could also involve establishing medical camps and extending technical support for military equipment. India is apparently already reviving its interest in securing basing rights to Ayni air base and seeking to open a military hospital at Farkhor air base in Tajikistan. [35]

Politically, New Delhi could be expected to develop closer links with the Northern Alliance's other supporters, Russia and Iran. However, such a renewed international alliance is complicated. There are obstacles to overcome if New Delhi is to build confidence with Moscow: the latter's opposition to NATO's role in Afghanistan and its concern over India's emerging strategic relationship with Washington. New Delhi's relations with Tehran have also suffered deeply as it voted against Iran three times in the International Atomic Energy Agency (IAEA). But, India and Iran have already begun to discuss Afghanistan, while seeking trilateral Afghanistan–Iran–India trade and transit interactions aimed at ending Afghanistan's dependence on Pakistan to reach the sea.

For India, two eventualities are of particular concern. The first is Pakistan's role in Afghanistan; the second is the influence of Taliban hardliners in shaping any future peace process or entering a future government. To mitigate the negative consequences of these, India's government might court domestic controversy by engaging with Pakistan on Afghanistan, and reaching out to Afghan insurgents.

Engaging Pakistan

There are no official bilateral India–Pakistan talks on Afghanistan. This is due to New Delhi's reluctance to deal with Pakistan separately rather than as part of a regional dialogue, and the Pakistan army's refusal to raise India's prominence any further in Afghanistan by dealing with it separately, even as their bilateral dialogue resumed in February 2011.

Yet, it is not inevitable that India and Pakistan will be locked into an unending cycle of rivalry and competition in Afghanistan. The risk of a civil war is a 'worst-case' scenario with negative implications for both. Both countries have an interest in discussing stability in Afghanistan, and share the objective of enhancing economic and trade links to help Afghanistan emerge as an economic hub linking south and central Asia. There is now greater realisation in the Pakistani security establishment that it needs Afghanistan to be peaceful for its own domestic stability and security, not just vis-à-vis India. It will not serve Pakistani interests for the Afghan Taliban to regain power in Kabul, as this could inspire the 'home-grown' Tehrik-e-Taliban Pakistan (TTP) militant group, which is dedicated to fighting the Pakistani state.

Therefore, the possibility of both the Indian and Pakistani governments engaging in a series of 'unilateral' initiatives in

Afghanistan – in an attempt to alleviate mutual suspicions and concerns over each other's activities – is very real. This may already, tentatively, be under way.

The Indian government has made it clear that it has no intention of deploying army troops or military trainers in Afghanistan, a sign of assurance to Pakistan. There are signs that India is perhaps reducing its diplomatic staff in Afghanistan: Indian officials in the Jalalabad and Kandahar consulates increasingly find themselves 'hunkered and bunkered'. Since no major Indian construction projects have started since 2008, there has been less need for paramilitary troops to protect Indian nationals (although this may change if an Indian consortium is awarded the Hajigak mining contract).

Pakistan, for its part, has taken apparent steps to avoid inflaming its traditional rivalry with India. It has withdrawn its opposition to India's participation in the international conference on Afghanistan in Turkey in November 2011 and has refrained from commenting officially on India's bolstered economic package for Afghanistan. Islamabad has also played down its strategic partnership agreement in October 2011,[36] in a move that did not sit well with the India–Pakistan strategic community. A bolstering of these 'unilateral' initiatives by both Islamabad and Delhi could well lead to a bilateral dialogue on Afghanistan, including between their intelligence agencies, thereby preventing any future confrontation in the country.

At the same time, India–Pakistan cooperation is probably indispensable to the mutual objective of building up the Afghan economy. Preliminary agreements on the TAPI gas pipeline project are a good start, although the project is unlikely to be feasible until stability returns to Afghanistan. A good first step by India and Pakistan could be engaging together in road construction projects in Pashtun-dominated areas of Khost, the city of Gardez in Paktia, and Nangarhar.

Reaching out to the Taliban?

The Indian government refuses to deal with the Afghan Taliban.[37] Yet, its policy towards the 'reconciliation' and 'reintegration' of the Taliban has undergone a significant change since early 2010, which mirrors the growing international shift. At the London Conference on Afghanistan in January 2010, India's External Affairs Minister S.M. Krishna told Britain's Foreign Secretary David Miliband that Delhi did not recognise 'good' Taliban, just as there were no 'good' terrorists.[38] India's Foreign Secretary Nirupama Rao spelled out the pre-conditions for reconciliation at the IISS in London in February 2010:

> Any integration process in Afghanistan should be Afghan-led, and should include ... those who abjure violence, give up armed struggle and terrorism and are willing to abide by the values of democracy, pluralism and human rights as enshrined in the Afghan Constitution.[39]

Krishna publicly reiterated this at the Kabul Conference on Afghanistan in July 2010.[40]

During his visit to Kabul in May 2011, Prime Minister Singh for the first time expressed his support for Karzai's peace plan for reconciliation with the Taliban. At the official banquet on the evening of his arrival on 12 May, Singh said: 'We strongly support the Afghan people's quest for peace and reconciliation.' The following month India put aside its concerns about diluting the existing sanctions regime to vote along with the 14 other members of the UN Security Council to split a key sanctions list. In effect, UN Security Council Resolution 1988 distinguished for the first time between al-Qaeda and the Taliban, which had previously been considered part of the same terrorist threat. The US Ambassador to the UN Susan Rice said: 'the new sanctions regime for Afghanistan will serve as an important tool to promote reconciliation, while isolating extremists. Resolution 1988 sends a clear message to the Taliban that there is a future for those who separate from al-Qaeda, renounce violence and abide by the Afghan constitution.'[41]

India is unlikely to accept reconciliation without a real commitment from the insurgents to renounce violence, end its links with al-Qaeda and abide by the Afghan constitution. Signs of compromise from the US, such as Secretary of State Hillary Clinton's February 2011 recasting of the 'red lines' as 'necessary outcomes', have deeply concerned India.[42] Foreign Secretary Rao reaffirmed the country's position at the IISS in June 2011, when she said that 'the red lines that were defined at the Afghanistan conference here in London last year in our mind are still very relevant. Whatever semantics you may use in this regard, whether it is a pre-condition or whether it is an outcome ... India's concerns about those principles have in no way abated. They are still very important to us.'[43]

But with its sights set on the drawdown of Western combat forces by the end of 2014, the international community is encouraging an Afghan-led political settlement with the Taliban, even though it is not clear if this will eventually succeed. In rare interviews with senior Indian journalists, a former Taliban Minister, Maulvi Abdul Wakeel Ahmed Muttawakil, urged India to support the peace process.[44] The group's former ambassador to Pakistan Abdul Salam Zaeef said: 'we have never taken part in any attack in India ... The Taliban aren't in any direct conflict with India ... It's possible for the Taliban and India to reconcile with each other.'[45] It is not clear, however, if these politicians still have significant influence in the Taliban.[46]

If New Delhi is to retain a say in the political future of Afghanistan, or to avoid being forced from the country, it needs to quietly reach out to the Taliban's Quetta Shura and other select militant groups, such as Gulbuddin Hekmatyr's Hizb-e-Islami, to assess views towards India.[47] It needs to ascertain whether there is any scope for setting 'pre-conditions' for its own future bilateral talks with the Afghan insurgents. These 'pre-conditions' would essentially focus on ensuring, along with Western powers, that the Taliban cut off all ties with the LeT and that no terror training camps targeting India are set up in Afghanistan, in return for India's diplomatic recognition.

India's pragmatic policy towards Afghanistan is undergoing a significant shift. From a maximalist position of seeking to make a strategic impact in Afghanistan with its reconstruction and development activities, it has scaled down its ambitions on the basis of the drawdown of NATO forces from Afghanistan and the internal political dispensation within Afghanistan. Yet, New Delhi is confident of its ability to persevere and adapt to the changing situation on the ground. India and the Indian development partnership in Afghanistan have high approval ratings among the Afghan people. With a very light physical footprint in terms of the number of its personnel in the country, future adjustments will be far easier. Adaptability will be the hallmark of India's future role in Afghanistan.

CHAPTER TWELVE

Saudi Arabia

Emile Hokayem

The Western interventions in Afghanistan and Iraq from 2001 and 2003 respectively profoundly changed the wider Middle East, as seen from Riyadh. Under Saddam Hussein, a well-resourced Iraq was a direct competitor to Saudi Arabia. The Iraq that emerged from the occupation was, in Saudi eyes, merely a pawn of the kingdom's greatest rival, Iran, which has grown more confident that it can challenge for ideological and geopolitical dominance in the region.

Saudi Arabia's initial interest in Afghanistan came from a desire to roll back Communism, an atheist ideology the kingdom saw as a potent threat in the Muslim world. After the Soviet Union entered Afghanistan to prop up a Communist regime there, the United States, Pakistan and Saudi Arabia joined hands to fund, equip and organise the disparate resistance groups. Alongside a variety of warlords that took Saudi money but did not embrace Wahhabi beliefs, there operated religiously driven jihadi factions, including the precursor of al-Qaeda.

The Taliban rose to dominance with discreet Saudi and Pakistani assistance. Riyadh extended formal diplomatic recognition to the regime after it seized Kabul in 1996. By 1998, Saudi

Arabia had become so concerned with the increasingly hostile rhetoric of Osama bin Laden that it sought to obtain his extradition from Afghanistan; the Taliban refused. This showed the limitations of Saudi influence over the Taliban.

Interests and policy

Saudi Arabia views Afghanistan through three interlinked prisms: its religious agenda, its relations with Pakistan and its rivalry with Iran. After the 2001 US-led invasion, Saudi Arabia punished the Taliban for harbouring bin Laden by recognising the Karzai government and adopting a hands-off approach. In 2008, as it became clear that the Taliban insurgency was recovering from its initial setbacks and that a political settlement would be needed, the Afghan government requested Saudi mediation with the Taliban. Initial contacts were low-key and inconclusive. When the United States adopted a new counter-insurgency strategy in 2010, Afghan President Hamid Karzai appealed again for Saudi help in dealing with the Taliban and its affiliates. In particular, Karzai hoped to leverage the influence Saudi Arabia enjoys over Jalaluddin Haqqani, whose terrorist group has emerged as a main security threat to both ISAF and the Afghan government and who relies significantly for his funding on Gulf donors.

For Saudi Arabia, however, relations with the Taliban are conditional on a break between that group and al-Qaeda, which Saudi Arabia views as an existential threat after its ideological and armed attacks against the ruling family. 'So long as the Taliban doesn't stop providing shelter for terrorists and bin Laden and end their contacts with them, I don't think the negotiations will be positive or feasible,' Prince Saud al-Faisal, the Saudi foreign minister, said in 2010.[1] The killing of Bin Laden in May 2011 may yet change Saudi calculations about involvement in the Afghan political process.

It is unclear how much leverage Saudi Arabia has over the Taliban. US officials claim private Gulf and Saudi funding fuels the Taliban insurgency. Richard Holbrooke, US special envoy to Afghanistan and Pakistan, said in 2009 that 'more money is coming from the Gulf than is coming from the drug trade to the Taliban ... The money is coming in from sympathisers from all over the world with the bulk of it appearing to come from the Gulf.'[2] Holbrooke was careful to add a caveat to his allegation: 'I am not – repeat, not accusing the governments of the region.'[3] US officials have repeatedly approached Saudi and Gulf counterparts asking for greater scrutiny of money movements into Afghanistan and Pakistan. It remains uncertain whether Gulf authorities are capable of cutting this flow and even whether doing so would decisively weaken the insurgency.

Saudi religious influence is another ambiguous instrument. While Saudi clerics can assuredly incite more violence against the Karzai government or NATO forces, it is doubtful that religious Saudi calls for reconciliation can have a significant impact given the fractious nature of Sunni clerical authority.

The main Saudi lever in Afghanistan is Pakistan, which has emerged as one of its closest allies. Despite occasional tensions (Riyadh has favourites in Islamabad), their relations are deep and multifaceted. Saudi Arabia has extended financial and economic support to its impoverished partner. Remittances from its workers in Saudi Arabia are essential to Pakistan's economy. Pakistan has allowed Saudi preachers to operate on its territory. In the 1970s and 1980s, Pakistan stationed several thousand troops on Saudi soil at Riyadh's request. Media reports citing Western intelligence sources insist that Saudi Arabia financed the Pakistani nuclear programme as an insurance policy, should it need to acquire or develop its own nuclear-weapons capability.[4]

Saudi and Pakistani interests in Afghanistan converge, although they are not completely aligned. The two countries seek the reintegration of the Taliban in politics as part of an agreement that gives the Pashtun community preponderance. Both aim to check the rise of a neighbour (India in the case of Pakistan, Iran in the case of Saudi Arabia). And both want to make sure any integration project linking Central Asia to the Persian Gulf and the subcontinent includes rather than bypasses them.

Ultimately, Saudi influence is largely a matter of will and coordination with Pakistan. Riyadh appears unconvinced that the US strategy will bear fruit without outreach to the Taliban and has proved unwilling to come to its rescue. But Riyadh is also concerned about Iranian inroads in Afghanistan and fears that its absence from the Afghan political scene would reinforce factions aligned with Tehran. Though it may be flush with money, Saudi Arabia lacks the human resources, territorial access and operational capabilities to operate without Pakistani partnership.

Concerned about being challenged in the Arab world by spreading Iranian power, Saudi Arabia has recently revitalised its foreign policy. It has sought to counter Iranian reach in the Levant, the Gulf and Iraq, with mixed results. But Afghanistan gives it the possibility to play Iran's own strategy of encirclement.

Policy after 2014

While ISAF remains in Afghanistan, there is no pressing need for Saudi Arabia to invest itself significantly there. The possibility of a Taliban return would put Saudi Arabia under pressure to engage more deeply. In particular, the Karzai government would request its support. As the ISAF presence declines, Karzai will need new allies with leverage over the

Taliban. To this end, he has already initiated a rapprochement with Pakistan after years of hostility and mutual recriminations. Further requests for Saudi assistance are therefore likely. Saudi Arabia may be more amenable to Afghan requests for help since the killing of bin Laden in Pakistan has removed a significant hurdle. Saudi Arabia will be prompted to act by the concern that al-Qaeda may surface anew and that renewed civil war will once again energise cohorts of men in search of jihadi opportunities.

At the same time, the Saudi role as a broker of a political settlement, with its capacity to lure the Taliban, may become more valuable, particularly with regard to the reintegration of combatants into society and government. Saudi Arabia is well placed to try to appeal to Taliban commanders and other anti-US warlords individually to weaken the Taliban front. The Taliban has not signalled a willingness to engage directly with Karzai, but some commanders may put their objections aside if both Saudi Arabia and Pakistan were to sponsor a dialogue aimed at the reconciliation of former adversaries. For both states, this would have the added advantage of limiting Iranian influence in Afghanistan.

A greater Saudi role can only be achieved through increased coordination with, and even subcontracting to, Pakistan. The strength of that relationship will be tested as Pakistani ties to a number of Taliban factions are profound, sometimes symbiotic, because of its search for strategic depth in its rivalry with India. Deeper Saudi involvement in Afghanistan may well antagonise Iran and lead to a proxy war in which competing interests and rivalries spill over into open confrontation. Given the intensification of Saudi–Iranian rivalry, Riyadh may welcome this as it could stretch Iranian attention and resources away from the Gulf, and mire Tehran in a bruising and expensive sectarian conflict on its eastern borders. Both Riyadh and Tehran are, however, averse to a direct conflict: despite massive investment in their conventional capabilities, both estimate that proxies, money and religious connections are better instruments to check the other. The sectarian nature of Saudi–Iranian competition may be a double-edged sword for Riyadh, as it would revive the very forces that have questioned the legitimacy and credentials of Saudi rule after the 1980s Afghanistan war and the 1990 Gulf War. Indeed, Saudi reliance on the US angered many Saudi citizens, including Osama bin Laden, who had offered to help the kingdom counter Saddam Hussein's forces but was turned down by the Saudi royal family. This led to the rise of al-Qaeda and the alienation of bin Laden and other jihadis with Afghan experience. Managing the risk of a second anti-Saudi jihadi awakening, should Riyadh mobilise these forces again will amount to a massive challenge. It would also be difficult for Pakistan to orchestrate an anti-Iranian escalation in Afghanistan, because it relies on Iran for trade and energy supplies. Saudi strategic preferences will form a large part of Pakistan's calculations, tempering its aspirations and holding its rivalry with Iran in check. It is not clear that Pakistan could even afford to compete with Iran, but what is certain is that any attempt to do so would inflame its own Shia minority.

Provided that the Afghan government is perceived to be viable after 2014, the Saudi perception of the Iranian challenge will be the primary determinant of its policy. A need for greater involvement would translate into increased political and economic support for the Karzai government in an attempt to outdo Tehran. There will, however, be few reasons for Saudi Arabia to step up its mediation efforts unless the Taliban meets its demand and breaks with al-Qaeda.

CONCLUSION

Adam Ward, Nicholas Redman and Toby Dodge

The Soviet Union fought in Afghanistan for nearly ten years and then left behind a client government. That government managed to last for just over three years, only being toppled by the country's warlords once Moscow had cut off its access to external financial support. Years of chaos and brutality ensued. By the end of 2014, the US and its allies will have fought in Afghanistan for 13 years. Thereafter, the government established by the Western powers and built up by Hamid Karzai faces a battle to avoid a similar fate to that suffered by the Najibullah administration, violently removed from power in the face of external neglect and indifference.

The principal conclusion arising from this volume is that Kabul will prevail, because the central government has probably amassed sufficient power to ensure that the centre will hold, even if it must curtail its ambitions after 2014. This broadly positive judgement also applies in the security sphere, considering the progress made to date in building up ANSF capability and the plans for 2012–14, as well as the likelihood of Western military support and funding for the years thereafter. The regional picture is also more promising than it was in

1989–92, in spite of the myriad risks residing in Pakistan. All but one of the neighbouring states support the Afghan central government, rather than their traditional ethnic client groups. This strengthens the hand of the central government in Kabul and reduces the support for actual and potential opponents.

As Alexander Nicoll notes in Chapter One, the Taliban regime collapsed swiftly in late 2001 in the face of a Northern Alliance ground assault backed by US air power and special forces. The Northern Alliance backed Hamid Karzai's appointment as national leader at the subsequent Bonn conference, at a time when power in Afghanistan lay with the militias rather than NATO forces. The US-led coalition did not have enough troops thereafter to hold the entire country. With Western attention soon distracted by preparations for the invasion of Iraq, and the execution of that plan, insurgents were afforded the breathing space to organise in areas of weak security, where tribal structures had been fragmented, educational attainment was low and territorial control was contested. Only in 2006 did Western policymakers begin to give due attention to the challenge, but by that time the Taliban had reconstituted itself and was offering fierce resistance. And it took another three years until the US, under a new administration, was prepared to commit to a surge that would provide commanders with sufficient troops to implement a counter-insurgency strategy.

The increased US commitment, as Dana Allin observes, was hedged. President Barack Obama came to office having argued that Afghanistan was a just war that the previous administration had largely ignored, but found himself caught between generals calling for an ambitious counter-insurgency plan linked to extensive nation-building, and civilian advisers who favoured a less ambitious approach focused on counter-terrorism. Obama's decision to approve a surge but with time and geographical limitations reflected a choice to return to a more limited, though still leading, US role in the world, in light of fiscal challenges, operational constraints and a desire to repair the country's legitimacy. Domestic support in the US for the war in Afghanistan has fallen in recent years, and Obama has shown that he has no intention of being diverted from the target of handing over responsibility to the Afghan state by the end of 2014. Yet while the US is war-weary, there is a recognition in Washington that it will have to retain a substantial commitment to Afghanistan for years to come in the form of aid, military training and the maintenance of one or two bases in the region for counter-terrorism purposes.

Turning to Afghan domestic politics, Toby Dodge argues that Hamid Karzai has built a state system that is tenacious, ambitious but also deeply corrupt. To an unprecedented degree, Karzai's vision of Afghanistan is highly centralised: this is embodied in the constitution and the way he has ruled, amassing huge resources along the way to fund a patronage system that has created an elite bound closely to the president by ties of corruption as opposed to loyalty or affection. The centralising ambitions of the Afghan constitution mean anyone taking over from Karzai after 2014 will in theory inherit remarkably wide-ranging power. However, the legitimacy of Karzai's government has fallen markedly over time, and corruption is a daily menace for the country's citizens. Yet Karzai has also used corruption as a tool of government, sanctioned at the highest level. He has made little progress on peace talks with the Taliban and shows a preference for reintegrating elements of the insurgency rather than seeking full national reconciliation. This is consistent with Karzai's desire to maintain an extraordinary degree of power. The challenge he – or the new president who replaces him – faces after 2014 is that the financial resources on which this style of government depends will dwindle as international attention moves elsewhere. This has to mean Karzai's ability to impose Kabul's will in the provinces will also drop. The solution will be for Karzai to embrace the rules of Afghan politics that existed prior to 1979, whereby the centre returns to a mediating role between the regions. This transition may be slow and painful, but there appears to be no alternative in light of the unavoidable reductions in Western military and financial support. With this in mind, the big question facing the Afghan presidency after 2014 is whether it will have the resources to tie Afghan's political elite to its president and hence to Kabul.

Developments in the economy will, as Nicholas Redman suggests, set the parameters in which this post-2014 government will operate. The Afghan economy in the decade since 2001 has shown strong but volatile GDP growth, with foreign aid playing a major role. The growth volatility is, however, principally a consequence of the varied fortunes of the agricultural sector, which is by far the country's largest source of employment. Developing other sectors will be difficult in light of the country's myriad troubles: insecurity, poor health, weak education, insufficient supplies of power and water, inadequate roads and railways, and rampant corruption. The best prospect for correcting the country's huge trade imbalance and providing the tax revenue that will be essential to empowering the central government lies in development of the country's mineral resources. In this regard, a great deal rests on the success of the Aynak copper mine and the Hajigak iron ore mine. However, there is little doubt that opium production will remain a mainstay of the economy for years to come. This has obvious negative effects, ranging from public-health troubles in Afghanistan and consuming states, to lawlessness and corruption in Afghanistan and transit states. Yet at the same time, opium production keeps a swathe of the Afghan population in employment and out of food poverty. It employs more people, and puts more money into the rural economy, than cereals production could.

The ANSF is likely to maintain the majority of the territorial gains achieved by ISAF at the time of writing, according to Ben Barry. The ANSF and its ISAF allies hold the cities and have obtained a sustained presence in most of the northern and western regions. In 2010–11 they made demonstrable progress in the south and southwest, but they lacked the strength to wrest decisive control in eastern Afghanistan. The ANSF faces an insurgency that draws mainly from the Pashtun community but encompasses many groups with a mixture of motives. At the time of writing, the ANSF was already some 300,000-strong, with 13 of the army's 20 brigades being assessed as 'semi-capable'. The target for the end of 2014 is that a majority of the brigades must be able to act independently or with advisory assistance only, pitting the ANSF and its ISAF trainers in a race against the clock. This means the ANSF will need Western military aid and support in-country for years after 2015, but this has already been publicly acknowledged in the US. Unless there is a marked increase in insurgent activity after 2014, which seems unlikely, the Afghan National Army will probably be able to maintain security in most populated areas.

The Western desire to counter the terrorist threat from Afghanistan was the reason for military intervention, as Nigel Inkster reminds us. Al-Qaeda and its affiliates have been weakened severely in the decade since the 11 September 2001 terror attacks on the US, but they remain a threat to Afghanistan, Pakistan and others. A key question for Western states as they looked for an exit from Afghanistan was whether al-Qaeda could be separated from their Taliban hosts. The relationship between the two was often fractious, for cultural reasons and because of the different strategic aims of the Afghan Taliban and the mainly Arab al-Qaeda. Today, al-Qaeda has little to

offer the Taliban, which has signalled a willingness to sever
ties. However, al-Qaeda can still rely on the support of the
Haqqani network which, from its base in Pakistan, controls the
eastern approaches to Kabul and has helped to facilitate extra-
regional terrorism. Within the spectrum of non-state groups,
the Haqqani network enjoys a unique position because it lies
beyond the reach of the Afghan military and is sympathetic
to international terrorism for ideological and tactical reasons,
but does not directly threaten Pakistan and hence enjoys the
support of the ISI. Whether the Haqqani network can be either
neutralised or negotiated with is open to doubt. It is probable that a hard core of non-Afghan fighters and terrorists will
continue to operate around the Afghanistan–Pakistan border,
and that US drone strikes and Pakistani army assaults will
be a recruiting sergeant for them. The US withdrawal from
Afghanistan will most likely remove an irritant, but it will
also constrain the ability of Western powers to tackle terrorist
capabilities. The constraints would be even more biting, potentially, if a future Afghan government followed the Iraqi model
of refusing to permit an extended US military presence on its
territory (this might conceivably be a Pakistani condition for
helping to end or curb the insurgency). For American leaders,
the transition could prove uncomfortable.

Pakistan is the neighbouring state with the greatest leverage in Afghanistan, as Rahul Roy-Chaudhury notes, but it is
also the neighbour most distrusted by the Afghan government
and people. This has come about despite ethnic ties between
the two states and Pakistan's role as an aid provider for and
major trade partner to Afghanistan. For Pakistan, affairs in
Afghanistan are inextricably linked with its own security.
Islamabad frets that an Afghan government or Afghanistan's
Pashtuns might seek to claim Pakistan's majority-Pashtun
border areas. Even though the Taliban was a creation of

Pakistan's security services, it did not reassure its sponsor on this question when it took power in Kabul. The other principal security concern for Pakistan in Afghanistan is the quest for strategic depth vis-à-vis India and the desire to avoid Indian encirclement. This explains Pakistan's suspicion of the Indian-educated Karzai, whose principal supporters in the early 2000s were the ethnic Tajiks and Uzbeks, rather than the Pashtun community that Pakistan regards as its principal allies and clients in Afghanistan. The imperative to support Pashtun groups in order to check Indian influence has led Pakistan deeper into the mire, for the encouragement of militants fighting in Afghanistan has unwittingly encouraged the growth of insurgents committed to the overthrow of the Pakistani state. Pakistan thus simultaneously finds itself engaged in a ferocious conflict with militant groups, while facing the building fury of the US for aiding terror groups that operate in Afghanistan. There were signs in 2010–11 that Pakistan's military recognised the depth of its predicament, and was willing to explore ways out of it. Stability in Afghanistan would ease Pakistan's internal security problems.

Iran's security is also closely bound with the security of Afghanistan, as Emile Hokayem argues, but in contrast to Pakistan Tehran has played a cautious and broadly constructive role. Iran is anxious to prevent the radical Sunni Taliban returning to power in Afghanistan, partly for confessional reasons. It has a further interest in a peaceful and stable Afghanistan, because this will allow the hundreds of thousands of Afghan refugees still living in Iran to return home, and because it offers the best hope of action against the opium trade. Iran is a transit state for Afghan opium and heroin, but it is also one of the largest end-user markets. In addition to these concerns for the stability of a neighbour, Iran also has geopolitical interests in Afghanistan. It is eager to check the influence of the Saudi–

Pakistani alliance on the government of Afghanistan, and wishes to see US military bases in Afghanistan and Central Asia closed as quickly as possible. In light of these interests, Iran has given political and financial support to Karzai, while hedging its bets by maintaining ties with other non-Pashtun constituencies. In a post-ISAF Afghanistan, an Iran that has less to fear from US bases *could* become a powerful ally, providing financial aid and opening trade routes as well as opening its large labour market to Afghanistan's growing and underemployed population.

Russia and the states of former Soviet Central Asia, in particular Tajikistan and Uzbekistan, also seem well placed to exert more influence in post-2014 Afghanistan, according to Oksana Antonenko. However, the legacy of the Soviet Union's exhausting and traumatic intervention in Afghanistan during the 1980s all but rules out direct military involvement. Russia and its former Soviet regional allies share a common interest in the stability of Central Asia, which would be threatened by a Taliban victory in Afghanistan. They are also deeply concerned about the pernicious effects on their own populations of the flood of opium from Afghanistan. However, differences between Russia and the Central Asian states are also apparent: the latter have welcomed the presence of US and NATO forces in their region, because it has given them greater leverage vis-à-vis Russia and China, as well as income and diplomatic legitimacy. Russia and China, by contrast, are uneasy about the prospect of a long-term US military presence close to their borders in Central Asia. Russia has, however, since 2010 put that reservation on hold, opening a major transit corridor for ISAF in order to support the stabilisation of Afghanistan in the run up to the end-2014 handover. Russia and the Central Asians have long-standing clients in Afghanistan among the ethnic Uzbek and Tajik communities. Nevertheless, they too have thrown their support behind Karzai, seeing in him the best chance to prevent the Taliban from reclaiming power.

India has deep historic and cultural ties to Pakistan, argues Rahul Roy-Chaudhury, but is hindered by its geographic detachment and the legacy of its backing for the 1979 Soviet invasion and the pro-Moscow government established in its wake. Indian interests were directly harmed by the Taliban takeover in 1996 and the expansion of terrorist training camps in Afghanistan. In the wake of the Taliban's ouster, India established a sizeable diplomatic and developmental presence in Afghanistan in order to boost security and to exert its soft power. Partly this was a matter of seeking to check the activities of anti-India terrorist groups that the Indian authorities suspect are supported by the ISI; yet it was also intended to establish an Afghan government that excluded pro-Pakistan elements, in order to deny Pakistan the strategic depth it so deeply desired. In response to a growing number of attacks on Indian interests in Afghanistan, New Delhi from 2008 reduced its activities in Afghanistan. However, it remains committed to engaging with all of Afghanistan's ethnic groups, rather than simply the non-Pashtun elements that might be considered its natural constituency. Whether it will persist with this approach remains to be seen. At the present time India appears willing to reduce its presence in Afghanistan as a way of easing Pakistan's fears and so allowing for Afghanistan to be stabilised. While it remains uneasy about the prospect of the Taliban entering Afghanistan's government, it might be willing to accept such an outcome if Afghanistan ejected al-Qaeda and closed all terrorist camps.

As Gary Li, Christian Le Mière and Nigel Inkster note, China is a neighbour of Afghanistan but has relatively little contact with it. For China, the key concern is the stability of its westernmost province, Xinjiang. Discontent on the part of the native Muslim Uighurs with Beijing's rule and an influx of Han Chinese designed to change the province's ethnic balance has the potential to establish a self-perpetuating insurgency. Thus China's primary interest is in insulating Xinjiang from any militant threat from Afghanistan. Although a direct threat is possible, the more likely scenario is that Afghan instability would reach China via former Soviet Central Asia. To bolster security in that region, China works through the Shanghai Cooperation Organisation, which includes Russia and four of the five Central Asian states, and is dedicated to combating extremism and separatism in Central Asia. That region is also becoming an increasingly important source of raw materials for China, which underscores the importance of maintaining security. China, like Russia, is anxious about the presence of US bases in Central Asia and Afghanistan. Although China desires to see ISAF succeed in stabilising Afghanistan before the end of 2014, it refused to open the Wakhan corridor to ISAF for supply purposes. With regard to security assistance, China has limited itself to some low-key measures to protect its own workers. Chinese companies will expand their operations in Afghanistan's mineral-rich economy if the security situation permits. Ultimately, China is playing a waiting game in Afghanistan: it has cordial relations with the Karzai government but provides little aid and will not take any steps to alienate the Taliban while there is a chance that the insurgency might triumph. This non-committal policy stance is also informed by the different stances that its allies take towards Afghanistan: Russia and the Central Asian states support Karzai and the ethnic Tajiks and Uzbeks that formed the Northern Alliance, whereas Pakistan backs the Pashtun Taliban.

For Saudi Arabia, Emile Hokayem argues, Afghanistan is a key battleground in its competition for influence with Iran.

Saudi Arabia has a religious agenda in Afghanistan but is also concerned about the potential security risk arising from a continued al-Qaeda presence. Its engagement in Afghanistan is also related to its alliance with Pakistan, which complements Saudi financial muscle with a range of operational capabilities. Saudi Arabia has some leverage over the Taliban which could be useful to facilitate peace talks, but if it does use this leverage it will do so in tandem with Pakistan. To date, Saudi Arabia has not offered much direct support to the Karzai government. However, this could conceivably change after 2014. It is possible that Saudi Arabia could use its oil wealth to initiate a bidding war with Iran for the support of the Afghan government. For Saudi Arabia, the prospect of cultivating a friendly state on Iran's eastern flank is attractive in the context of the battle for supremacy with Tehran.

Outlook

Compared with the Najibullah regime, the Afghan state can confidently expect to retain Western military assistance for many years after 2015, as well as financial aid to support its economy and help to pay the wages of large security forces. Even if Western financial aid tails off more rapidly than expected, there are potential alternative sources of support in the form of Iran, Saudi Arabia and the Gulf states. Domestically, the Karzai government has more power than Najibullah's did in 1989–92, because of the way Karzai has used his financial resources to build an elite that is tied to him through financial and political dependence. His government has also made some inroads into the Pashtun community. This has the potential, after 2015, to limit the Taliban's capacity to successfully launch a sustainable political and military offensive.

Compared with the early 1990s, the regional environment is also more favourable for the Afghan authorities. As the noted

Afghan expert Olivier Roy observed in an IISS *Adelphi* written in mid-1991:

> Afghanistan is divided, exhausted and open to foreign encroachment. Regional actors are playing the Afghan game by exploiting ethnic constraints, even under ideological banners, such as fundamentalism.[1]

By contrast, in 2011 most of Afghanistan's neighbours and the regional powers were supporting the Karzai government, rather than supporting traditional allies among the country's ethnic groups. As a result, neighbouring states (aside from Pakistan) are giving legitimacy to Karzai, rather than seeking to undermine him. This is a dramatic difference: instead of the neighbouring powers seeking to meddle and divide Afghanistan, they are engaging with an Afghan government that has the ability – despite its weaknesses and shortcomings – to leverage these relationships to its advantage.

Policy implications

What does this mean for Western policy? Three lessons stand out. Firstly, the US and its allies must continue to deliver substantial and sustainable aid flows to the Afghan state. This will help to cushion the economy from the fiscal contraction that will inevitably follow the drawdown of Western forces. This will matter primarily in the cities, which have been the principal beneficiaries of foreign spending in Afghanistan since 2001. Just as importantly, several billion dollars of foreign aid will be needed each year to sustain the ANSF. Even under optimistic scenarios, Afghanistan's government will be unable to pay for a 400,000-strong ANSF out of its own revenue until at least 2020 and most likely until 2025. Any shortfall in external support for the Afghan state will oblige the government to make potentially ruinous choices between cutting back on the armed forces or cutting back on the provision of basic services such as health and education. The state-building project after 2015 will only succeed if security can be maintained and the provision of government services extended.

Secondly, the provision of military and civilian training by the US and other external powers must continue. While the ANSF is developing the capacity to replace ISAF ground forces, the air arena poses an even greater challenge. The provision of manned and unmanned airborne intelligence, surveillance and reconnaissance, along with fixed and rotary wing close air support – often in integrated packages – has proved of immense value to the NATO-led operation. The nascent Afghan air force has a limited number of medium transport aircraft and helicopters, as well as combat support helicopters. It will be inherently incapable of delivering comparable support to that now available to ground forces. Addressing this weakness via a continuing alliance air effort coupled with mentoring the Afghan air force, and changes in combat tactics on the ground to accommodate the reduction in air assets will probably be necessary. In the civilian sphere too, the Afghan state will be a work in progress for years to come. Western states only belatedly addressed the question of capacity-building and so there is still much work to be done, mentoring state officials and helping to build indigenous institutions that reach beyond the city limits of Kabul and other major urban areas.

Thirdly, the US and its allies will need to increase the conduct of a muscular regional diplomacy after most of their troops leave Afghanistan. This applies principally to Pakistan, which at the time of writing was the primary external source of instability in Afghanistan. Continued engagement with neighbouring states could increase the prospects of peace talks in Afghanistan, or (less ambitiously) curb the potential for destabilisation.

This applies particularly to eastern Afghanistan, which is likely to be an ungoverned territory up to 2014 and beyond, with control contested between warlord factions. Most likely, it will become a base for attacks on government-controlled territory and a recruiting ground for militants, as well as an area of increasing opium cultivation. Potentially, it could also be a base for international terrorist groups. In light of that threat, the US is likely to continue to use special forces and proxies to counter the threat. Terrorist groups in turn are likely to reach for an asymmetric response abroad. However, their capacity to do so has been curbed by the atomisation of terror groups and much better intelligence on their capabilities and intentions. Even if the Kabul government cannot subjugate eastern Afghanistan, a degree of military pressure upon them will be vital in order to prevent those provinces becoming part of an extended territory in which terror groups can operate comfortably. At the time of writing, eastern Afghanistan differs in this respect from North Waziristan.

Overall, the years immediately after the handover will be crucial. If the Afghan authorities can maintain security or slowly extend it, to roll out basic services to the population and to continue to reintegrate elements of the insurgency, they will gain credibility at home and abroad. This will also create more space for a licit economy that will support stability. If the authorities fail in these tasks, control could quickly slip from their grasp. Thus it is vital for Western states to ensure the government has a good start in 2015. The most likely scenarios are either slow, uneven progress or a relatively rapid descent into disorder.

Attendant risks

External shocks have the clear potential to undermine Afghanistan's progress after 2014. The first is an attack on Iran and its nuclear facilities by either the US or Israel. This would have far-reaching and very destabilising effects well beyond Afghanistan. Iran has already made it clear that its response to such an attack, whether authorised in Tel Aviv, Washington or both, would be to strike back where America and its allies are most vulnerable. The potential ramifications of such a strategy in Afghanistan could see Iran rapidly and decisively increasing its support for the Taliban and Haqqani network. This support could certainly be financial but would also include advanced weaponry and training. In addition, Iran would remove its financial support for the presidency in Kabul and use the influence it has built up among Afghanistan's wider ruling elite to foment instability. The aftermath of an attack on Tehran would also see its strategic rivalry with Saudi Arabia increase, with consequences for Afghanistan. Overall, such a scenario would not in itself stop Afghanistan's process to stability but would make it harder to achieve this in the timeframe envisaged.

The second potentially ruinous external shock is state collapse in Pakistan. If that happened, the militant threat to Afghanistan would multiply and Afghanistan's principal trade route would be thrown into jeopardy. Although Pakistan has been criticised for aiding Afghan insurgent groups, it has nevertheless sustained hefty losses in a fight against militancy. The true value of the Pakistani military to Afghanistan's security may only be recognised in a situation where it is no longer able to play any role at all. Moreover, a collapse of state power in Pakistan would have devastating regional implications that Afghanistan could not hope to avoid.

The internal risks are just as great. Firstly, a collapse in foreign aid or the failure to realise modest development goals for the agricultural and mining sectors could undermine social stability and the state's budget revenues. That could fatally weaken the Afghan government's capacity. Secondly, if the ANSF were to splinter along ethnic lines, fail to recruit and retain sufficient troops or lack funding, then the hard-won security gains of recent years would be put at risk. Thirdly, a new state president after 2014 may well not follow the same political strategy as Hamid Karzai. For all Karzai's faults, his inconsistencies and irascibility, he succeeded in developing a coherent strategy for governing Afghanistan. His successor may simply try to reproduce this approach. However, ties of patronage and political and financial dependence are by their very nature personal. Any successor to Karzai would have to slowly rebuild his relationship with the country's wider ruling elite. This would undoubtedly take time, cause doubt and instability and would perhaps not result in a similar ruling strategy to the one pursued by Karzai himself. It is possible that a new president could attempt to rule the country in a legal-rational, transparent way. This in itself would represent a major transformation of and systemic shock to the country with all the attendant risk. He may also fail to acknowledge the financial, political and military limits of his power in the years immediately following 2014. A national leader who overreached in circumstances where his patronage powers are reduced would risk alienating core constituencies and so weakening the authority of the government.

If any of these risks were to materialise, it is likely that a contagion effect would be observed in short order. For instance, a collapse in foreign aid would increase the strains on the ANSF, while a decline in security would adversely affect the economy as well as confidence in the government. The cumulative effect would be a rapid weakening of the national government that would undermine the confidence of the Afghan people and neighbouring states. The latter would be far more likely to return to the established practice of backing their traditional allies in the country's ethnic communities, rather than a national government.

Lessons for leaders

The disquiet about Afghanistan's prospects after 2014 is partly a consequence of the country's chronic weaknesses and divisions, yet it has been exacerbated by the absence until relatively recently of a coherent plan for Afghanistan that was realistic with regard to local conditions, the resources that Western states were prepared to commit, and the amount of time that they were willing to invest. The initial intention behind the intervention in 2001 was counter-terrorism. However, the US and its allies then drifted inconsistently into a state-building mission almost by default, but failed to give sufficient resources or attention to that project. The fact that US attention quickly turned to planning for the invasion of Iraq, then executing the mission and struggling to deal with the consequences, created huge problems in Afghanistan. In particular, it gave the Taliban the strategic space to reconstitute itself. Yet the critique must go well beyond the security sphere. Policymakers did not give Afghanistan sufficient attention until 2007 or later, and there was a failure to align military and civilian objectives and timelines. The oft-uttered remark from ISAF officials from 2010 onwards that Afghanistan was 'never going to be a Jeffersonian democracy', while evidently sensible, could not dismiss the suspicion that Western objectives – to the extent that they had been coherently articulated – were decidedly utopian.

For instance, the US and British insistence on Karzai replacing corrupt governors was understandable if the goal was to build a modern state on Western lines, but as the Afghan president forcefully remarked, this ran counter to Afghan practice:

> You are trying to pick and choose tribal chiefs (who will expand the presence of the central government into rural areas), but that is not how the tribal system works. A tribal chiefdom is jealously guarded. It

cannot be taken by force and it cannot be imposed from the outside. When we distort tribal structures, the vacuum is filled by the Taliban, and that is exactly what has happened in Helmand and Uruzgan.[2]

Similarly, a desire to limit corruption was one of the reasons why foreign donors disbursed funds directly, rather than through the Afghan government, even though this hindered the build-up of domestic capacity. The unifying theme of these and other examples is that the US and its allies set ambitious objectives for Afghanistan, without making commitments of sufficient magnitude. In short, after the surprisingly quick removal of the Taliban, the occupying powers failed to match their objectives for the Afghan state to their willingness to expend blood, treasure and time in the country. The decision to draw down provided an answer to some of these questions, but it was undertaken primarily with regard to domestic Western considerations rather than Afghan conditions. Had the US and its allies set some firm parameters on their commitment in 2004–05 – with regard to the amount of time they were willing to remain in the country, the number of soldiers they were willing to commit and the amount of money they were willing to spend – and had they matched those with an appreciation of prevailing Afghan conditions to identify a set of political, economic and security objectives for the country that were achievable, the plan might not have looked very different from the one we now have, but the prospects for achieving it would almost certainly have been better. The need for a clear exit strategy should have been apparent in 2001, but it was nonetheless neglected. Belatedly, these plans have been produced; it is imperative for Afghanistan's stability that they are executed properly and that support for the Afghan government continues without interruption from 2015.

NOTES

Chapter One

1 Human Rights Unit of the United Nations Assistance Mission in Afghanistan (UNAMA Human Rights), '2010 Annual Report on the Protection of Civilians in Armed Conflict in Afghanistan', available at http://unama.unmissions.org/Default.aspx?tabid=4538.

2 NATO Lisbon Summit Declaration, 20 November 2010, http://www.nato.int/cps/en/natolive/official_texts_68828.htm?selectedLocale=en; and http://www.nato.int/cps/en/natolive/official_texts_68828.htm.

3 'David Cameron defends Afghan withdrawal deadline', BBC News, 20 November 2010, http://www.bbc.co.uk/news/uk-politics-11804205.

4 Joshua Partlow quoting David H. Petraeus, 'COMISAF assessment', 'Petraeus Offers Optimistic Assessment of War in Afghanistan', *Washington Post*, 25 January 2011, p. A13, http://www.documentcloud.org/documents/29586-comisaf-assessment.html.

5 United Nations, 'The situation in Afghanistan and its implications for international peace and security: Report of the Secretary-General', 10 December 2010, http://daccess-dds-ny.un.org/doc/UNDOC/GEN/N10/667/78/PDF/N1066778.pdf?OpenElement.

6 Paul Wolfowitz, on CBS television, 'Face the Nation', 18 November 2001, quoted in Adam Roberts, 'Doctrine and Reality in Afghanistan', *Survival*, vol. 51, no.1, February–March 2009, p. 29.

7 Thomas Barfield, *Afghanistan: A Cultural and Political History* (Princeton, NJ: Princeton University Press, 2010), p. 69.

8 Gary C. Schroen, *First In: An Insider's Account of How the CIA Spearheaded the War on Terror in Afghanistan* (New York: Presidio Press, 2005).

9 United Nations Security Council, 'Agreement on Provisional Arrangements in Afghanistan Pending the Re-Establishment of Permanent Government Institutions ("Bonn Agreement")', S/2001/1154, 5 December 2001, http://daccess-dds-ny.un.org/doc/UNDOC/GEN/N01/678/61/IMG/N0167861.pdf?OpenElement.

10 United Nations Security Council Resolution 1386, 20 December 2001,

http://daccess-dds-ny.un.org/doc/UNDOC/GEN/N01/708/55/PDF/N0170855.pdf?OpenElement.

11 Seth G. Jones, *In the Graveyard of Empires: America's War in Afghanistan* (New York: W.W. Norton & Co., 2009), p. 125. For a summary of the policy debate in Washington, see Chapter Seven, 'Light Footprint', pp. 109–33.

12 For a clear summary, see Barfield, *Afghanistan*, pp. 23–32.

13 Barnett R. Rubin, *The Fragmentation of Afghanistan: State Formation and Collapse in the International System* (New Haven, CT: Yale University Press, 1995), pp. 19–20.

14 This term for the Russian–British strategic struggle was coined by Arthur Conolly, a Bengal cavalry officer and British intelligence agent. Peter Hopkirk writes that Conolly was, at the age of 22 in 1829, 'the first of Lord Ellenborough's young bloods to be sent into the field to reconnoitre the military and political no-man's-land between the Caucasus and the Khyber, through which a Russian army might march'. Lord Ellenborough was then the senior official in London dealing with Indian affairs. Peter Hopkirk, *The Great Game: On Secret Service in High Asia* (Oxford: Oxford University Press, 1990), pp. 123–31, 278–9.

15 Rubin, *The Fragmentation of Afghanistan*, p. 47.

16 Barfield, *Afghanistan*, pp. 161–2. The preceding paragraph draws heavily from Barfield, pp. 146–63.

17 Amin Saikal, 'Afghanistan after the Loya Jirga', *Survival*, vol. 44, no. 3, Autumn 2002, pp. 48–9.

18 See, for example, John F. Burns, 'Gratitude and Doubt in the New Life of Afghans', *New York Times*, 11 September 2002, p. G32; and Pamela

Constable, 'Delegates Give Karzai a Diversity of Advice', *Washington Post*, 15 June 2002, p. A18.

19 Peter Marsden, *The Taliban: War and Religion in Afghanistan* (London: Zed Books, 2002), p. 40.

20 *Ibid.*, pp. 60–2.

21 Antonio Giustozzi, *Koran, Kalashnikov and Laptop: The Neo-Taliban Insurgency in Afghanistan* (London: Hurst & Company, 2007), pp. 18–19.

22 *Ibid.*, p. 42.

23 Graeme Smith, 'What Kandahar's Taliban Say', in Antonio Giustozzi (ed.), *Decoding the New Taliban: Insights from the Afghan Field* (London: Hurst & Company, 2009), pp. 191–210. The book, giving accounts of the Taliban's spread in many different areas of Afghanistan, demonstrates the dangers involved in making generalisations about this complex insurgency.

24 David Kilcullen, 'Taliban and Counter-Insurgency in Kunar', in Giustozzi (ed.), *Decoding the New Taliban*, pp. 238–9.

25 *Ibid.*, p. 240.

26 Giustozzi, *Koran, Kalashnikov and Laptop*, p. 111.

27 This paragraph draws heavily on Giustozzi, *Koran, Kalashnikov and Laptop*, Chapter 4, 'The Taliban's Strategy', pp. 97–146.

28 United Nations Security Council Resolution 1510, 13 October 2003, http://daccess-dds-ny.un.org/doc/UNDOC/GEN/N03/555/55/PDF/N0355555.pdf?OpenElement.

29 'UK Troops "to Target Terrorists"', BBC News, 24 April 2006, http://news.bbc.co.uk/1/hi/uk/4935532.stm.

30 Carlotta Gall, 'Taliban Threat is Said to Grow in Afghan South', *New York Times*, 3 May 2006, p. A1.

31 Pamela Constable and Javed Hamdard, 'Accident Sparks Riot in Afghan

Capital', *Washington Post*, 30 May 2006, p. A1.

32 See, for example, James Fergusson, *A Million Bullets: The Real Story of the British Army in Afghanistan* (London: Random House, 2008; Corgi edition, 2009), Chapter Four, 'The Joint UK Plan for Helmand' pp. 195–254.

33 See, for example, David Ucko, 'The Role of Economic Instruments in Ending Conflict', Report on IISS Roundtable at the National Press Club, Washington DC, 6 May 2009, pp. 7–8, an account of remarks by Colonel Christopher Kolenda, http://www.iiss.org/about-us/offices/washington/iiss-us-events/iiss-us-iiss-economics-and-conflict-resolution-programme-inaugral-roundtable-meeting/.

34 NATO Riga Summit Declaration, 29 November 2006, http://www.nato.int/docu/pr/2006/p06-150e.htm.

35 The White House, 'White Paper of the Interagency Policy Group's Report on US Policy towards Afghanistan and Pakistan', 27 March 2009, http://www.whitehouse.gov/assets/documents/Afghanistan-Pakistan_White_Paper.pdf.

36 Commander, NATO ISAF, 'Commander's Initial Assessment', 30 August 2009. Published with redactions agreed with the US Department of Defense, *Washington Post*, 21 September 2009, http://media.washingtonpost.com/wp-srv/politics/documents/Assessment_Redacted_092109.pdf?sid=ST2009092003140.

37 The debate is recounted in Bob Woodward, *Obama's Wars* (New York, Simon & Schuster, 2010).

38 *Ibid.*, p. 150.

39 Barack Obama, 'Remarks by the President in Address to the Nation on the Way Forward in Afghanistan and Pakistan', 1 December 2009, http://www.whitehouse.gov/the-press-office/remarks-president-address-nation-way-forward-afghanistan-and-pakistan.

Chapter Two

1 For my own extended contribution to the debate about how the Cold War ended, see Dana H. Allin, *Cold War Illusions: America, Europe and Soviet Power, 1969-1989* (New York: St. Martin's Press, 1994).

2 Brian Whitaker, 'Al-Qaida Is Bleeding US to Bankruptcy, Bin Laden Claims', *Guardian*, 3 November 2004, http://www.guardian.co.uk/world/2004/nov/03/usa.alqaida.

3 Ezra Klein, 'Osama bin Laden Didn't Win, but He Was "Enormously Successful"', *Washington Post*, 3 May 2011, http://www.washingtonpost.com/business/economy/osama-bin-laden-didnt-win-but-he-was-enormously-successful/2011/05/02/AFexZjbF_story.html.

4 As Francis Fukuyama wrote at the outset of the Iraq War, 'Neither American political culture nor any underlying domestic pressures or constraints have determined the key decisions in American foreign policy since Sept. 11. In the immediate aftermath of the 9/11 attacks, Americans would have allowed President Bush to lead them in any of

several directions, and the nation was prepared to accept substantial risks and sacrifices. The Bush administration asked for no sacrifices from the average American, but after the quick fall of the Taliban it rolled the dice in a big way by moving to solve a longstanding problem only tangentially related to the threat from Al Qaeda – Iraq. In the process, it squandered the overwhelming public mandate it had received after Sept. 11. At the same time, it alienated most of its close allies, many of whom have since engaged in "soft balancing" against American influence, and stirred up anti-Americanism in the Middle East.' Francis Fukuyama, 'Invasion of the Isolationists', *New York Times*, 31 August 2005.

5 Ezra Klein, 'Osama bin Laden Didn't Win, but He Was "Enormously Successful"'.

6 Barack Obama, 'Remarks by the President in Address to the Nation on the Way Forward in Afghanistan and Pakistan', 1 December 2009, http://www.whitehouse.gov/the-press-office/remarks-president-address-nation-way-forward-afghanistan-and-pakistan.

7 The US justified its invasion of Afghanistan under Article 51 of the UN charter, the right to self-defence. According to the UN Human Rights Council Report of the Special Rapporteur on extrajudicial, summary or arbitrary executions, the right to self-defence extends to the extra-territorial use of drones, as long as the target is deemed 'lawful' by drone pilots, and the 'requirements of necessity, proportionality and discrimination are met'. See 'Report of the Special Rapporteur on extrajudicial, summary or arbitrary executions, Philip Alston,

Study on targeted killing', UN Human Rights Council Report to the UN General Assembly, A/HRC/14/24/Add.6, 28 May 2010, paragraph 93, http://www2.ohchr.org/english/bodies/hrcouncil/docs/14session/A.HRC.14.24.Add6.pdf.

8 Barack Obama, speech given in Chicago, IL, 2 October 2002, transcript available at http://www.economics.utoronto.ca/munro5/ObamaonIraqOct2002.pdf.

9 Commission on Presidential Debates, '2004 Debate Transcript', 30 September 2004, http://www.debates.org/index.php?page=september-30-2004-debate-transcript.

10 Commission on Presidential Debates, '2008 Debate Transcript', 26 September 2008, http://www.debates.org/index.php?page=2008-debate-transcript.

11 David E. Sanger, 'Hawk Sightings Could Be Premature', *New York Times*, 21 November 2004, http://query.nytimes.com/gst/fullpage.html?res=9C03E0DC1E3FF932A15752C1A9629C8B63&pagewanted=all.

12 Commission on Presidential Debates, '2008 Debate Transcript: The Second Gore–Bush Presidential Debate', 11 October 2000, http://www.debates.org/index.php?page=october-11-2000-debate-transcript.

13 Bob Woodward, *Bush at War: Inside the White House* (New York and London: Simon & Schuster, 2002).

14 James Dobbins et al., *The Beginner's Guide to Nation-Building* (Santa Monica, CA: RAND, 2007), available at http://www.rand.org/content/dam/rand/pubs/monographs/2007/RAND_MG557.pdf.

15 H.R. McMaster, 'On War: Lessons to be Learned', *Survival*. vol. 50, no.1, February–March 2008, pp.19–30.

16 Steve Miller, 'The Flawed Case for Missile Defence', *Survival*, vol. 43, no. 3, Autumn 2001, pp. 95–109.

17 Woodward, *Obama's Wars*.

18 Bob Woodward, 'McChrystal: More Forces or "Mission Failure"', *Washington Post*, 21 September 2009, http://www.washingtonpost.com/wp-dyn/content/article/2009/09/20/AR2009092002920.html.

19 Gordon M. Goldstein, *Lessons in Disaster: McGeorge Bundy and the Path to War in Vietnam* (New York: Henry Holt & co., 2008).

20 General Stanley McChrystal, Address, at IISS London, 1 October 2009, http://www.iiss.org/recent-key-addresses/general-stanley-mcchrystal-address/.

21 Woodward, *Obama's Wars*, p. 194.

22 For example, Andrew J. Bacevich, 'Non-Believer', *The New Republic*, 7 July 2010, http://www.tnr.com/node/76091.

23 See, for example, Eliot A. Cohen, 'Why McChrystal Has to Go', *Wall Street Journal*, 23 June 2010, http://online.wsj.com/article/SB10001424052748704853404575322800914018876.html; and John McCain, 'The Surge and Afghanistan', *Wall Street Journal*, 31 August 2010, http://online.wsj.com/article/SB10001424052748703618504575455998369001946 8.html.

24 See, for example, Bacevich, 'Non-Believer'.

25 Woodward, *Obama's Wars*, p. 390.

26 For US statistics on government spending see http://www.whitehouse.gov/omb/budget/Historicals.

27 Letting all Bush tax cuts expire at the end of 2012 would cut $3.9 trillion off the national debt by 2020, reducing that debt to about 2.5% of GDP, meaning, under reasonable economic conditions, the debt would no longer be growing faster than the economy.

Jonathan Cohen, 'Want to Reduce the Debt? Then Talk About Taxes', *The New Republic*, 16 Febuary 2011, http://www.tnr.com/blog/jonathan-cohn/83600/debt-deficit-republican-bush-tax-cut-entitlement.

28 Robert Pear, 'Administration Offers Health Care Cuts as Part of Budget Negotiations', *New York Times*, 4 July 2011, http://www.nytimes.com/2011/07/05/us/05deficit.html?_r=1&scp=1&sq=federal%20budget%20military&st=cse. See *Budget of the US Government, fiscal year 2012* (Washington DC: US Printing Office, 2010), pp. 64 and 175–6. Discretionary spending is US government expenditures which are subject to annual review and authorisation by Congress, as opposed to entitlements or mandatory spending, which is authorised by previously enacted laws. In 2011, the total discretionary budget for government was estimated at (CBO adjusted baseline) $1,231bn, of which the DoD's share is estimated at approximately $708bn.

29 The World Bank, http://data.worldbank.org/country/afghanistan.

30 Rajiv Chandrasekaran, 'Cost of War in Afghanistan Will Be Major Factor in Troop-reduction Talks', *Washington Post*, 31 May 2011.

31 *Ibid.*

32 US Department of State, 'FY 2012 State and USAID – core budget', http://www.state.gov/s/d/rm/rls/fs/2011/156553.htm.

33 Mitt Romney, 2011 Republican Debate, New Hampshire, 13 June 2011, http://transcripts.cnn.com/TRANSCRIPTS/1106/13/se.02.html.

34 See 'Statistical information about casualties of the Vietnam War', National Archives, http://www.archives.gov/

research/military/vietnam-war/casualty-statistics.html#year; and 'Coalition Deaths by Year', iCasualties.

org, http://icasualties.org/OEF/ByYear.aspx.

35 Woodward, *Obama's Wars*, p. 325.

Chapter Three

1 I would like to thank Clare Day, Karl Eikenberry, Clare Lockhart, H.R. McMaster and Janis Lee for their close reading of the text and extensive comments. Needless to say, the remaining disagreements they have and all the errors of fact and judgement in the resulting paper are my responsibility alone.

2 Barack Obama, 'Remarks by the President on the Way Forward in Afghanistan', The White House, 22 June, 2011, http://www.whitehouse.gov/the-press-office/2011/06/22/remarks-president-way-forward-afghanistan.

3 See Bob Woodward, *Obama's Wars* (London: Simon & Schuster, 2010).

4 See Ambassador Karl W. Eikenberry to Secretary of State Hillary Clinton, 6 October, 2009, http://documents.nytimes.com/eikenberry-s-memos-on-the-strategy-in-afghanistan.

5 See, for example, Stanley McChrystal, 'COMISAF's initial assessment', Kabul, 30 August, 2009, http://www.washingtonpost.com/wp-dyn/content/article/2009/09/21/AR2009092100110.html.

6 See Ian F.W. Beckett, 'Insurgency in Iraq: an historical perspective', January 2005, Strategic Studies Institute, p. 51, available at http://www.carlisle.army.mil/ssi/; and Lorenzo Zambernardi, 'Counterinsurgency's Impossible Trilemma', *The Washington Quarterly*, vol. 33, no. 3, July 2010, p. 21.

7 David Kilcullen, 'Counter-insurgency Redux', *Survival*, vol. 48, no. 4, Winter 2006–07, p. 112–13.

8 Stanley McChrystal, 'Ends and means: balancing a complex counter-insurgency effort', talk given in London, 5 May 2011.

9 According to David Petraeus, 'Of the many books that were influential in the writing of [FM] 3-24, perhaps none was as important as David Galula's *Counterinsurgency Warfare: Theory and Practice*', quoted in Douglas C. Lovelace, 'Forward', in Ann Marlowe, *David Galula; his life and intellectual context*, (Carlisle, PA: Strategic Studies Institute, 2010), p. iii.

10 David Galula, *Counter-insurgency Warfare: Theory and Practice*, (London: Pall Mall Press, 1964), p. 27.

11 Stathis N. Kalyvas, 'The New U.S. Army/Marine Corps Counterinsurgency Field Manual as Political Science and Political Praxis', *Perspectives on Politics*, vol. 6, no. 2, June 2008, p. 351.

12 Department of the Army, *Counterinsurgency FM 3-24*, December 2006, Chapter 2, paragraph 6 (2–6), http://www.fas.org/irp/doddir/army/fm3-24.pdf.

13 See, for example, James Risen, 'Karzai's Kin Use Ties to Gain Power in Afghanistan', *New York Times*, 5 October 2010, http://www.nytimes.com/2010/10/06/world/asia/06karzai.html?_r=1.

14 Fred Kaplan, 'It's not about the troops; only a legitimate Afghan government can beat the Taliban', *Slate*, 22 September 2009, http://www.slate.com/id/2229227/.

15 See Thomas Barfield and Neamatollah Nojumi, 'Bringing More Effective Governance to Afghanistan: 10 Pathways to Stability', *Middle East Policy*, vol. 17, no. 4, Winter, 2010, pp. 43–4.

16 See Afghanistan Research and Evaluation Unit, *How government works in Afghanistan: a Summary of findings and recommendations*, (Kabul: Afghanistan Research and Evaluation Unit, October, 2003), p. 8.

17 Thomas Barfield, *Afghanistan; a Cultural and Political History* (Princeton, NJ: Princeton University Press, 2010), p. 337.

18 Barfield and Nojumi, 'Bringing More Effective Governance to Afghanistan', pp. 40–4.

19 See Barnett R. Rubin, *The Fragmentation of Afghanistan: State formation and collapse in the international system*, (New Haven, CT: Yale University Press, second edition, 2002), pp. 65, 75; and Antonio Giustozzi, 'Afghanistan; transition without end: An analytical narrative on state making', Crisis States Research Centre, Working Paper 40, November 2008, p. 20.

20 See Ahmed Rashid, *Taliban; the story of the Afghan warlords*, (London: Pan, 2001), p. 101.

21 Giustozzi, 'Afghanistan: transition without end', p. 31.

22 Rubin, *The Fragmentation of Afghanistan*, pp. 117–23.

23 See Clare Lockhart, 'Learning from Experience; Afghanistan stabilized after 9/11', *Slate*, 5 November 2008, http://www.slate.com/id/2203650/.

24 Afghanistan Research and Evaluation Unit, *How government works in Afghanistan*, p. 7.

25 Lockhart, 'Learning from Experience', and Ahmed Rashid, *Descent into chaos: The United States and the failure of nation building in Pakistan, Afghanistan and central Asia* (New York: Viking, 2008), p. 184.

26 Seth G. Jones, *In the graveyard of empires: America's war in Afghanistan* (New York: W.W. Norton and Company, 2009), pp. 118, 131.

27 See Donald Rumsfeld, 'Beyond nation building', New York City, 14 February 2003, http://www.defense.gov/speeches/speech.aspx?speechid=337.

28 Astri Suhrke, Kristian Berg Harpviken and Arne Strand, 'Conflictual peacebuilding: Afghanistan two years after Bonn', in Chr. Michelsen Institute, *Development Studies and Human Rights*, 2004, p. 16, http://www.cmi.no/publications/file/1763-conflictual-peacebuilding.pdf.

29 Lockhart, 'Learning From Experience'.

30 Sarah Lister, 'Understanding State-Building and Local Government in Afghanistan', Crisis States Research Centre Working paper no. 14, May, 2007, p. 4.

31 Barfield and Nojumi, 'Bringing More Effective Governance to Afghanistan', p. 48.

32 International Crisis Group, 'Afghanistan's flawed constitutional process', ICG Asia Report no. 56, 12 June 2003, p. 34.

33 Jones, *In the graveyard of empires*, p. 172.

34 Joshua Partlow and Karen DeYoung, 'Afghan Government Falters in Kandahar', *Washington Post*, 3 November 2010, http://www.

washingtonpost.com/wp-dyn/content/article/2010/11/02/AR2010110206608.html; and Bashir Ahmad Naadem, 'Death Threats, Low Salaries Leave Kandahar Government Understaffed', Pajhwok Afghan News, 17 October 2010, http://www.pajhwok.com/en/2010/10/17/death-threats-low-salaries-leave-kandahar-government-understaffed.

35 See US Senate Foreign Relations Committee, 'Evaluating US foreign assistance to Afghanistan, a Majority Staff Report prepared for the use of the Committee on Foreign Relations', United States Senate, 112th Congress, 1st Session, 8 June 2011, p. 8.

36 Josh Boak, 'In Afghanistan, U.S. "Civilian Surge" Falls Short in Building Local Government', Washington Post, 8 March 2011, http://www.washingtonpost.com/wp-dyn/content/article/2011/03/08/AR2011030805351.html.

37 US Senate Foreign Relations Committee, 'Evaluating US foreign assistance to Afghanistan', p. 7.

38 Department of Defense, 'Report on Progress toward Security and Stability in Afghanistan', October 2009, Report to Congress in accordance with the National Defense Authorization Act 2008, (Section 1230, Public Law 110-181), p. 57.

39 Greg Jaffe and Karen DeYoung, 'Afghanistan's Karzai To Urge Caution as U.S. Pushes To Empower Local Leaders', Washington Post, 12 May 2010, http://www.washingtonpost.com/wp-dyn/content/article/2010/05/11/AR2010051105114_pf.html.

40 See 'The Constitution of the Islamic Republic of Afghanistan', http://www.embassyofafghanistan.org/constitution.html.

41 See Ahmed Rashid, Descent into chaos, p. 216.

42 Barfield, Afghanistan, p. 332.

43 International Crisis Group, 'Afghanistan: Elections and the Crisis of Governance', Policy Briefing, Asia Briefing No. 96, Kabul/Brussels, 25 November 2009, pp. 8–9.

44 International Crisis Group, 'Afghanistan: Elections and the Crisis of Governance', p. 1.

45 See, for example, Dexter Filkins, 'Letter from Kabul; the Afghan Bank Heist', The New Yorker, 14 February, 2011, http://www.newyorker.com/reporting/2011/02/14/110214fa_fact_filkins.

46 International Crisis Group, 'Afghanistan's Elections Stalemate', Update Briefing Asia Briefing no. 117, Kabul/Brussels, 23 February 2011.

47 Jon Boone, 'Election Commission Says it has No Option but to Turn Away Voters in Some of the Most Violent Parts of Afghanistan', Guardian, 17 August 2010, http://www.guardian.co.uk/world/2010/aug/17/afghanistan-election-polling-stations-shut.

48 Thomas Ruttig, 'Afghanistan's elections: political parties at the fringes again', Foreign Policy, 13 September 2010, http://afpak.foreignpolicy.com/posts/2010/09/13/afghanistans_elections_political_parties_at_the_fringes_again.

49 Tina Blohm, 'Campaign Trail 5: A pre-election visit to Paktika', Afghanistan Analysis Network, 23 August 2010, http://aan-afghanistan.com/index.asp?id=990.

50 Scott Worden, 'Why the West should care about Afghan election fraud', Foreign Policy, 2 September 2010, http://afpak.foreignpolicy.com/posts/2010/09/02/why_the_west_

should_care_about_afghan_election_ fraud.

51   Katherine Tiedemann, 'Daily brief: Afghanistan votes', *Foreign Policy*, 20 September, 2010, http://afpak. foreignpolicy.com/posts/2010/09/20/ daily_brief_afghanistan_votes; and Jon Boone, 'Afghanistan Elections "More Violent" than Last Year's Presidential Poll', *Guardian*, 23 September, 2010, http://www. guardian.co.uk/world/2010/sep/23/ afghanistan-election-violence.

52   Associated Press, 'Quarter of Afghan Election Ballots Thrown out for Fraud', *Guardian*, 20 October 2010, http:// www.guardian.co.uk/world/2010/ oct/20/afghanistan-election-fraud.

53   See International Crisis Group, 'Afghanistan's Elections Stalemate', p. 2.

54   Martine Van Bijlert, 'Afghanistan's elections: let's talk turnout', *Foreign Policy*, 20 September, 2010, http://afpak. foreignpolicy.com/posts/2010/09/20/ afghanistans_elections_lets_talk_ turnout.

55   Joshua Foust, 'You would cry too: in defense of Hamid Karzai', *Foreign Policy*, 28 September 2010, http://afpak. foreignpolicy.com/posts/2010/09/28/ you_would_cry_too_in_defense_of_ hamid_karzai.

56   Cable from the Deputy Chief of Mission Kabul, Valerie C. Fowler, to the Secretary of Defense, Robert Gates, 9 December, 2008, available at http://www.guardian.co.uk/world/ us-embassy-cables-documents/181930; and Jon Boone, 'WikiLeaks Cables Portray Hamid Karzai as Corrupt and Erratic', *Guardian*, 2 December 2010, http://www. guardian.co.uk/world/2010/dec/02/ wikileaks-cables-hamid-karzai-erratic.

57   Jon Boone, 'Hamid Karzai Admits Office gets "Bags of Money" from Iran', *Guardian*, 25 October 2010, http:// www.guardian.co.uk/world/2010/ oct/25/hamid-karzai-office-cash-iran.

58   Kate Clark, 'Who will replace Saleh and Atmar?', *Foreign Policy*, 8 June 2010, http://afpak.foreignpolicy.com/ posts/2010/06/08/the_aftermath_of_ karzais_cabinet_shakeup_0.

59   Dexter Filkins, 'Letter from Kabul'.

60   Aunohita Mojumdar, 'Afghan citizens Paid $1bn in Bribes for Public Services Last Year, Study Finds', *Guardian*, 8 July, 2010, http://www. guardian.co.uk/world/2010/jul/08/ afghanistan-bribes-corruption-taliban.

61   See Department of Defence, 'Report on Progress toward Security and Stability in Afghanistan', November 2010, p. 62.

62   See Filkins, 'Letter from Kabul'; Greg Miller and Ernesto Londoño, 'U.S. Officials Say Karzai Aides are Derailing Corruption Cases Involving Elite', *Washington Post*, 28 June, 2010, http://www.washingtonpost.com/ wp-dyn/content/article/2010/06/27/ AR2010062703645.html; and Jon Boone, 'Karzai "Fired" Anti-corruption Lawyer after Top Official Stung', *Guardian*, 30 August 2010, http://www. guardian.co.uk/world/2010/aug/30/ karzia-fired-fazel-aqiryar-corruption.

63   Matthew Rosenberg, 'Corruption Suspected in Airlift of Billions in Cash From Kabul', *Wall Street Journal*, 25 June 2010, http://online.wsj.com/ article/SB100014240527487046385045753 18850772872776.html.

64   See Department of Defence, 'Report on Progress toward Security and Stability in Afghanistan', November 2010, p. 10.

65   Robert Dreyfuss, 'Revenge of the Puppet: Rolling Stone's 2010 Story on Hamid Karzai', *Rolling*

Stone, 28 April 2010, http://www.rollingstone.com/politics/news/revenge-of-the-puppet-20100428.

66 *Ibid.*

67 *Ibid.*

68 Jaffe and DeYoung, 'Afghanistan's Karzai to Urge Caution as U.S. Pushes to Empower Local Leaders'.

69 Jon Boone, 'Afghan Opposition Leader Abdullah Abdullah Vows to Boycott "Peace Jirga"', *Guardian*, 1 June 2010, http://www.guardian.co.uk/world/2010/jun/01/afghan-opposition-leader-abdullah-abdullah-boycott-peace-jirga; and Thomas Ruttig, 'Why Afghanistan's Jirga Will Fail', *Foreign Policy*, 2 June 2010, http://afpak.foreignpolicy.com/posts/2010/06/02/the_karzai_show.

70 Boone, 'Afghan Opposition Leader Abdullah Abdullah Vows to Boycott "Peace Jirga"'.

71 Clark, 'Who will replace Saleh and Atmar?'.

72 Ewen MacAskill and Simon Tisdall, 'White House Shifts Afghanistan Strategy towards Talks with Taliban', *Guardian*, 19 July 2010, http://www.guardian.co.uk/world/2010/jul/19/obama-afghanistan-strategy-taliban-negotiate; Aunohita Mojumdar and Chris McGreal, 'Hamid Karzai in Tearful Plea for Peace with Taliban', *Guardian*, 28 September 2010, http://www.guardian.co.uk/world/2010/sep/28/hamid-karzai-taliban-afghanistan; Katherine Tiedemann, 'Daily brief: nine dead in Kandahar blasts', *Foreign Policy*, 6 October 2010, http://afpak.foreignpolicy.com/posts/2010/10/06/daily_brief_nine_dead_in_kandahar_blasts.

73 Mojumdar and McGreal, 'Hamid Karzai in Tearful Plea for Peace with Taliban'.

74 Dreyfuss, 'Revenge of the Puppet'; Mojumdar and McGreal, 'Hamid Karzai in Tearful Plea for Peace with Taliban'; Katherine Tiedemann, 'Daily brief: Karzai confirms Taliban "contacts"', *Foreign Policy*, 11 October 2010, http://afpak.foreignpolicy.com/posts/2010/10/11/daily_brief_karzai_confirms_taliban_contacts; 'Afghan Peace Talks in a Holidaymakers' Paradise', BBC News, 23 November 2010, http://www.bbc.co.uk/news/world-south-asia-11811285.

Chapter Four

1 This seems a reasonable assumption, even though progress on the Turkmenistan–Afghanistan–Pakistan–India (TAPI) gas pipeline project prompted Iran in early 2011 to block fuel supplies to Afghanistan from Russia and other third parties in protest. If realised, TAPI would cut Iran out of the emerging gas trade between Caspian producers and energy-hungry South Asian markets. Economist Intelligence Unit, *Country Report: Afghanistan*, April 2011.

2 *Warlord, Inc: Extortion and Corruption along the US Supply Chain in Afghanistan*, US Congressional report, Washington DC, June 2010, http://www.globalsecurity.org/military/library/congress/2010_rpt/warlord-inc_100622.htm.

3 The figures were quoted by Karl Eikenberry, former US ambassador to Afghanistan, at the IISS 2011 Global Strategic Review in Geneva on 10 September 2011.

4 Islamic Republic of Afghanistan, *Afghanistan National Development Strategy 1387–1391 (2008–13)*, Kabul, April 2008, http://www.cfr.org/afghanistan/afghanistan-national-development-strategy-2008-2013/p16450.

5 The Soviets helped develop a gas industry that produced 3bn cubic metres per year at peak, which provided sizeable exports to the USSR as well as supporting the production of chemical fertilisers at Mazar-e-Sharif. Cotton mills and textile, sugar and cement plants were also established during the 1980s. Economist Intelligence Unit, *Country Profile: Afghanistan*, 1996–97.

6 Islamic Republic of Afghanistan, *Afghanistan National Development Strategy*.

7 Islamic Republic of Afghanistan, *Afghanistan National Development Strategy*.

8 Afghanistan's standing on other basic metrics of human development is equally poor. For instance, ADB data show that 39% of Afghan children under five are underweight, which puts the country in a similar development bracket to Cambodia, Laos and Pakistan. The country also has the lowest ratio of girls to boys in primary, secondary and tertiary education across the ADB region. Asian Development Bank, *Basic Statistics 2011* (ADB, April 2011).

9 Jean-Francois Arvis, Monica Alina Mustra, Lauri Ojala, Ben Shepherd and Daniel Saslavsky, *Connecting to Compete 2010: Trade logistics in the global economy* (Washington DC: World Bank, 2010).

10 International Monetary Fund (IMF), World Economic Outlook Database, September 2011 update, http://www.imf.org/external/pubs/ft/weo/2011/02/weodata/index.aspx. Fiscal years run from 21 March to 20 March.

11 For harvest data, See UN Food and Agriculture Organisation, http://www.fao.org/giews/countrybrief/country.jsp?code=AFG. For GDP data, see IMF World Economic Outlook Database, September 2011 update, http://www.adb.org/documents/books/key_indicators/2011/pdf/AFG.pdf.

12 Asian Development Bank, Key Indicators for Asia and the Pacific 2011.

13 *Ibid.*

14 Economics Intelligence Unit, *Country Report: Afghanistan*, April 2010.

15 Islamic Republic of Afghanistan, *Afghanistan National Development Strategy*.

16 Asian Development Bank, 'Afghanistan', *Asian Development Outlook 2011*.

17 Anthony Cordesman anticipates a 60% fall in military and civilian spending between the end of 2014 and the end of 2016. See Cordesman, *Afghanistan win or lose: transition and the coming resource crisis* (Washington DC: Center for Strategic and International Studies, 23 August 2011).

18 Special Inspector General for Afghan Reconstruction (SIGAR), *Quarterly report to the US Congress*, 30 July 2011.

19 Development spending was also a notable feature of budgets after 2007: capital spending's share in fiscal outlays rose from 15% in 2004/05 to 27% in 2008/09. See Yoichiro Ishihara, *Public expenditure trends and fiscal sustainability*, working paper no. 2 for

the 2010 Afghan Public Expenditure Review, World Bank, 2010.

20 World Bank data quoted in SIGAR, *Quarterly report to the US Congress*, 30 July 2010.

21 Ishihara, *Public expenditure trends and fiscal sustainability*.

22 *Ibid*.

23 IMF, 'Islamic Republic of Afghanistan: program note', updated 15 April 2011.

24 James K. Boyce, 'Aid and Fiscal Capacity Building in Post-Conflict Countries', in Mats Berdal and Achim Wennmann (eds), *Ending Wars, Consolidating Peace: Economic Perspectives* (Abingdon: Routledge for IISS, 2010), pp. 102–5.

25 Ashraf Ghani, Clare Lockhart, Nargis Nehan and Baqer Massoud, 'The Budget as the Linchpin of the State: Lessons from Afghanistan', in James Boyce and Madeleine O'Donnell (eds), *Peace and the public purse: Economic Policy for Postwar Statebuilding* (Boulder, CO: Lynne Reiner, 2007), pp. 153–84.

26 Capacity shortcomings have already proved costly in Afghanistan. In 2006–10, just 40–55% of the core development budget was executed. This inflicted annual losses equivalent to 8–10% of GDP. See Ishihara, *Public expenditure trends and fiscal sustainability*.

27 Islamic Republic of Afghanistan, *Afghanistan National Development Strategy*.

28 SIGAR, *Quarterly report to the US Congress*, 30 July 2011.

29 Islamic Republic of Afghanistan, *Afghanistan National Development Strategy*.

30 SIGAR, *Quarterly report to the US Congress*, 30 July 2010.

31 Islamic Republic of Afghanistan, *Afghanistan National Development Strategy*.

32 'First Major Afghan Railway Opens', *Railway Gazette*, 25 August 2011, http://www.railwaygazette.com/nc/news/single-view/view/first-major-afghan-railway-opens.html; and US Embassy Cables, 'Rail Projects Underway but a Uniform Network Remains Elusive', 1 February 2010, http://www.cablegatesearch.net/cable.php?id=10KABUL388.

33 Christophe Jaffrelot, 'A Tale of Two Ports', *Khaleej Times Online*, 12 January 2001.

34 Asian Development Bank, *Basic Statistics 2011* (ADB, April 2011).

35 *Ibid*.

36 Economics Intelligence Unit, *Country Profile: Afghanistan*, 1996–97.

37 United Nations Development Programme, *Human Development Indicators*, 2010.

38 A survey of 1,066 firms across ten provinces in 2008 identified numerous weaknesses, including weak property rights, inefficient regulations, arbitrary enforcement, inadequate institutions and high levels of corruption. It noted that corruption had worsened and security had deteriorated compared with 2005. See World Bank, *The Afghanistan Investment Climate in 2008: growth despite poor governance, weak factor markets and lack of innovation*, 2009.

39 US Embassy Cables, 'Chinese Firm Rethinks Afghan Mining Contract after Difficulties of the Aynak Copper Mine Project', 10 December 2009, http://www.cablegatesearch.net/cable.php?id=09BEIJING3295.

40 Islamic Republic of Afghanistan, *Afghanistan National Development Strategy*.

41 James Risen, 'US Identifies Vast Mineral Riches in Afghanistan', *New York Times*, 13 June 2010.

42 SIGAR, *Quarterly report to the US Congress*, 30 July 2010.

43 US Geological Survey, *Preliminary assessment of the non-fuel mineral resources of Afghanistan*, 2007.

44 SIGAR, *Quarterly report to the US Congress*, 30 July 2011.

45 Islamic Republic of Afghanistan, *Afghanistan National Development Strategy*.

46 Asian Development Bank, 'Afghanistan', *Asian Development Outlook 2011*.

47 US Embassy Cables, 'Chinese Firm Rethinks Afghan Mining Contract'.

48 US Embassy Cables, 'Aynak Copper Mine Technical Negotiations Complete', at http://www.cablegatesearch.net/cable.php?id=08KABUL1047.

49 Reuters, 'Afghan Leader Signs Deal To Deepen Ties With India', 4 October 2011, available at http://in.reuters.com/article/2011/10/04/india-afghanistan-idINL3E7L41PV20111004.

50 US Geological Survey, *Preliminary assessment of the non-fuel mineral resources of Afghanistan*, 2007.

51 US Embassy Cables, 'Chinese Firm again Frontrunner for Major Afghan Mining Contract', 7 November 2009, available at http://wikileaks.org/cable/2009/11/09KABUL3574.html.

52 Asian Development Bank, 'Afghanistan', *Asian Development Outlook 2011*.

53 Adam Pain and Paula Kantor, 'Beyond the market: can the AREDP transform Afghanistan's rural economy?', AREU Briefing paper, February 2011.

54 SIGAR, *Quarterly report to the US Congress*, 30 July 2011.

55 Ministry of Defence, *Helmand Annual Review 2010*.

56 Adam Pain, 'Opium poppy strikes back: the 2011 return of opium in Balkh and Badakhshan provinces', AREU July 2011.

57 AREU, 'Decline and stagnation: why rural Afghans are staying poor', 27 November 2010.

58 Pain, 'Opium poppy strikes back'.

59 Citha D. Maas, *Afghanistan's drug career: evolution from a war economy to a drug economy*, Stiftung Wissenschaft und Politik, March 2011.

60 As a result, wheat cultivation in Helmand (Afghanistan's premier opium-producing province) almost doubled in 2008–09. See David Mansfield, 'Managing concurrent and repeated risks: explaining the reductions in opium production in central Helmand between 2008 and 2011', AREU, August 2011.

61 US Embassy Cables, 'The 2009 Afghanistan Opium Survey: UNODC Costa Briefs NATO and Partner Nations', http://www.cablegatesearch.net/cable.php?id=09USNATO397.

62 It is becoming accepted that counter-narcotics enforcement only succeeds in a sustainable manner when eradication is undertaken in conjunction with agricultural support for farmers (irrigation, fertiliser, seeds and loans), viable rural development plans and the maintenance of security and the authority of the government. See United Nations Office on Drugs and Crime (UNODC), *Afghanistan opium survey 2011: summary findings*, October 2011, http://www.unodc.org/documents/crop-monitoring/Afghanistan/Executive_Summary_2011_web.pdf.

63 David Mansfield, 'Managing concurrent and repeated risks: explaining the reductions in opium production in central Helmand between 2008 and 2011', AREU, August 2011.

64 Jalili quoted in Maas, 'Afghanistan's drug career'.

65 Mark Shaw, 'Drug trafficking and the development of organized crime in post-Taliban Afghanistan', in Doris Buddenberg and William A. Byrd (eds), *Afghanistan's Drug industry: structure, functioning, dynamics and implications for counter-narcotics policy*, UNODC/World Bank, November 2006.

66 UNODC, *Afghanistan opium survey 2010*; UNODC, *World drug report 2011*, http://www.unodc.org/unodc/en/data-and-analysis/WDR-2011.html.

67 UNODC, *World Drug Report 2011*, Statistical Annex 6.2.

68 UNODC, *Afghanistan opium survey 2011: summary findings*.

69 Edouard Martin and Steven Symansky, 'Macroeconomic impact of the drug economy and counter-narcotics efforts', in Buddenberg and Byrd (eds), *Afghanistan's Drug industry*.

70 UNODC, *Afghanistan opium survey 2010*.

71 Martin and Symansky, 'Macroeconomic impact of the drug economy and counter-narcotics efforts', in Bud-denberg and Byrd (eds), *Afghanistan's Drug industry*.

72 UNODC, *World Drug Report 2011*.

73 UNODC, *Global Afghan Opium Trade: a threat assessment*, July 2011.

74 UNODC, *Afghanistan opium survey 2011: summary findings*.

75 Martin and Symansky, 'Macroeconomic impact of the drug economy and counter-narcotics efforts'.

76 Pain, *Opium poppy strikes back*.

77 For a comprehensive analysis of the impact of the drug trade in producing and transit states on security and state capacity, see the forthcoming *Adelphi* by Nigel Inkster and Virginia Comolli, *Drugs, insecurity and failing states: the problems of prohibition* (London: IISS, forthcoming).

78 Shaw, 'Drug trafficking and the development of organized crime in post-Taliban Afghanistan'.

79 Maas, *Afghanistan's drug career*.

80 *Warlord, Inc.*

81 IMF, Islamic Republic of Afghanistan: program note, updated 15 April 2011.

82 *Ibid.*

83 SIGAR, *Quarterly report to the United States Congress*, 30 July 2010.

Chapter Five

1 'Citing Rising Death Toll, UN Urges Better Protection of Afghan Civilians', UN News Centre, 9 March 2011, http://www.un.org/apps/news/story.asp?NewsID=37715&Cr=Afghan&Cr1.

2 See http://www.isaf.nato.int/images/media/PDFs/11-10-15%20data%20release_finalv2.pdf.

3 The International Council of Security and Development, *Afghanistan transition: the death of Bin Laden and local dynamics*, May 2011, p. 13, http://www.icosgroup.net/static/reports/bin-laden-local-dynamics.pdf.

4 UNAMA Afghanistan Mid-year Report, 'Protection Of Civilians In Armed Conflict', July 2011, http://unama.unmissions.org/Portals/UNAMA/Documents/2011%20Midyear%20POC.pdf.

5   There has also been a significant increase in similar teams working with the ANP. Over 300 Police Operational Mentoring and Liaison teams have been deployed, 90% of them provided by US military police battalions using similar techniques to those applied in Iraq from 2008.

6   Briefings by UK MOD officials to author May 2011.

7   Briefing by Brig. James Chiswell at IISS, London, 16 June 2011, http://www.iiss.org/events-calendar/2011-events-archive/june-2011/brigadier-james-chiswell-on-operations-in-helmand-province-afghanistan-2010-11/.

8   UNDP, *International Human Development Indicators*, accessed at http://hdrstats.undp.org/en/countries/profiles/AFG.html.

9   See slides used by LTG Caldwell commander NTM-A in video address to the Royal United Services Institute, 23 September 2011, http://www.rusi.org/downloads/assets/110923_-_U_-_Think_Tank_VTC_Script_RUSI.pdf.

10 See 'Statement on Afghanistan by the prime minister David Cameron to the House of Commons', 6 July 2011, http://www.number10.gov.uk/news/latest-news/2011/07/statement-on-afghanistan-65349.

11 Admiral Mike Mullen US Chairman of the Joint Chiefs of Staff, testimony to the US Senate Armed Services Committee 22 September 2011, http://armed-services.senate.gov/statemnt/2011/09%20September/Mullen%2009-22-11.pdf.

12 Senate Armed Services Committee Hearing on Iraq and Afghanistan September 22, 2011 at http://www.jcs.mil/speech.aspx?ID=1651.

13 Department of Defense, *Report on Progress toward Security and Stability in Afghanistan*.

14 *Ibid.*

15 Discussions with MoD personnel, May-October 2011.

16 Rodriguez, 'Leaving Afghanistan to the Afghans'.

Chapter Six

1   Fedayeen attacks are typified by the 2008 coordinated shooting and bombing attack in Mumbai, in which several members of Lakshar-e-Taiba shot indiscriminately before turning their rifles on themselves or detonating devices.

2   By the latter part of 2009, US intelligence officials were briefing that al-Qaeda had no more than 100 operatives in Afghanistan. See 'President Obama's Secret: Only 100 al-Qaeda Now in Afghanistan', ABC News, 2 December 2009, http://abcnews.go.com/Blotter/president-obama-secret-100-al-qaeda-now-afghanistan/story?is=9227861. See also Bob Woodward, *Obama's Wars: the Inside Story* (New York: Simon and Schuster, 2010).

3   John Prados, *Safe for Democracy: the Secret Wars of the CIA* (Chicago, IL: Ivan R. Dee, 2006), pp. 488–90.

4   Peter Bergen, *The Osama bin Laden I Knew* (New York: Free Press, 2006), pp. 73–6.

5   The 9/11 Commission Report (New York: W.W. Norton and Company, 2004), pp. 57–9.

6   Bergen, The Osama bin Laden I Knew, p. 164.

7   Brynjar Lia, Architect of Global Jihad: the Life of Al Qaida Strategist Abu Musab al Suri (New York: Columbia University Press, 2008), p. 289. Suri was a veteran of the failed uprising by the Syrian Muslim Brotherhood who subsequently made his way to London, where he worked as a journalist and strategist of jihad. Believing himself – erroneously – to be in imminent danger of arrest by the British authorities, Suri moved in the mid-1990s first to Pakistan, then to Afghanistan. He is now thought to be in US custody, possibly in Bagram air base.

8   Ibid., page 287.

9   Steve Coll, Ghost Wars: The Secret History of the CIA, Afghanistan and bin Laden from the Soviet Invasion to September 10, 2001 (London and New York: Penguin, 2004), p. 401.

10 Ibid., p. 514.

11 Lia, Architect of Global Jihad, pp. 247–50.

12 Vahid Brown, 'The Façade of Allegiance: Bin Laden's Dubious Pledge to Mullah Omar', Sentinel, vol. 3, no. 1, January 2010, p. 3, http://www.ctc.usma.edu/sentinel/CTSSentinel.

13 Ibid., page 5. Takfiri practices are those which accuse other Islamic subsets of apostasy.

14 'Al-Qaeda "Plotted Nuclear Attacks"', BBC News, 8 September 2002, http://news.bbc.co.uk/1/hi/world/middle_east/2244146.stm.

15 B. Rahman, 'Musharraf's Ban', South Asia Analysis Group paper 395, 18 January 2002, http://www.southasiaanalysis.org/%5Cpapers4%5Cpaper395.htlm.

16 Bergen, The Osama bin Laden I Knew, p. 371.

17 Rashid, Descent into Chaos (London: Allen Lane, 2008), p. 268.

18 UN High Commissioner for Refugees in Pakistan, 'Afghan Refugee Statistics', 6 May 2001, http://www.un.org.pk/unhcr/Afstats-stat.htm.

19 Zahid Hussain, Frontline Pakistan: The Struggle with Militant Islam (New York: Colombia University Press, 2007), p. 72.

20 Peter Chalk, 'Pakistan's Role in the Kashmir Insurgency', Jane's Intelligence Review, 1 September 2001.

21 'Musharraf Declares War on Extremism', BBC News, 12 January 2002, http://news.bbc.co.uk/1/hi/world/south_asia/1756965.stm.

22 Private discussion with Western intelligence officer, March 2009.

23 Jim Hoagland, 'Pakistan: Pretence of an Ally', Washington Post, 28 March 2002.

24 Rashid, Descent into Chaos, p. 147.

25 Alex Strick van Linschoten and Felix Kuehn, 'Separating the Taliban from al-Qaeda: the Core of Success in Afghanistan', New York: NYU Center on International Co-operation, February 2011, p. 6.

26 'FATA: recent developments', glogalsecurity.org, http://www.globalsecurity.org/military/world/pakistan/fata.hm.

27 A.G. Sulzberger and William K. Rashbaum, 'Guilty Plea Made in Plot to Bomb New York Subway', New York Times, 22 February 2010, http://www.nytimes.com/2010/02/23/nyregion/23terror.html.

28 For details of Pakistani military operations in FATA, see C. Christine Fair and Seth Jones, 'Pakistan's War Within', Survival, vol. 51, no. 6,

December 2009 January 2010, pp. 165–77.

29   Declan Walsh, 'Red Mosque Siege Declared Over', *Guardian*, 11 July 2007, http://www.guardian. co.uk/world2007/jul/11/pakistan. declanwalsh.

30   Hassan Abbas, 'A Profile of the Tehrik-i-Taliban Pakistan', *Sentinel*, vol. 50, no. 2, January 2008.

31   See Ma Liyao and Qin Jize, 'Pakistan Confident of Winning Anti-terror War', *China Daily*, 10 May 2011, http://usa. chinadaily.com.cn/epaper/2011-05/10/content_12480708.htm.

32   Bill Roggio and Alexander Mayer, 'Charting the data for US missiles in Pakistan', *The Long War Journal*, 17 March 2011, http://www. longwarjournal.org/pakistan-strikes. php.

33   Peter Bergen and Katherine Tiedemann, 'The Year of the Drone', New America Foundation, 24 February 2010, http:// counterterrorism.newamerica.net/ sites/newamerica.net/files/policydocs/ bergentiedemann2.pdf.

34   Salman Mahsoud, 'Pakistani General, in Twist, Credits Drone Strikes', *New York Times*, 9 March 2011, http:// www.nytimes.com/2011/03/10/world/ asia/10drones.html.

35   Bill Roggio, 'US killed al-Qaeda Lashkar al Zil commander in airstrike', *The Long War Journal*, 7 January 2010, http://www.longwarjournal.org/ archives/2010/01/us_killed_al_qaedas. php.

36   Private conversation with senior Western intelligence officer, March 2011.

37   See 'Message of Felicitation of the Esteeemed Amir-ul-Momineen on the Eve of Eid-ul-Fitr', TheUnjustmedia.com, http://
theunjustmedia.com/Afghanistan/ Statements?Sep10?message of Felicitation of the Esteeemed Amir-ul-Momineen on the Eve of Eid-ul-Fitr. htm.

38   van Linschoten and Kuehn, 'Separating the Taliban from al-Qaeda: the Core of Success in Afghanistan', p. 7.

39   http://www.newslinemagazine. com/2011/03/spy-or-intermediary/.

40   Carlotta Gall, 'Taliban Arrest May Be Crucial for Pakistanis', *New York Times*, 16 February 2010, http://www.nytimes. com/2010/02/17/world/asia/17intel. html.

41   Headley, of mixed US and Pakistani parentage, was a narcotics trafficker who also allegedly worked for the US Drugs Enforcement Administration (DEA). Between 2002 and 2008 Headley was a member of Lashkar-e-Tayiba, during which period he carried out reconnaissance in Mumbai in preparation for the November 2008 LeT attack on the city. He was also involved in a plot led by Harakat-ul-Jihad-ul-Islami (HUJI) commander and al-Qaeda associate Ilyas Kashmiri to prepare an attack on the Danish newspaper *Jyllands-Posten*, which had published cartoons of the Prophet Mohammed, for which he was arrested by the FBI in 2009. See Ginger Thompson, 'Terror Trial Witness Ties Pakistan to 2008 Attacks', *New York Times*, 23 May 2011, http:// www.nytimes.com/2011/05/24/ world/asia/24headley.html?_ r=1&ref=global-home. See also Paul Cruickshank, 'Terror Made in Pakistan', *Foreign Policy*, 4 May 2010.

42   Private comment by former senior Pakistani official close to Pakistani military thinking.

43 Gregg Carlstrom, 'Afghan Talks Raise Speculation', *al-Jazeera* English news, 27 June 2010, http://aljazeera.net/news/asia/2010/06/2010627202528829196.html.

44 Conversations with Western intelligence officials.

45 David Kilcullen, *The Accidental Guerrilla* (Oxford: Oxford University Press, 2009).

Chapter Seven

1 Asian Development Bank, 'Key Indicators for Asia and the Pacific 2011', p. 4.

2 Frederic Grare, 'Pakistan–Afghanistan Relations in the Post-9/11 Era', Carnegie Papers, no. 72, October 2006, p. 3.

3 Rizwan Hussain, *Pakistan and the emergence of Islamic Militancy in Afghanistan* (Aldershot: Ashgate, 2005), p. 78.

4 *Ibid.*, pp. 79–80.

5 *Ibid.*

6 Barnett R. Rubin, *The Fragmentation of Afghanistan* (New Haven, CT: Yale University Press, 2002), p.100.

7 Hilary Synnott, *Transforming Pakistan: Ways out of instability* (Abingdon: Routledge for IISS, 2009), p. 28.

8 Armen Georgian, 'Commentary', *France 24*, http://www.france24.com/en/20080909-pakistan-afghanistan-really-twins-conjoined-zardari-karzai.

9 'Karzai's visit', *Daily Times*, 13 March 2010, http://www.dailytimes.com.pk/default.asp?page=2010\03\13\story_13-3-2010_pg3_1.

10 Ambassador Mohammad Sadiq, 'Pakistan–Afghanistan Relationship: a Journey of Friendship', Embassy of Pakistan in Afghanistan, http://www.mofa.gov.pk/afghanistan/contents.aspx?type=statements&id=6.

11 UNHCR, 'Pakistan Helping Communities that have Helped Afghan Refugees', 24 August 2011, http://www.unhcr.org.uk/news-and-views/news-list/news-detail/article/pakistan-helping-communities-that-have-hosted-afghan-refugees.html.

12 Julie Ray and Rajesh Srinivasan, 'Afghans Assess Roles for NATO, U.N., Regional Actors', 20 November 2009, http://www.gallup.com/poll/124445/afghans-assess-roles-nato-regional-actors.aspx.

13 The survey was conducted for ABC News, the BBC and ARD by the Afghan Center for Socio-Economic and Opinion Research (ACSOR), a D3 Systems Inc. subsidiary based in Kabul. Interviews were conducted in person, in Dari or Pashto, among a random national sample of 1,534 adults from 11–23 December 2009. See BBC, 11 January 2010, http://news.bbc.co.uk/2/shared/bsp/hi/pdfs/11_01_10_afghanpoll.pdf, pp. 22 and 24.

14 In 1893, Sir Henry Mortimer Durand of the Indian Civil Service agreed the boundary with the Emir of Afghanistan, Abdul Rahman Khan.

15 See Satinder Kumar Lambah, *The Durand Line*, Policy Paper no. 4, Aspen Institute India, September 2011, pp. 8–16.

16 Grare, 'Pakistan–Afghanistan Relations in the Post-9/11 Era', pp. 8–9.

17 Stephen Tankel, 'The Threat to the U.S. Homeland Emanating from Pakistan', Testimony to the U.S. House Committee on Homeland Security (Subcommittee on Counterterrorism and Intelligence), Washington DC, 3 May 2011, http://www.carnegieendowment.org/files0503_testimony_tankel.pdf, pp. 1 and 5.

18 'Obama kills Osama', *Spearhead Analysis*, 3 May 2011, http://spearheadresearch.org.

19 See, for example, 'RAW training 600 Baloch in Afghanistan', *Dawn*, 16 April 2006, http://www.dailytimes.com.pk/default.asp?page=2006\04\16\story_16-4-2006_pg1_4.

20 'Qureshi Accuses India of Aiding Insurgents', *Dawn*, 23 November 2009, http://archives.dawn.com/archives/35808.

21 'India Must "Decrease Footprint in Afghan" to Gain Pak Trust: Gilani', *Economic Times*, 2 December 2010, http://articles.economictimes.indiatimes.com/2010-12-02/news/28493347_1_balochistan-prime-minister-gilani-syed-yousaf-raza-gilani.

22 See Pamela Constable, 'Pakistan's Army Chief Seeks Stable Afghanistan', *Washington Post*, 2 February 2010, http://www.washingtonpost.com/wp-dyn/content/article/2010/02/01/AR2010020102506_pf.html; and Zahid Hussain, 'Kayani Spells out Terms for Regional Stability', *Dawn*, 2 February 2010, http://archives.dawn.com/archives/38741.

23 Syed Talat Hussain, 'Policy Paper Catches Obama's Attention', *Dawn*, 2 December 2010, http://www.dawn.com/2010/12/02/policy-paper-catches-obamas-attention.html.

24 See Tahir Khan, 'News Analysis: Pakistan Plays Down Afghan–

India Strategic Pact', Xinhua, http://news.xinhuanet.com/english2010/world/2011-10/06/c_131177071.htm. Pakistan's Foreign Ministry spokesperson cautioned its neighbours to avoid doing anything that may destabilise the region. See Imtiaz Ahmad, 'Avoid Steps that Destabilise Region: Pak to Neighbours', *Hindustan Times*, 5 October 2011, http://www.hindustantimes.com/StoryPage/Print/754044.aspx.

25 Constable, 'Pakistan's Army Chief Seeks Stable Afghanistan'.

26 'Emerging Strategy', *Spearhead Analysis*, 7 April 2011, http://spearheadresearch.org.

27 Qaiser Butt, 'Pakistan Drops Opposition to India's Participation at Ankara Moot', *Express Tribune*, 5 April 2011, http://tribune.com.pk/story/143291/afghanistan-conference-pakistan-drops-opposition-to-indias-participation-at-ankara-moot/?print=true.

28 See Secretary Robert Gates's remarks, CEO Council 2010 Meeting, 16 November 2010, http://www.defense.gov/transcripts/transcript.aspx?transcriptid=4720.

29 Synnott, *Transforming Pakistan*, p. 32.

30 Constable, 'Pakistan's Army Chief Seeks Stable Afghanistan'.

31 Talk by Pakistan's Interior Minister Rehman Malik at the IISS, London, 28 July 2011.

32 Stephen P. Cohen, *The Future of Pakistan* (Washington DC: Brookings Institution, 2010), http://www.brookings.edu/~/media/Files/rc/papers/2011/01_pakistan_cohen/01_pakistan_cohen.pdf, pp. 13–14; and Amir Mir, '2010: Suicides Drop by 35pc, Deaths Up by 1pc', 24 December 2010, *The News*, http://www.

thenews.com.pk/TodaysPrintDetail. aspx?ID=21975&Cat=2. I have also included the Bajaur suicide bombing of 25 December 2010, which killed 47 people.

33 See Ma Liyao and Qin Jize, 'Pakistan Confident of Winning Anti-terror War', *China Daily*, 10 May 2011, http://usa. chinadaily.com.cn/epaper/2011-05/10/ content_12480708.htm.

34 Malik, talk at IISS.

35 Rahimullah Yusufzai, 'Pakistan Wild West Frontier', *Rediff*, 7 April 2004, http://www.rediff.com/news/2004/ apr/07spec.htm.

36 Benazir Bhutto, 'The Future of Democracy', talk given at IISS, London, 20 July 2007.

37 Carlotta Gall, 'At Border, Signs of Pakistani Role in Taliban Surge', *New York Times*, 21 January 2007, http:// www.nytimes.com/2007/01/21/world/ asia/21quetta.html.

38 Grare, 'Pakistan–Afghanistan Relations in the Post-9/11 Era', p. 3.

39 *IISS Strategic Survey 2009* (Abingdon: Routledge for IISS, 2009), p. 302.

40 Lieutenant-General Tariq Majid, 'Counter-terrorism and Counter-insurgency Efforts by Pakistan: Progress and Prospects', address at the 7th IISS Shangri-La Dialogue, Singapore, 31 May 2008, p. 3.

41 'Overview of the Afghanistan and Pakistan Annual Review', White House Office of the Press Secretary, 16 December 2010, http://www.whitehouse.gov/the-press-office/2010/12/16/overview-afghanistan-and-pakistan-annual-review.

42 Stanley McChrystal, Unclassified assessment leaked to the *Washington Post*, September 2009, http://media. washingtonpost.com/wp-srv/ politics/documents/Assessment_ Redacted_092109.pdf?hpid=topnews.

43 Matt Waldman, *The Sun in the Sky: The relationship between Pakistan's ISI and Afghan insurgents*, Crisis States Research Centre, London School of Economics, June 2010, p. 1, http:// eprints.lse.ac.uk/id/eprint/28435.

44 'South Asia still beset by violent extremism', IISS *Strategic Comments*, vol. 17, January 2011, http://www.iiss. org/publications/strategic-comments/ past-issues/volume-17-2011/january/ south-asia-still-beset-by-violent-extremism/.

45 Lister and Kassim, 'Pakistanis Strike Back at U.S. Accusations of Ties to Haqqani Network'.

46 *Ibid.*

47 'Opening remarks of the Prime Minister at the conference of the leaders of the Political Parties', Islamabad, 29 September 2011, http:// www.mofa.gov.pk/mfa/pages/article. aspx?id=943&type=1.

48 Matt Waldman, Testimony to the Foreign Affairs Committee, House of Commons Report, 'The UK's foreign policy approach to Afghanistan and Pakistan', p. 33, http://www. publications.parliament.uk/pa/ cm201011/cmselect/cmfaff/514/514.pdf.

49 'UK PM cautions Pakistan over "terror exports"', BBC, 28 July 2010, http://www.bbc.co.uk/news/ world-south-asia-10791182.

50 Dexter Filkins, 'Pakistanis Tell of Motive in Taliban Leader's Arrest', *New York Times*, 22 August 2010, http:// www.nytimes.com/2010/08/23/world/ asia/23taliban.html.

51 Waldman, 'The UK's foreign policy approach to Afghanistan and Pakistan', p. 31.

52 *Ibid.*, p. 36.

53 Declan Walsh, 'WikiLeaks Cables: US Aid Will Not Stop Pakistan Supporting Militants', *Guardian*, 30 November 2010, http://www.guardian.co.uk/world/2010/nov/30/wikileaks-us-aid-pakistan-militants.

54 Press Trust of India, 'Supply to Afghanistan through Pakistan Reduced to 35 per cent', *The Hindu*, 22 July 2011, http://www.thehindu.com/news/international/article2284207.ece?css=print.

55 'Osama bin Laden Must Have Had Pakistan Support Network, Says Obama', *Guardian*, 9 May 2011, http://www.guardian.co.uk/world/2011/may/08/osama-bin-laden-pakistan-obama; and 'Investigations to Uncover Truth Behind Osama bin Laden's Support Network', *DNA India*, 29 May 2011, http://www.dnaindia.com/world/report_investigations-to-uncover-truth-behind-osama-bin-laden-s-support-network_1548955.

56 Matthew Rosenberg, 'Karzai Told to Dump US', *Wall Street Journal*, 27 April 2011, http://online.wsj.com/article/SB10001424052748704729304576287041094035816.html#.

57 Julian E. Barnes, 'Efforts to Recruit Pashtuns in Afghan South Falter', *Wall Street Journal*, 12 September 2010, http://online.wsj.com/article/SB10001424052748704621204575487720827425774.html.

58 In October 2010, the Pakistan cabinet approved the Pakistan–Afghanistan Transit Trade Agreement. It provided for an increase in the number of border crossing points and allowed Afghan trucks extended access beyond the Torkham border on the Durand Line to Wagha on the Pakistan–India border, but with the proviso that they would carry only Pakistani export goods back to Afghanistan. UNCTAD, 'UNCTAD-supported Afghanistan–Pakistan transit trade agreement to take effect on 14 February', http://www.unctad.org/templates/webflyer.asp?docid=14422&intItemID=1634&lang=1.

59 'Pakistani PM Gilani Meets Afghanistan's Karzai in Kabul', BBC News, 16 April 2011, http://www.bbc.co.uk//news/world-south-asia-13105007.

60 See Hamid Shalizi and Omar Sobhani, 'Afghanistan Says Rabbani's Killer was Pakistani', Reuters, 2 October 2011, http://uk.reuters.com/article/2011/10/02/uk-afghanistan-pakistan-idUKTRE7911W120111002.

61 Synott, *Transforming Pakistan*, p. 94.

62 See Maleeha Lodhi, 'Crux of the Crisis', *The News*, 4 October 2011, http://thenews.com.pk/TodaysPrintDetail.aspx?ID=70711&Cat=9&dt=10/4/2011.

Chapter Eight

1 'Pak-Iran Gas Pipeline to Bring Industrial Revolution: Envoy', *Tehran Times*, 15 October 2011, http://www.tehrantimes.com/index.php/component/content/article/3563.

2 Douglas Jehl, 'For Death of Its Diplomats, Iran Vows Blood for Blood', *New York Times*, 12 September 1998, http://www.nytimes.com/1998/09/12/world/for-death-of-its-diplomats-iran-vows-blood-for-blood.html.

3   UNHCR *2005 Statistical Yearbook*, p. 231.

4   UNHCR, 'UNHCR seeks $18 million to assist Afghan refugees in iran', 1 June 2010, http://www.unhcr.org.uk/resources/monthly-updates/may-2010-copy-1/unhcr-seeks-us18-million-to-assist-afghan-refugees-in-iran.html.

5   Delegates at a conference held by PRIO and the Chr. Michelsen Institute in 2003 heard that educational opportunities have been decreasing for refugees since 2003, and that Iranian women who married Afghan men could, along with their entire families, face the risk of deportation as the lines between voluntary repatriation become blurred. Iranian women who marry Afghan men immediately lose their Iranian citizenship. See Arne Strand, Astri Suhrke and Kristian Berg Harpviken, 'Afghan refugees in Iran: from refugee emergency to migration management', PRIO and CMI Policy Brief, 16 June 2004, http://www.cmi.no/pdf/?file=/afghanistan/doc/CMI-PRIO-AfghanRefugeesInIran.pdf.

6   'Joint Programme between the government of the Islamic Republic of Iran, the Islamic Republic of Afghanistan and UNHCR for voluntary repatriation of Afghan refugees and displaced persons', statement issued 8 March 2006.

7   'Research study on Afghan deportees from Iran', Altai consulting, Kabul, 1 August 2008.

8   UNODC, 'Addiction, crime and insurgency: the transnational threat of Afghan opium', October 2009, pp. 1 and 11.

9   Dexter Filkins, 'Afghan Leader Admits His Office Gets Cash from Iran', *New York Times*, 25 October 2010, http://www.nytimes.com/2010/10/26/world/asia/26afghan.html.

10   'Iran, US Spar over Afghanistan', CBC News, 10 March 2010, http://www.cbc.ca/news/world/story/2010/03/10/afghan-iran.html.

11   Michael Kamber and Taimoor Shah, 'Iran Stops Fuel Delivery, Afghanistan Says, and Prices Are Rising, 22 Decembre 2010, *New York Times*, http://www.nytimes.com/2010/12/23/world/asia/23afghan.html.

12   Conversation with a US official working on Afghanistan–Pakistan, Washington DC, April 2011.

13   Simon Tisdall, 'Afghanistan War Logs: Iran's Covert Operations in Afghanistan', *Guardian*, 25 July 2010, http://www.guardian.co.uk/world/2010/jul/25/iran-backing-taliban-alqaida-afghanistan.

14   John Ward Anderson, 'Arms Seized in Afghanistan Sent From Iran, NATO Says', *Washington Post*, 21 September 2007, http://www.washingtonpost.com/wp-dyn/content/article/2007/09/20/AR2007092001236.html.

15   'NATO confirm Iranian support to the insurgency in Afghanistan', Foreign and Commonwealth Office, 9 March 2011, http://www.fco.gov.uk/en/news/latest-news/?view=News&id=562991482.

16   Dean Nelson, 'WikiLeaks Afghanistan: Iran Accused of Supporting Taliban Attacks', *Telegraph*, 27 July 2010, http://www.telegraph.co.uk/news/worldnews/asia/afghanistan/7910926/Wikileaks-Afghanistan-Iran-accused-of-supporting-Taliban-attacks.html.

17   Ali Sheikholeslami, 'Iran–Afghanistan Trade Is More Than $1.5 Billion, President Karzai Says', *Bloomberg*, 5 August 2010, http://www.bloomberg.com/news/2010-08-05/iran-afghanistan-trade-is-more-than-1-5-billion-president-karzai-says.html.

Chapter Nine

1 Roman Kozhevnikov, 'Al Qaeda Ally Claims Tajik Attack, Threatens More', Reuters, 23 September 2010.

2 Kozhevnikov, 'Tajikistan Kills 20 Taliban Fighters at Border', Reuters, 11 September 2010.

3 Kozhevnikov, 'Bomb Blast Wounds Five in Tajikistan Nightclub', Reuters, 6 September 2010.

4 In March ISAF forces killed several senior IMU commanders in Baghlan Province (see http://www.dvidshub. net/news/66925/isaf-joint-command-morning-operational-update) and others were targeted in Balkh Province (http://news.xinhuanet. com/english2010/world/2011-03/11/c_13772775.htm).

5 'Northern route eases supplies to US forces in Afghanistan', IISS Strategic Comments, August 2010, http://www.iiss.org/publications/strategic-comments/past-issues/volume-16-2010/august/.

6 UNODC, 'The Global Heroin Market', World Drug Report 2010, pp. 44 and 46, http://www.unodc.org/documents/wdr/WDR_2010/1.2_The_global_heroin_market.pdf.

7 The project was discussed again at the summit of the Presidents of Russia, Tajikistan, Afghanistan and Pakistan in August 2011. The Russian president reportedly asked his counterparts to expedite the project, but disagreements with Uzbekistan over the impact of the Rogun hydropower station on water supply for the region and a World Bank's request to conduct environmental assessment are likely to delay the implementation of the project. See Mushtaq Ghumman, 'CASA-1000 Project in the Doldrums?', http://www.brecorder.com/fuel-a-energy/single/630/193:pakistan/1228417:casa-1000-project-in-the-doldrums/?date=2011-09-04.

8 'TAPI Gas Pipeline Talks Begin', The Hindu, 26 April 2011.

9 On the Amu Darya river, upstream, Tajikistan is focused mainly on the expansion of irrigated land in its territory and on the development of its hydropower potential, whereas downstream, Turkmenistan and Uzbekistan are mainly concerned with food security and water-intensive cotton production. Tensions over the Syr Darya River further complicate Central Asian relations. UN-sponsored programmes on 'alternative livelihoods assistance', for example, replacing poppy fields in Northern Afghanistan with food crops, are also putting increased pressure on the Amu Darya river.

10 'Northern Route Eases Supplies to US Forces in Afghanistan'.

11 White House Office of the Press Secretary, 'U.S.-Russia Relations: "Reset" Fact Sheet', 24 June 2010, http://www.whitehouse.gov/the-press-office/us-russia-relations-reset-fact-sheet.

12 See Catherine A. Fitzpatrick, 'Turkmenistan: Secret U.S. Base For Afghanistan, Iraq, Iran Campaigns: Is the U.S. Violating Turkmenistan's Neutrality with the NDN?', http://www.globalresearch.ca/index.php?context=va&aid=20411.

13 Deirdre Tynan, 'Uzbekistan: Veil is Lifted on German Payments for Termez Base', http://www.eurasianet.org/node/63148.

14 Michael Schwirtz and Clifford J. Levy, 'In Reversal, Kyrgyzstan Won't Close a US Base', *New York Times*, 23 June 2009. Under the US deal to lease the base, Washington has agreed to provide more than $100m in a one-off investment to Kyrgyzstan. See 'Tulips Squashed', *Economist*, 30 July 2009, http://www.economist.com/node/14140310; and Deirdre Tynan, 'US Air Base at Manas Busier Now than Before', 11 August 2009, http://www.eurasianet.org/departments/insightb/articles/eav081209a.shtml.

15 Vitaliy Skrinnik, first secretary at the Russian embassy in Bishkek, quoted in 'Kyrgyzstan: Moscow withholding promised aid to Bishkek', Eurasianet, 15 February 2010, http://www.eurasianet.org/departments/insightb/articles/eav021610.shtml.

16 Figure cited in EIU, 'Russia – Losing Central Asia to China?', Viewswire, 18 December 2009.

17 Rayhan Demytrie, 'Struggle for Central Asian Energy Riches', BBC News, 3 June 2010, http://www.bbc.co.uk/news/10175847.

18 In contrast, the year before, Russian firms (led by LUKOIL) extracted just 6.4m tonnes of oil from Kazakhstan. See Cholpon Orozobekova, 'Beijing's Stealthy Expansion in Central Asia', Eurasia Internet, 13 January 2011, http://www.eurasia.org.ru/en/events-and-opinions/beijing-s-stealthy-expansion-in-central-asia.

19 Alisher Ikhamov, 'Profit Not Patronage: Chinaese Interests in Uzbekistan', Jamestown Foundation, *China Brief*, vol. 5, no. 20, September 2005, http://www.jamestown.org/programs/chinabrief/archivescb/cb2005/.

20 EIU, 'Russia – Losing Central Asia to China?'.

21 'Karzai Visit to Russia Irks US', *al-Jazeera* English, 20 January 2011, http://english.aljazeera.net/news/europe/2011/01/201112014297833879.html.

22 See James Risen, 'Reports Link Karzai's Brother to Heroin Trade', *New York Times*, 5 October 2008.

23 For a transcript of the question and answer session during which Ivanov made his comments, see http://www.iiss.org/conferences/the-shangri-la-dialogue/shangri-la-dialogue-2010/plenary-session-speeches/fifth-plenary-session/qa/.

24 See 'Afghan President Karzai Criticises US-Russia Drugs Raid', BBC News, 31 October 2010, http://www.bbc.co.uk/news/world-south-asia-11659814.

25 See http://www.regnum.ru/news/fd-abroad/tajik/polit/1443295.html (Russian language).

26 See http://www.regnum.ru/news/fd-abroad/tajik/polit/1441656.html (Russian Language).

27 Such are the severity of claims and counterclaims that President Rahmon told his counterparts in the US embassy in December 2005 that Russian border guards had been 'more involved in trafficking heroin than stopping [drugs trafficking]', according to a leaked cable from WikiLeaks, http://www.guardian.co.uk/world/us-embassy-cables-documents/4662). Quoted in Alexander Sodiqov, 'Moscow Blackmails Dushanbe to Return to the Afghan Border', *Eurasia Daily Monitor*, vol. 8, no. 158, 16 August 2011.

28 See Roger McDermott, 'Tashkent and Dushanbe Cautious on CSTO Forces', *Eurasia Daily Monitor*, vol. 6, no. 27, 10 February 2009.

29 These talks will include Uzbekistan, Tajikistan, Turkmenistan, Pakistan, China, Iran, the United States, Russia and NATO.

Chapter Ten

1 Steve Coll, *Ghost Wars* (London: Penguin Books, 2004), p. 66.

2 For a timeline of the unrest, see Radio Free Asia, 'Unrest Timeline', http://www.rfa.org/english/multimedia/unresttimeline-07072009122503.html; Peter Foster, 'China Executes Two Muslims for pre-Olympics Attack', *Daily Telegraph*, 9 April 2009; 'China Investigating Terrorist Links in Xinjiang Attack', Reuters, 11 August 2008; 'Police Killed in new Xinjiang Clash', Radio Free Asia, 28 August 2008.

3 'Turkistan Islamic Party Claims Responsibility for Xinjiang Attacks', *Jane's Intelligence Weekly*, 9 September 2011; and 'Separatists Launch Attacks in Xinjiang', *Jane's Intelligence Weekly*, 1 August 2011.

4 Aaron L. Friedberg, *A Contest for Supremacy* (New York: W.W. Norton and Company, 2011), p. 170.

5 'China's Russian Invasion', thediplomat.com, http://thediplomat.com/2010/02/19/china's-russian-invasion/.

6 'Russia backs Afghan entry into SCO', Tajikistan Newswire, 24 October 2011, http://www.universalnewswires.com/centralasia/tajikistan/viewstory.aspx?id=10512.

7 Colonel Dai Xu, *C xingbaowei* (Beijing: Wei Hui Publishing, 2010).

8 Private conversation with the individual cited.

9 Russell Hsia and Glen E. Howard, 'China Builds Closer Ties to Afghanistan through Wakhan Corridor', Jamestown Foundation, *China Brief*, vol. 10, no. 1, 7 January 2010.

10 Richard Galpin, 'Struggle for Central Asian Energy Riches', BBC, 2 June 2010.

11 Bin Laichun, *Afuhan duiyu woguo nengyuan zhanlue de zhongyao yiyi* (Beijing: China Ministry of Land, Oil and Gas Resources, July 2009).

12 Raymond Gilpin and Ashley Pandya, 'Improving High-Value Resource contracting in Afghanistan, United States Institute of Peace', 16 August 2010.

13 Steven A. Zyck, 'Afghanistan: the Re-Tendering of Hajigak Mining Rights', Civil-Military Fusion Centre, 17 November 2010.

14 Michelle Nichols, 'Afghan Mine Development Seen Costly, Risky and Slow', Reuters, 5 July 2011.

15 'Chinese enjoy a peaceful existence in Afghanistan', interview with Chinese business people in Kabul, Sina.com , 11 May 2011.

16 'Zhongguo zhengfu wei afuhan, yilake juban rendaozhuyi saolei peixunban', Xinhua, 15 September 2009, http://www.gov.cn/jrzg/2009-09/15/content_1417854.htm.

17 The English-language blog 'China Defense' carries a repost of the original blog and photographs. See http://china-defense.blogspot.com/2009/09/follow-up-on-my-earlier-blog-entry-of.html.

18 Hussein Haqqani, cited in Esther Pan, 'China and Pakistan: a Deepening Bond', Council on Foreign Relations, 8 March 2006.

19 Robert Shuey and Shirley Kan, 'China Missile and Nuclear Proliferation: Issues for Congress', CRS Report (Washington DC: Congressional Research Service, 29 September 1995).

20 Thomas Reed and Danny B. Stillman, *The Nuclear Express: A Political History of the Bomb and its Proliferation*

(Minneapolis, MN: Zenith Press, 2009), pp. 249–50.

21 Jamal Afridi and Jayshree Bajaria, 'China–Pakistan Relations', Council on Foreign Relations, 6 July 2010.

22 Farhan Bokhari and Kathrin Hille, 'Pakistan Turns to China for Naval Base', *Financial Times*, 21 May 2011.

23 Li Xiguang, 'Zhongguo Junjing yu Taliban Zuozhan Keneng Daozhi Xinjiang Luanju', *Global Times*, 30 December 2009.

Chapter Eleven

1 B. Raman, 'U.S. Bombing of Terrorist Camps in Afghanistan', South Asia Analysis Group Papers, 3 November 1998, http://www.southasiaanalysis. org/%5Cpapers%5Cpaper10.html.

2 Sudha Ramachandran, 'India's Foray into Central Asia', *Asia Times*, 12 August 2006, http://www.atimes.com/ atimes/South_Asia/HH12Df01.html.

3 'India's role in Afghanistan', IISS Strategic Comments, vol. 17, no. 22, June 2011, http://www.iiss.org/ publications/strategic-comments/ past-issues/volume-17-2011/june/ indias-role-in-afghanistan/.

4 See 'US Embassy Cables: No Power-sharing with the Taliban, Holbrooke Pledges', *Guardian*, 2 December 2010, http://www.guardian.co.uk/ world/us-embassy-cables-documents/245980.

5 See Shanthie Mariet D'Souza, 'What India Needs to Do in Afghanistan', *Rediff News*, 21 October 2009, http:// news.rediff.com/slide-show/2009/ oct/21/slide-show-1-securing-indias-interests-in-afghanistan.htm.

6 Sheela Bhatt, 'The Security of Indian Workers is our Foremost Responsibility', *Rediff Special*, 26 February 2009, http://specials.rediff. com/news/2009/feb/26sld3-interview-with-indias-afghan-envoy-jayant-prasad.htm; and Government of India, Ministry of External Affairs, *India and Afghanistan: a development relationship* (New Delhi: Press Information Bureau, 2009), http://meaindia.nic.in/staticfile/ Report.pdf.

7 Rahul Roy-Chaudhury, 'India Needs Taliban Talks to Stay Relevant', *Times of India*, 15 May 2011, http://articles. timesofindia.indiatimes.com/2011-05-15/all-that-matters/29545566_1_ afghan-taliban-quetta-shura-taliban-talks.

8 See Asian Development Bank, 'Key Indicators for Asia and the Pacific 2011', p.4, http://www.adb.org/documents/ books/key_indicators/2011/pdf/AFG. pdf.

9 Prasad made the comments when questioned about India's perceptions of US policy in Afghanistan. See

http://specials.rediff.com/news/2009/feb/26sld2-interview-with-indias-afghan-envoy-jayant-prasad.htm.

10 See Government of India, Ministry of External Affairs, 'India and Afghanistan – A Development Partnership', http://meaindia.nic.in/mystart.php?id=8400.

11 Interview with senior Indian official, New Delhi, 13 June 2011.

12 'India's Role in Afghanistan'.

13 'Shunning Pakistan, Afghans Rush to India for Quality Healthcare', *Deccan Herald*, 30 May 2011, http://www.deccanherald.com/content/164900/shunning-pakistan-afghans-rush-india.html.

14 *Ibid.*

15 Interview with senior Indian official, New Delhi, 13 June 2011.

16 Julie Ray and Rajesh Srinivasan, 'Afghans Assess Roles for NATO, UN, Regional Actors', 20 November 2009, http://www.gallup.com/poll/124445/afghans-assess-roles-nato-regional-actors.aspx.

17 See BBC News, 11 January 2010, p.23, http://news.bbc.co.uk/2/shared/bsp/hi/pdfs/11_01_10_afghanpoll.pdf.

18 See US diplomatic cable 250737, 'NSA Menon Discusses Regional Security and Trade Issues with Codel McCaskill', *The Hindu*, 21 May 2011, http://www.thehindu.com/news/the-india-cables/the-cables/article2035456.ece.

19 Press Trust of India, 'ISI Involved in Kabul Attack, Says Narayanan', *The Hindu*, 13 July 2008, http://www.hindu.com/2008/07/13/stories/2008071359580800.htm.

20 See AFP, 'India Blames Pak Militants for Kabul Attack', *Hindustan Times*, 1 April 2010, http://www.hindustantimes.com/India-blames-Pak-militants-for-Kabul-attack/

Article1-525786.aspx; and 'Guesthouses Used by Foreigners in Kabul Hit in Deadly Attacks', *New York Times*, 26 February 2010, http://www.nytimes.com/2010/02/27/world/asia/27kabul.html.

21 Shashank Joshi, 'With allies like this: what the WikiLeaks war logs say about Pakistan', RUSI, 28 July 2010, http://www.rusi.org/go.php?s tructureID=commentary&ref=C4C4FFEDD32F02; http://www.bbc.co.uk/news/world-south-asia-13191241.

22 'Haqqani Network is a "veritable arm" of ISI: Mullen'", *Dawn*, 22 September 2011, http://www.dawn.com/2011/09/22/haqqani-network-is-a-%E2%80%9Cveritable-arm%E2%80%9D-of-isi-mullen.html; and Tim Lister and Aliza Kassim, 'Pakistanis Strike Back at US Accusations of Ties to Haqqani Network', CNN, 23 September 2011, http://edition.cnn.com/2011/09/23/world/asia/pakistan-haqqani-network/index.html?iref=allsearch.

23 See 'NSA Echoes Pillai on ISI Role in 26/11', *Times of India*, 21 July 2010, http://articles.timesofindia.indiatimes.com/2010-07-21/india/28293270_1_orf-heritage-foundation-dialogue-headley-clearer-picture-today.

24 For a contrary view see Associated Press, 'Indo-Pakistan Proxy War Heats up in Afghanistan', Fox News, 25 April 2010, http://www.foxnews.com/world/2010/04/25/indo-pakistan-proxy-war-heats-afghanistan/.

25 Shyam Saran, 'How to Fashion a Fork', *Outlook*, 16 August 2010, http://www.outlookindia.com/article.aspx?266557.

26 Government of India, Ministry of External Affairs, 'Factsheet on Indian Assistance to Afghanistan', March 2007, p. 6.

27 Closing remarks, Centre for Land Warfare Studies (CLAWS) seminar on 'Afghanistan: Emerging Scenarios', 14 January 2011.

28 Arun Sahgal, 'US Af-Pak Strategy and Afghanistan's Alternative Futures: Options for India', in R.K. Sawhney, Arun Sahgal and Gurmeet Kanwal (eds), *Afghanistan: A Role for India* (New Delhi: KW Publishers Pvt. Ltd., 2011), pp. 131–2.

29 See 'Indian para-military forces deployed in Afghanistan', *Press Trust of India*, 7 February 2006, http://www.india-defence.com/reports/1320.

30 See 'US embassy cables: No Power-sharing with the Taliban, Holbrooke Pledges'; and Government of India, 'Factsheet on Indian Assistance to Afghanistan', p. 6.

31 Elizabeth Roche, 'India, Afghanistan sign pacts on security forces, minerals', *Live Mint*, 5 October 2011, http://www.livemint.com/2011/10/05001259/India-Afghanistan-sign-pacts.html.

32 'Indians Scale Down in Afghanistan, Fearing Attacks', *Dawn*, 31 March 2010, http://archives.dawn.com/archives/98946.

33 Archis Mohan, 'Afghanistan? Babus Won't Go – Pay of Half-a-crore a Year without Tax, but Officials Don't Respond', *Telegraph* (Calcutta), 23 March 2011, http://www.telegraphindia.com/1110323/jsp/frontpage/story_13752971.jsp.

34 D. Suba Chandran, 'Af-Pak Diary: Now a Peace Council to Negotiate with the Taliban', Institute of Peace and Conflict Studies, 30 September 2010, http://www.ipcs.org/article/Terrorism/Af-Pak-diary-now-a-peace-council-to-negotiate-with-3249.html.

35 M.K. Bhadrakumar, 'India Promises to Prop up Karzai', *Asia Times*, 6 October 2011, http://www.atimes.com/atimes/South_Asia/MJo6Dfo4.html.

36 Tahir Khan, 'News Analysis: Pakistan plays down Afghan-India strategic pact', Xinhua, http://news.xinhuanet.com/english2010/world/2011-10/06/c_131177071.htm.

37 See Jyoti Thottam, 'Afghanistan: India's Uncertain Road', *Time*, 11 April 2011, http://www.time.com/time/magazine/article/0,9171,2062364,00.html.

38 Rahul Roy-Chaudhury, 'Shared Interests in "AfPak" Issues and Counter-Terrorism', in Jo Johnson and Rajiv Kumar (eds), *Reconnecting Britain and India: Ideas for an Enhanced Partnership* (New Delhi: Academic Foundation, 2011), p. 70.

39 Nirupama Rao, 'Perspectives on Foreign Policy for a 21st Century India', Keynote Speech at the 3rd IISS–Ministry of External Affairs (MEA) Dialogue, 22 February 2010, http://www.iiss.org/programmes/south-asia/conferences-and-seminars/iiss-mea-foreign-policy-dialogue/third-iiss-mea-dialogue/nirupama-rao-address/.

40 See Statement by External Affairs Minister S.M. Krishna at Kabul Conference, 20 July 2010, http://www.indianembassy.org/prdetail1559/statement-by-external-affairs-minister-mr.-s.m.-krishna-at-kabul-conference.

41 'Statement by Ambassador Susan E. Rice, Permanent Representative to the UN, on the adoption of resolutions 1988 and 1999', New York, 17 June 2011, http://usun.state.gov/briefing/statements/2011/166468.htm.

42 'India's role in Afghanistan'.

43 Nirupama Rao, 'Key Priorities for India's Foreign Policy', Q&A Session at the IISS, London, 27 June 2011, http://www.iiss.org/events-calendar/2011-

events-archive/june-2011/
nirupama-rao/qa-session/.

44 Jyoti Malhotra, 'India Should Recognise the Taliban', *Business Standard*, 12 July 2009, http://www.business-standard.com/india/news/india-should-recognisetaliban/363608/.

45 Surya Gangadharan, 'Taliban Not Anti-India: Former Taliban Leader', CNN-IBN, 15 March 2010, http://ibnlive.in.com/news/taliban-not-antiindia-former-taliban-leader/111513-2.html.

46 Syed Saleem Shahzad, 'War and Peace: A Taliban View', *Asia Times*, 26 March 2010, http://www.atimes.com/atimes/South-Asia/LC26Df03.html.

47 Roy-Chaudhury, 'India needs Taliban talks to Stay Relevant'.

Chapter Twelve

1 Abeer Allam, 'Karzai in Saudi Arabia to Seek Help with Taliban', *Financial Times*, 3 February 2010.

2 'Funds for Taliban Largely Come from Abroad: Holbrooke', Dawn.com, 29 July 2009 http://archives.dawn.com/archives/40446.

3 Special Briefing on July 2009 Trip to Pakistan, Afghanistan, and Brussels with Richard Holbrooke, US Department of State, 29 July 2009.

4 Julian Borger, 'Pakistan's Bomb and Saudi Arabia', *Guardian*, 11 May 2010, http://www.guardian.co.uk/world/julian-borger-global-security-blog/2010/may/11/pakistan-saudiarabia.

Conclusion

1 Olivier Roy, *The Lessons of the Soviet/Afghan War* (Adelphi Paper 259; IISS/Brasseys, 1991), p. 67.

2 Karzai put forward the specific example of Sher Mohammed Akhundzada: 'The question is why do we have Taliban controlling these areas now when two years ago I had control of Helmand? When Sher Mohammad was governor there, we had girls in schools and only 160 foreign troops. The international community pushed me to remove him and now look where we are.' US Embassy Cables, 'Boucher and Karzai, Spanta on Jirgas, Drugs, Econ Cooperation, Governance', 8 September 2007, available at http://www.guardian.co.uk/world/us-embassy-cables-documents/121457.

Adelphi books are publis̶h̶e̶d̶ ̶e̶i̶g̶h̶t̶ ̶t̶i̶m̶e̶s̶ ̶a̶ ̶y̶e̶a̶r̶ ̶b̶y̶ ̶R̶o̶u̶t̶l̶e̶d̶g̶e̶ ̶jo̶u̶rnals, an imprint of
Taylor & Francis, 4 Park S̶q̶u̶a̶r̶e̶,̶ ̶M̶i̶l̶t̶o̶n̶ ̶P̶a̶r̶k̶,̶ ̶A̶b̶i̶n̶g̶d̶o̶n̶,̶ Oxfordshire OX14 4RN, UK.

A subscription to the institution print edition, ISSN 1944-5571, includes free access for
any number of concurrent users across a local area network to the online edition, ISSN
1944-558X

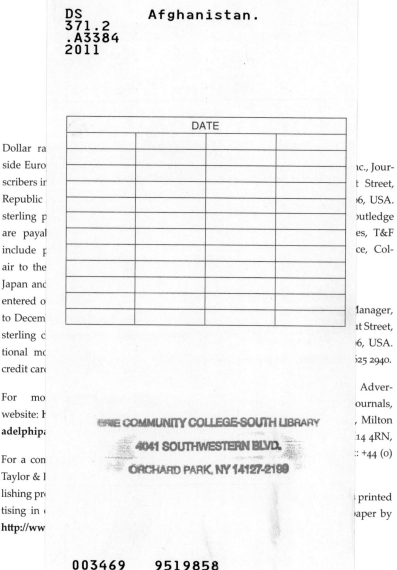

Dollar ra
side Euro   ic., Jour-
scribers in   t Street,
Republic   )6, USA.
sterling p   outledge
are payal   es, T&F
include p   ce, Col-
air to the
Japan and
entered o
to Decem   Ianager,
sterling c   it Street,
tional mo   )6, USA.
credit car(   )25 2940.

For   mo   Adver-
website: F   ournals,
adelphip: , Milton

For a con   14 4RN,
Taylor & I   :: +44 (0)

lishing pro   : printed
tising in (aper by
http://ww